HIBERNIAN
The Players and Managers
1946–2009

HIBERNIAN
The Players and Managers 1946–2009

Jim Jeffrey

First published in Great Britain in 2009 by The Breedon Books Publishing Company Limited, Breedon House, 3 The Parker Centre, Derby, DE21 4SZ.
ISBN 978-1-85983-712-2

Paperback edition published in Great Britain in 2012 by The Derby Books Publishing Company Limited, 3 The Parker Centre, Derby, DE21 4SZ.

© Jim Jeffrey, 2009

All Rights Reserved. No part of this publication may be reproduced, stored in a retrieval system, or transmitted in any form, or by any means, electronic, mechanical, photocopying, recording or otherwise without the prior permission in writing of the copyright holders, nor be otherwise circulated in any form or binding or cover other than in which it is published and without a similar condition being imposed on the subsequent publisher.

A catalogue record for this book is available from the British Library.

Front cover images:
Top row left to right: Franck Sauzee, John Collins, Willie Ormond, Joe Baker.
Bottom row: Lawrie Reilly, Russell Latapy, Pat Stanton, Mixu Paatelainen.

Back cover images:
Top: The Hibs squad pictured in 1957. Bottom: The Hibs squad in 1979.

ISBN 978-1-78091-116-8

Printed and bound by Copytech (UK) Limited, Peterborough.

CONTENTS

Acknowledgements 6
Introduction 7
Hibernian Players   A 9
                               B 17
                               C 38
                               D 53
                               E 62
                               F 64
                               G 71
                               H 80
                               I 94
                               J 95
                               K 101
                               L 106
                               M 116
                               N 150
                               O 152
                               P 163
                               Q 169
                               R 170
                               S 182
                               T 202
                               V–X 209
                               Y 219
                               Z 221
Hibernian Managers 223
Hibernian Stats 229

ACKNOWLEDGEMENTS

My thanks go to Brian Johnson, Rikki Raginia, Dave Beaton (Hibernian), Alastair MacLachlan (St Mirren), Duncan Carmichael (Ayr United), Rob Mason (Sunderland), Graham Barnstaple, John Swinburne (Motherwell), Robert McElroy (Rangers), Peter Rundo (Dundee United), David Hardie, John Gibson (*The Edinburgh Evening News*), David Thomson (Scottish Football League).

The staff of the National Library in Edinburgh who lugged enormous volumes to and from me with good patience, the staff at Perth AK Bell Library likewise.

Players too numerous to mention who answered questions and provided snippets of information at the eleventh hour, and finally the staff at Breedon Books, who treated my continual tweaking and revisions with good humour and considerable patience.

The images in this book have come from a variety of sources, including my own collection of memorabilia and that held by Brian Johnson and the players themselves. Wherever possible I have tried to establish and acknowledge the source of any image included but the author would like to hear from any copyright holder who has been unintentionally missed out to allow for inclusion in future editions.

I would welcome additional information on any of the players included within via Breedon Books, 3 The Parker Centre, Mansfield Road, Derby DE21 4SZ.

INTRODUCTION

The seeds of this book were sewn when I was the editor of the Hibernian match programme. Of all the articles I put together for that publication the historical features were among my favourites. Interviewing old players was a particular pleasure and started me off researching their careers in more detail than the programme would allow. Some of these were of the one club variety, others were incredibly convoluted…they were all interesting and a challenge to piece together. Thus I set off on a project to gather as much information as I could and publish it in book form.

The following pages are essentially an A to Z of every Hibernian player who has made a competitive outing for the club since the 1946–47 season. I've gleaned as much detail as I can from old programmes, handbooks and newspaper reports, but inevitably I haven't had sight of every source that is out there. What I have had however, is great assistance from a number of people. I'd like to thank Brian Johnson of Almondvale Programmes who has allowed me generous access to his huge collection of Hibernian materials, Rikki Raginia (Hibernian's *de facto* historian and number one supporter), who put his encyclopaedic knowledge at my disposal, and Dave Beaton of Arbroath who compiles a most comprehensive and fact-packed Hibernian web site and allowed me access to his statistical archive. Nevertheless, in the pages that follow there will inevitably be errors; these lie firmly at my door.

An exercise of this nature requires detail on what happened to players before and after they played with Hibs. Unfortunately there is no Scottish equivalent to the comprehensive records held on players by the English Football League. Therefore no ready source exists to tap into player dates and places of births or subsequent career moves (especially in the immediate post-war period) and I'd be extremely grateful if anyone noticing omissions contacts me so that I can revise future editions.

I hope this book will appeal to Hibernian supporters and indeed fans of the Scottish game in general. Easter Road has been part of Edinburgh's fabric for over a century now and some wonderful afternoons and evenings have been provided by the many players to serve the club. If I've captured and preserved some of that excitement then the book will be worthwhile.

ADAIR, Gerry

Defender

Born: 16 February 1955.
Career: Edinburgh Schools, West Bromwich Albion 1970, HIBERNIAN 1973, Dunfermline 1975, Meadowbank 1976, Cowdenbeath 1979, Armadale Thistle 1979.

■ A promising schoolboy player, Gerry had gone to West Bromwich Albion straight from school as an apprentice. However, in a setup dominated by quality players like Cyrille Regis and Bryan Robson, his task of breaking into a very strong side was a huge one. Thus, he snapped up the chance to join Hibs in 1973. He made his bow in a 3–1 win at Dundee and looked a solid prospect at centre-half, but the competition at Easter Road was still too stiff for an inexperienced youngster. Four matches in the League preceded a move to Dunfermline where he fared a little better, making 20 League outings. A June 1976 transfer saw him return to Edinburgh to join Meadowbank Thistle (the forerunners to Livingston).

ADAMS, Willie

Goalkeeper

Born: Prestonpans, 1936.
Career: Tranent Juniors, Ormiston Primrose, HIBERNIAN 1955.

■ Imagine sitting down with your grandchildren and saying 'I only ever played the one match for Hibs – it was in the European Cup; a semi-final.' Yet that is the strange career enjoyed by Willie Adams. When Tommy Younger was fog-bound in Germany on his way back to Hibs for the second leg against Rheims in April 1956, young Willie was drafted in for a debut. Although the European Cup was in its infancy and nothing like the global phenomenon it is now, it is still a wonderful story that Willie Adams has. He was freed by Hibernian in April 1956 and appears to have dropped out of the senior game at that point. His only game ended in a 1–0 defeat but there was never any suggestion that he contributed to that defeat.

AGATHE, Didier

Winger

Born: Saint-Pierre, France, 16 August 1975.
Career: Montpellier, 1992, Olympique Ales (loan) 1996, Raith Rovers 1999, HIBERNIAN 2000, Celtic 2000, Aston Villa 2006, JS Saint-Pierroise 2007.

■ Hibernian supporters, and then manager Alex McLeish, have to view Didier as 'the one who got away'. Didier may only have played five games as a Hibee but what joy he brought to the club. Here was a player who had lightening speed and wonderful close control. He missed a sitter on his debut against Hearts at Tynecastle but then scored two goals against both Dundee and their city rivals United. Alas, he was only signed on a short-term deal, and before Hibs could extend his contract the 25-year-old was lured to Celtic on a three-year deal. The only compensation for Hibernian was a paltry £50,000 transfer fee, and Hibs boss McLeish remarked that Agathe was

destined for the Celtic reserves. Rather surprisingly he was used as a wing-back by Celtic (where he won four Championships), and the Parkhead faithful rarely saw the Didier that had 'wowed' Easter Road. In September 2006 he was reunited with his former Celtic boss, Martin O'Neill, at Aston Villa.

AIRD, Peter

Centre-half

Born: 29 August 1921.
Career: Lochee Harp, Bowhill Rovers, HIBERNIAN 1943, East Fife 1951, Llanelly 1954.

■ Peter, who was distinctively tall and red-headed, signed for Hibs in 1943 from Fife junior club Bowhill Rovers and made his debut in the 1944–45 wartime Southern League. He was a regular in the 1945–46 campaign and helped the club reach the 1946 Victory Cup Final, which sadly ended in defeat to Rangers. In the immediate post-war era Peter Aird was a regular in the Hibernian side. He missed just a handful of matches in the first full season after World War Two and formed a formidable partnership with Willie Finnegan and Sammy Kean. However, thereafter he gradually slipped out of the side, and by the time he left the club in January 1951 for East Fife he had only made 44 peacetime appearances as a Hibee and had missed out on the championship medals which were part and parcel of being a Hibernian player in this era. He was a regular for East Fife from signing until being injured early in 1952 after which he missed the entire 1952–53 season. A couple of games thereafter preceded a move to Welsh football with Llanelly in July 1954.

AITKEN, Andy

Inside-forward

Born: Edinburgh, 21 August 1934.
Career: Cliftonville, British Army, HIBERNIAN 1956, West Bromwich Albion 1959, Falkirk 1961, Raith Rovers 1961, Gala Fairydean.

■ There may be several reasons why Hibs lost the 1958 Cup Final to Clyde. But it would be a

brave man to deny that the loss of clever inside-forward Andy Aitken through injury early in the match was a key factor. In the days before substitutes were allowed Aitken had to stay on and was reduced to the role of 'passenger'. His loss was too much for the Hibernian side, already shorn of the talents of Lawrie Reilly. Clyde went on to win 1–0 and Hibs' dreadful ill-fortune in the Scottish Cup continued. Raised in the Edinburgh district of Craigmillar, Andy was signed while carrying out his national service and making fleeting appearances for Northern Irish side Cliftonville. Aitken made his Hibernian debut against Falkirk as an outside-right but really caught the eye when deputising for Willie Ormond on the left wing. Slim and light on his feet he was a creative player rather than a muscular midfield engine-room player. But his influence was considerable and when he was 'on song' Hibs positively purred. Never the most confident of players, he was perhaps guilty of being over-awed at times when in reality he should really have been 'bossing' the midfield. Thus, unable to stamp his authority in a team of mixed talents, he headed for West Bromwich Albion in September 1959 while Hibs were desperately seeking a replacement for the much missed Bobby Johnstone. Aitken did not stay long in the West Midlands and was back in Scotland in February 1961 as a Falkirk player. Teaming up with former Hibee Doug Moran, he helped the Bairns climb out of the Second Division but moved to Fife as the Bairns prepared for life in the top flight. As Andy's career wound down he played briefly with Raith Rovers and Gala Fairydean.

AITKENHEAD, Johnny

Winger

Career: Queen's Park 1941, HIBERNIAN 1946, Motherwell 1949, Hamilton Accies 1957.

■ Nicknamed 'The Daddler', Johnny was a tricky outside-left who ultimately lost out to Willie Ormond in a battle for the number-11 jersey. Signed from Queen's Park in 1945 he could well have been a Hibernian legend had his spell at Easter Road not coincided with the existence of the forward line known collectively as 'The Famous Five'. Aitkenhead did make his mark with Hibs but it was his 1949 transfer to Motherwell after recovering from a serious leg injury that provided him with trophies. Johnny joined Queen's Park in 1941 and was to rack up over 100 League outings for the Spiders before being lured to Edinburgh. He had scored against Hibs in a couple of games and clearly made an impression. A goal in the 1946 Victory Cup Final against Rangers proved he was a new signing of quality. When football returned to normal after World War Two he played in the opening match of season, and scored, as Hibs thumped Queen of the South 9–1. Aitkenhead was the regular number 11 until he was injured at St Mirren in November and lost his place to Ormond. Thus in season 1947–48 as Hibs landed the title he was a bit player, only finding a spot in the team near the end of the season when Ormond was himself injured. Aitkenhead hung around for most of 1948 but was off to George Stevenson's Motherwell when the chance came up just after Christmas. He made his Motherwell bow in a League match on New Year's Day 1949 and scored twice in the 3–1 win at Albion Rovers. For the following five seasons he was very much a regular and capable of contributing quite a few goals despite his wide berth; he even had two against Hibs in a December 1951 clash. League Cup goals were a speciality of his and it was fitting that he played in the side which beat Hibernian in the 1950 League Cup Final at Hampden Park. Indeed, en route to Hampden he had notched two goals in the pulsating 4–3 semi-final win against Ayr United. He missed out on a remarkable double that season as the 'Well lost 0–1 to Celtic in the Scottish Cup Final. However, he made up for the disappointment by playing in the 1952 team which won Motherwell's first ever Scottish Cup. Capped three times by the Scottish League, Johnny was a penalty expert and enjoyed a spell in which he netted 40 consecutive spot kicks. He brought the curtain down on his senior career with a brief spell at Hamilton Accies

ALLAN, Thomson

Goalkeeper

Born: Longridge, 5 October 1946.
Career: Holycross Academy, Edina Hibs, HIBERNIAN 1963, Dundee 1971, Meadowbank (loan) 1979, Hearts 1979, Falkirk 1980, East Stirling 1983.

■ Thomson started his career at Hibernian, with a debut against Hearts in a Scottish Cup tie, and eventually racked up 70 outings. A competent, if unspectacular, goalkeeper he was an excellent shot-stopper and had good positional sense. Nevertheless, he was not able to fend off the challenge of Gordon Marshall. Thus Allan would make his most notable impact on the game while with Dundee, where he won two Scotland caps and a League Cup-winners' badge. He spent eight years on Tayside and in the mid-1970s was an ever present for two seasons. He did return to Edinburgh later in his career but only as emergency cover and never quite scaled the heights of 1969 when he served Hibs in the League Cup Final against Celtic. By the time his career came to a close he had added Falkirk and East Stirling to his list of senior clubs.

ALLAN, Willie

Winger

Born: Kelty, 19 March 1929.
Career: Lumphinnans, HIBERNIAN 1950, Stirling Albion 1952, Cowdenbeath 1952.

■ Season 1950–51 saw Willie make his Hibernian debut against Raith Rovers in a 3–1 victory at Kirkcaldy. One week later the club went top of the League and within a few weeks they would clinch the title. It should therefore have been the start of a glittering career for Willie. Alas as a winger he was up against Gordon Smith and Willie Ormond for a position in the first team, and his outing at Raith (when Ormond had a knee-injury) turned out to be his only game as a Hibee. In May 1952 Allen cut his losses and headed to Stirling Albion where he stayed for six months, making six appearances, before moving to Cowdenbeath prior to stepping down from senior football

ALLISON, Ken

Inside-forward

Born: Edinburgh, 6 January 1937.
Career: West Calder United, HIBERNIAN 1958, Dumbarton 1959, Cowdenbeath 1959, Darlington 1963, Lincoln City 1965.

■ In season 1958–59 Ken played five League games for Hibernian and scored four goals. He also scored in the 3–0 home friendly win over Bayern Munich. It is therefore rather surprising that he had such a short Easter Road career. When he moved away from Hibs he proved his worth by collecting career statistics of 96 goals in 220 League games. He was signed from West Calder United in 1958 and was listed as an inside-left. After Hibs his career took him to Dumbarton, Cowdenbeath, Darlington and Lincoln City. There was even a short stint in America with Rochester Lancers. His best days in Scotland were spent with Cowdenbeath in the early-1960s, where he twice returned double-figures in the 'goals for' column over a season, and between 1963 and 1966 he grabbed 39 goals in only 75 matches.

ANDERSON, Derek

Centre-half

Born: Paisley, 15 May 1972.
Career: Ferguslie United, Morton 1991, Kilwinning Rangers, Kilmarnock 1993, Ayr United 1998, HIBERNIAN (loan) 1998, Morton 1998, Alloa Athletic 2001, Queen of the South 2002, Stirling Albion 2003, Auchinleck Talbot.

■ Signed by Alex McLeish during Hibernian's brief stint in the First Division, Derek was a journeyman centre-half who figured in six games while on loan. Tall, strong and seemingly dependable, he perhaps lacked the creativity that Hibs were hoping for in the late-1990s. The last of his matches was a 3–3 draw with Ayr United and an error-ridden performance did little to enhance his chances of a permanent contract. He had played with Kilmarnock and Ayr United prior to his Easter Road adventure and he was clearly a popular player because both Morton and Ayr employed him twice. He went back to Greenock after his loan spell in Edinburgh ended and thereafter had stints with several clubs in the lower leagues.

ANDERSON, Des

Wing-half

Born: Edinburgh, 9 January 1938.
Career: Edinburgh Thistle, HIBERNIAN 1957, Millwall 1961, Tonbridge 1964.

■ A Schoolboy international, Des was lured to Hibs in 1957 from Edinburgh Thistle, a juvenile club with a clear link to Hibs. Sadly, two League outings in 1957–58 were the sum total of Des Anderson's career with Hibs. Although signed as a centre-forward he achieved more as a wing-half, but he was eventually frustrated by the lack of opportunity at Hibernian and in the summer of 1961 moved south of the border to join Millwall. He spent two seasons in London and made 46 League outings for the Lions.

ANDERSON, William

Outside-right

Born: Glencraig, Fife, 6 November 1926.
Career: Bishop Auckland, HIBERNIAN 1952, Southend United 1953, Weymouth 1954.

■ Educated at the Queen Victoria School (Dunblane), Bill entered minor football south of the border, played for Bishop Auckland in the English Amateur Cup Final and was capped by Scotland as an amateur. He joined Hibs in 1952 but his Easter Road career has to enter the 'one game wonder' category. On 7 April 1954 he was in the Hibernian side that lost 2–1 at Stirling Albion thus halting a run of six consecutive League victories. Bill made 16 appearances for Southend before slipping into non-League football with Weymouth. His father had also played for Hibernian.

ANDERSSON, Daniel

Goalkeeper

Born: Bjuv, Sweden, 18 December 1972.
Career: Ramlosa 1991, Angelholm 1992, Kalmar 1994, Hogaborg 1995, Trelleborgs 1998, AIK Stockholm 2000, HIBERNIAN 2003, Helsingborgs IF 2004.

■ Daniel will be forever associated with his enthusiastic celebrations following Hibs' CIS semi-final penalty shoot-out win over Rangers in 2004; a game in which he saved two spot kicks in the finale and one in normal time! At the age of 31, Andersson was a solid goalkeeper and highly experienced by the time he came to Scotland. Indeed, he had played in two Swedish Cup Finals, even scoring a penalty in one when he experienced the other side of a penalty decider. However, for all his experience (he had one international cap for Sweden too) he never seemed entirely settled at Hibs. His debut came against Celtic in Glasgow on 2 March 2003, and although only youngster Alastair Brown vied with him for the first-team spot he did not establish himself. He had come to Edinburgh from Swedish football and that was the route he retraced when he left the club.

ANDREWS, Lyndon

Midfield

Born: Trinidad & Tobago, 20 January 1976.
Career: Superstar Rangers, Joe Public (Trinidad & Tobago), HIBERNIAN 2000, Western Connection.

■ An international with Trinidad & Tobago, Lyndon joined Hibernian from Joe Public in the summer of 2000; his previous club was the equally exotically named Superstar Rangers. A tricky midfield schemer, many hoped his career would echo that of Russell Latapy, but Lyndon's spell at Easter Road never quite took off and despite some invigorating displays these were mainly as a substitute (most notably in the 6–2 demolition of Hearts) and he was never a permanent feature in the Hibs first XI. He made his debut against Stenhousemuir in a League Cup tie in August 2000 but was released in April 2002 and took up the opportunity to train in Belgium.

ANTOINE-CURIER, Mickael

Striker

Born: Orsay, France, 5 March 1983.
Career: Brentford 2003, Oldham Athletic 2003, Kidderminster Harriers 2003, Rochdale 2003, Sheffield Wednesday 2004, Notts County 2004, Grimsby Town 2004, Vard Haugesund 2004, FK Haugesund 2006, HIBERNIAN 2007, Dundee 2008.

■ Mickael scored four times for Hibs in a trial match against Livingston and thus secured his move to Edinburgh in the summer of 2007. A powerful French striker, he was recruited from Norwegian football but could list Oldham,

Kidderminster, Rochdale, Sheffield Wednesday, Notts County and Grimsby among the English sides with whom he had enjoyed short contracts. While plying his trade in Norway he scored 15 goals in 39 starts for FK Haugesund where former Hibee Kevin Nicol was among his teammates. But although he started the 2007–08 season with much promise he was clearly unsettled by the departure of the man who signed him – John Collins – and this culminated in a loan move to Dundee during the transfer window of January 2008. He seized that opportunity and scored a couple of goals early in his loan period.

ARCHIBALD, Steve

Striker

Born: Rutherglen, 27 September 1956.
Career: Fernhill Athletic, Clyde 1974, Aberdeen 1978, Tottenham Hotspur 1980, Barcelona 1984, Blackburn Rovers 1987, HIBERNIAN 1988, Espanyol 1990, St Mirren 1990, Reading 1992, Clyde 1992, Ayr United 1992, Fulham 1992, East Fife 1994.

■ A teenage sensation with Clyde, Archibald was lithe, quick and possessed an unerring accuracy around goal. He spent his formative years at Shawfield before joining Aberdeen in 1978. He was a huge success at Pittodrie under Alex Ferguson and it cost Tottenham £800,000 to lure him to London. Equally successful at Spurs, his next port of call was the mighty Spanish giants Barcelona where he fully justified a then huge £1.5 million transfer fee. He eventually returned to Britain on a short loan spell to the less salubrious Blackburn Rovers before Hibernian signed him. He made his Hibs debut in a Skol Cup tie against Stranraer in August 1988 and scored twice in a 4–0 win, and in his next game he helped the Hibees gather an unlikely early-season point at Ibrox. His value was clearly the great experience and good habits he brought to Easter Road. Younger players were bound to learn from him and many would later say that he was a huge influence on their career. There was an air of the wanderlust about Steve and he was not a Hibee for too long, but 13 goals in his first season showed enough to impress. After his stint at Hibs this often underrated Scotland international enjoyed a brief period with an array of clubs but he gave the air of merely marking time until he moved into management. He later became a successful football agent, managed East Fife and was also involved in the first bid to save Airdrie in 1999. His CV could also include an entry as a director at Portuguese giants Benfica.

ARPINON, Frederic

Midfield

Born: Nimes, France, 9 May 1969.
Career: Nimes 1989, Nice 1992, Sedan 1994, Metz 1995, Strasbourg 1997, Troyes 1999, HIBERNIAN 2000, Nimes 2003.

■ Signed by Alex McLeish in March 2001 from Troyes, Frederic had trained with Hibernian at the start of that season but was unable to obtain a release from his club. A vastly experienced midfielder, he had played for Strasbourg against both Rangers and Liverpool

Frederic Arpinon

and was a former teammate of David Zitelli; clearly his qualities were well known at Easter Road. Starting his career with his home-town club Nimes, he really made his mark at Metz before joining Strasbourg. When he finally arrived at Hibernian the club were heading for third place in the League and the Scottish Cup Final and he consequently found it hard to break into a settled side. A nippy midfielder, he was quite willing to 'put himself about' and was booked just minutes into his debut which came in a 2–0 defeat at St Johnstone. He later earned a degree of notoriety for being sent off at Dundee after spitting at an opponent.

AULD, Bertie

Inside-forward

Born: Maryhill, Glasgow, 23 March 1938.
Career: Maryhill Harp, Celtic 1955, Dumbarton (loan) 1956, Birmingham City 1961, Celtic 1965, HIBERNIAN 1971.

■ Bertie is one of the select band of players who went on from playing for Hibs to later managing the club. He had made his reputation with Celtic as a member of Jock Stein's all-conquering 1967 'Lisbon Lions' side and arrived at Easter Road in the early 1970s when he was clearly in the veteran stage of his playing career. This was a shrewd move on the part of Hibs manager Eddie Turnbull, for Auld was the perfect addition to the coaching team. However, he was still possessed of a shrewd footballing brain on the field and helped the club win 2–1 at Ibrox soon after arriving. His forte, however, was to be coaching and he earned his spurs at Easter Road before going on to make his name as manager of Partick Thistle. His achievement at Firhill was to keep an unfashionable club in the cut-throat, 10-club Premier League. This survival success was based largely on a defensive policy and thus when Bertie came to Hibs as boss in November 1980 and adopted these 'safety first' tactics he was not always popular. A cigar smoking, wise-cracking character he was loved by the press but never universally popular among his players, some of whom complained he was unable to accept that not every player could match his own high playing standards. After dismissal by Hibs in September 1982 he later managed both Hamilton Accies and Dumbarton, but it is as a wily and somewhat spiky Celtic midfielder that he is best remembered.

B

BAILEY, Lee

Forward

Born: Edinburgh, 10 July 1972.
Career: Tynecastle Boys Club, HIBERNIAN 1990, Meadowbank Thistle 1992, Livingston 1992, Queen of the South 1998, Brechin City 1999, Stirling Albion 2001, East Fife 2001, Bonnyrigg Rose, Rosyth Recreation, Arniston Rangers.

■ Despite a promising debut as a 17-year-old against Aberdeen, Lee was unable to establish himself at Easter Road as the club lifted the League Cup and re-established its credentials in the Scottish game. Away from Hibs he fared better and made over 200 outings in the senior Leagues and a further 70-plus as a substitute. At just 5ft 6in perhaps Lee was a little too small for the modern game but he made a good fist of life in the lower Leagues, starring with a succession of clubs before moving into the junior ranks with some style. Away from football he worked as a driving instructor.

BAILLIE, Jonothan

Centre-half

Born: Irvine, 2 September 1985.
Career: HIBERNIAN, Ayr United (loan) 2005, retired through injury.

■ Jonothan snuffed out the threat of Henrik Larsson and Chris Sutton on his debut as Hibs defeated Celtic in a League Cup quarter-final tie in 2003. Tall and strong, he looked the part at centre-half but was sent off in his very next game and soon began to suffer from the injuries that would end his career prematurely. A short loan period in his home county of Ayrshire was tried but it was injuries rather than lack of first team action that were proving problematic. Away from the game he wore glasses and seemed a rather unlikely looking stopper, yet on the field he was possessed of great determination and strength.

BAINES, Roy

Goalkeeper

Born: Derby, 7 February 1950.
Career: Derby County juniors, Dalry Amateurs, HIBERNIAN 1968, Morton 1972, Celtic 1976, Morton 1979, St Johnstone 1983.

■ Roy joined Hibernian in September 1968 and in the 1970–71 season played in 23 matches. However, he was unsettled by the lack of opportunities and moved to Morton in August 1972. He was a regular at Cappielow until Celtic signed him in October 1976 but Morton signed him back in March 1979. He was by now well on the way to his 344 Scottish League total and ended his career in Perth with St Johnstone. His spell with Hibs in the early-1970s coincided with that of Gordon Marshall which meant that the club rather oddly had two English goalkeepers on their books. Roy, for all his ability, never quite dominated the scene at Easter Road. When his playing career ended he became a publican in the Keeper's Arms in Tranent.

BAIRD, Sammy

Wing-half

Born: Denny, Stirlingshire, 13 May 1930.
Career: Rutherglen Glencairn, Clyde 1949, Preston North End 1954, Rangers 1955, HIBERNIAN 1960, Third Lanark 1962, Stirling Albion 1963.

■ Vastly experienced by the time he joined Hibs, Baird had won promotion with Clyde in 1952 and moved on to Preston North End before Scott Symon took him to Rangers (indeed Symon had also signed him for Preston). Sammy won League and Scottish Cup honours while at Rangers and had seven full Scotland caps when Hibernian signed him in 1960. His role was largely to fill the void left by the departure of Bobby Johnstone and encourage the youngsters at Easter Road. He reserved some of his best displays for European nights and would perhaps have stayed longer at

Hibernian had an old friend not come calling. He managed only 39 League games for Hibs when he moved back to the west of Scotland with George Young's Third Lanark.

BAKER, Gerry

Centre-forward

Born: New York, 11 April 1938.
Career: Larkhall Thistle, Chelsea, Motherwell 1956, St Mirren 1958, Manchester City 1960, HIBERNIAN 1961, Ipswich Town 1963, Coventry City 1967, Brentford 1969, Margate, Nuneaton Borough.

■ It is difficult to avoid the feeling that Gerard Austin Baker played much of his career in the considerable shadow of his brother Joe. His career verged upon the nomadic and while he could have been a star at any of the clubs he played with he seldom stayed long enough to make a genuine impression. With Motherwell he was impatient for an opening in a side dominated by the 'Ancell Babes' of Ian St John, Andy Weir, Pat Quinn and Willie Hunter. At St Mirren he was a scoring sensation with 19 goals in his first 21 League games. In 1959 he won a Scottish Cup-winners' badge with the Saints (scoring in the Final) and he followed that up with 10 goals in a 15–0 Scottish Cup win over Glasgow University the very next season. But still he could not settle. Wanderlust surfaced again and he was soon pulling on the colours of Manchester City; his single season there brought 14 goals in 37 starts. Miffed at being dropped from the first team he angled for a transfer and got his wish in November 1961 when Hibs paid £18,000 for his services. Gerry was an able marksman for Hibs and his 10 goals in season 1961–62 undoubtedly helped the club stay up. He had 13 the next season but was off to Ipswich Town in December 1963 for £17,000. Had he stayed he would surely have been a key performer at Easter Road. When his playing career ended he worked in the Jaguar plant in Coventry, and as a full American international he had much to reflect on. There was a sporting enthusiasm in his family and his daughters Karen and Lorraine were both notable athletes – Lorraine finishing fifth in the 800 metres race at the Los Angeles Olympics.

BAMBA, Souleymane

Central-defender

Born: Ivory Coast, 13 January 1985.
Career: PSG 2004, Dunfermline Athletic 2006, HIBERNIAN 2008.

■ Just as the 2008 summer transfer window was shutting, beleaguered Hibernian boss Mixu Paatelainen secured this powerful defender from Dunfermline. A 23-year-old Ivory Coast international, he had made more than 50 appearances for the Pars and had just returned from representing his country at the Beijing Olympics. Paatelainen was in no doubts about the qualities that Bamba brought to Easter Road: 'He is a player with tremendous pace and physical presence that will most definitely help bolster our defence.' Bamba cost Hibs £50,000 and was sent off in his debut at home to Dundee United in September 2008.

BANNERMAN, Scott

Defender

Born: Edinburgh, 21 March 1979.
Career: Hutcheson Vale BC, HIBERNIAN 1995, Morton 2001, Dumbarton 2005, Raith 2006.

■ Signed by Alex Miller, Scott played a handful of games for Alex McLeish but was unable to settle on a single position to make his own. Small and stocky, this blond-haired defender enjoyed his best season at Easter Road when the club won the First Division championship in 1999 and he featured in a dozen games. But as the club stepped up to the top flight he found himself out in the cold. Loan spells with Alloa and Airdrie preceded a move to Greenock Morton. A nephew of former Hearts favourite John Robertson, Scott was ultimately happiest patrolling a midfield beat.

BANNON, Eammon

Midfield

Born: Edinburgh, 18 April 1958.
Career: Links BC, Hearts 1975, Chelsea 1979,

JOE BAKER — HERO

Centre-forward
Born: Liverpool, 17 July 1940.
Career: Craigneuk Boys Club, Coltness United, Armadale Thistle, Chelsea 1955, HIBERNIAN 1955, Torino 1961, Arsenal 1962, Nottingham Forest 1966, Sunderland 1969, HIBERNIAN 1971, Raith Rovers 1972.

■ There is a genuine danger of running out of superlatives when describing the career of Joseph Henry Baker. From making his Hibernian debut in August 1957 until departing for Italian giants Torino in June 1961 he was the terror of defences up and down Scotland. His goalscoring feats were the stuff of legend and when he became the first player from outside the English Football League to be capped by England his reputation as a superstar was cemented.

Born in Liverpool, his family moved to Lanarkshire during World War Two and although Joe tried his luck down south at Chelsea as a schoolboy, it was in the industrial surrounds of Wishaw that he made his name. Capped by Scotland at schoolboy level he scored twice in a schools international fixture at Tynecastle Park and had scouts aplenty on his tail. He was dabbling on the fringes of the junior game with Coltness United when Hibernian stepped in and promptly farmed him out to their preferred local junior team – Armadale Thistle. Deep within the Hibernian Handbook for 1956–57 comes an early mention of the prowess of Joe Baker in front of goal. He is not named in the player profiles, nor is he one of the talented youngsters Hibs proudly list in the opening paragraphs, but tucked away under *Other Matches* is the result Hibernian 10, Armadale 1 and Baker has scored four of the goals. Joe does feature in the 1957–58 handbook and it is worth recalling how he was introduced to a curious Hibernian support...

J. BAKER
Called up this season from Armadale Thistle for whom he notched 51 goals last season. Like John Paterson could never play for Scotland as he was born in England, but played for Scotland as a schoolboy. Lives in Motherwell and joined Hibs after playing a great game for Lanarkshire Schools at Tynecastle. Centre-forward, 5'8½, 11st, Signed 1955 Lanarkshire Schools.

In the 1957–58 season Joe burst onto the Easter Road scene with a blaze of talent that stunned even a support weaned on the Famous Five. He made his debut at Airdrie in August, scored twice against Queen's Park in October and had a hat-trick against Tottenham two days later. He never looked back. He scored 14 goals in 25 League starts and seven in seven Scottish Cup ties. The latter haul included all four in a quite sensational 4–3 victory over city rivals Hearts at Tynecastle. Had Hibs gone on to win the Scottish Cup Final against Clyde the season would have been perfect. Undeterred, Joe was back

to his dazzling best at the start of the 1958–59 campaign. This time he scored 25 goals in only 26 League matches and had fans up and down the country eager to see him. How then to describe what happened the following season when he gathered the biggest haul ever by a Hibernian player in a single season? In scoring 42 goals (yes, 42!) from a mere 33 League games he left sportswriters at a loss as to how to portray his impact on the game. Sure, they could mention his blistering pace, and they could have a stab at describing his ability to hang in the air and bullet headers goalwards. His fearsome shooting was also capable of being captured in words, but nothing could quite sum up his uncanny ability to find time and space to bury chance after chance. Baker not only had awesome talent but also an easy style and in-built scoring radar. That 1959–60 season marked Baker out as something quite extraordinary. Here was a Hibernian side that finished in mid-table yet scored 106 League goals; four more than championship winning Hearts. It was a League campaign in which Hibs won games 7–4, 11–1 and 10–2; the latter two being away fixtures! Joe Baker scored no fewer than FIVE hat-tricks. He had played for England at Under-23 level in September 1958 and then scored on his full England debut against Northern Ireland at Wembley. It seemed that he could do no wrong. His achievements for England gave Hibernian claim to being the first Scottish club to have players capped for all five 'home' nations. Season 1960–61 was to bring the curtain down on his first spell at Easter Road and few could have been surprised. Indeed, Hibs had done well to hang onto such a prolific talent for so long. He did, however, reserve a couple of special treats for that farewell season. He scored five against Third Lanark in a League game and then stunned the nation by scoring nine in a Scottish Cup tie against Peebles Rovers. Add to this six goals against Barcelona and Roma in European ties and it is clear why his reputation was known the length and breadth of the footballing community. The inevitable came in July 1961 when he moved to Torino in a deal reputed to have earned Hibs £65,000. Although paired with Denis Law in Turin he did not settle, suffered appalling injuries in a near-fatal car-crash and in 1962 returned to Britain with Arsenal in August 1962 for £67,000. A star at Highbury, he then played for Nottingham Forest and Sunderland. He would grab over 100 goals in the Football League thus mirroring his achievements north of the border. In 1971 he returned to Hibernian, nine years and eight months on from his initial departure, and made a sensational second debut, scoring with a classic header in a 2–1 win over Aberdeen that ended the Dons' remarkable run of 15 straight wins. Injury, however, had caught up with Joe and he retired soon afterwards, although there was time for a brief sortie to Raith Rovers. Baker's career with Hibernian in summary is quite astonishing: 159 goals in only four seasons; A Scottish Cup Final appearance when only 17 having scored four times at Tynecastle in a 4–3 epic earlier in the competition; 42 League goals in a single season; 14 hat-tricks; and caps for England at full and Under-23 level. Little wonder that Hibs supporters loved the fabulous Baker Boy. When his playing career ended he dabbled in management with the likes of Fauldhouse United juniors and Albion Rovers. But ultimately he could not be kept away from Easter Road and he was a popular host on match days. Sadly, aged just 63, Joe died of a heart-attack while taking part in a charity golf event in 2003. A wonderful talent, a goalscoring sensation and thoroughly good company, Joe Baker was one of the all-time great Hibees.

Dundee United 1979, Hearts 1988, HIBERNIAN 1993, Stenhousemuir 1995.

■ Eammon enjoyed a marvellous playing career which took in Hearts, Chelsea, Dundee United and Scotland. Unfortunately, his stint with Hibs came as his career was drawing to a close and he played only one game as a Hibee – and even that was as emergency cover. At Tannadice Eammon really flourished and he was an integral part of Jim McLean's Championship and League Cup-winning sides. Moreover, he served Scotland 11 times and played in some wonderful United European nights, and his galloping goal against Borussia Mönchengladbach was arguably one of the finest goals by a Scottish player at this level. Very left footed, very good in possession and the owner of a wicked shot he had a lot going for him as a player. He was subsequently a player-coach at Hibs (playing one game in the 1993–94 season), then assistant manager at Hearts before donning his boots again for Terry Christie's Stenhousemuir. A fairytale ending saw him bow out with a Challenge Cup-winners' medal, ironically gained against Dundee United. His football career ended on a note of controversy as he was sacked as manager of Falkirk after the Bairns had used an unregistered player in a match against St Mirren, thus incurring a steep Scottish League fine. There are many who felt that the responsibility for fielding the player did not lie at Eammon's door.

BARRY, Roy

Defender

Born: Edinburgh, 19 September 1942.
Career: Musselburgh Athletic, Hearts 1961, Dunfermline 1966, Coventry City 1969, Crystal Palace 1973, HIBERNIAN 1975, East Fife 1976.

■ A powerful centre-half, Roy Alexander Barry came to Hibs in the latter stages of his career but helped the club finish second in the 1975 title race and third the following year. His career began with a move from Musselburgh Athletic to Hearts. Never quite an automatic pick at Tynecastle, he joined Dunfermline and was part of the Pars side that defeated Hearts in the 1968 Scottish Cup Final (Alex Edwards was also in that side). He then sampled life south of the border with Coventry City and Crystal Palace. At the end of January 1975 Eddie Turnbull signed Barry for Hibs following an injury to John Blackley. He made his debut in a 2–1 home win over Dundee. Barry had been on the verge of taking up a coaching spot in America but stayed at Hibs until the arrival of George Stewart consigned him to the reserves. In October 1976 he joined East Fife but he was only able to make a handful of appearances while in Methil.

BAXTER, John

Left-half

Career: Benburb, HIBERNIAN 1955, Falkirk 1966, Clydebank 1967.

■ At 5ft 11in and 12st, John was a powerful half-back who joined Hibernian from Glasgow junior side Benburb in 1955. He could defend with vigour but liked to get forward too and netted some memorable goals, including one against Rangers in the late-1950s. Indeed, in the 1959–60 season he

scored a season-best of seven goals, and he was on the score sheet in each of his Easter Road seasons. Dependability rather than flashy excess was the hallmark of John's game and thus his name, while well known to Hibs fans, rarely features in the list of all-time greats, despite his excellent appearance record. In April 1964 he caused mild controversy by being sent off in a League fixture at Dundee United; a rare event in that era. Capped by Scotland at Under-23 level against Wales in 1958, there was a feeling that John's career never quite reached the heights it threatened to. He stayed at Easter Road until June 1966 when he joined Falkirk. His Final season in senior football was in 1967–68 when he played in 26 League matches for Clydebank. John played in 245 matches in the Scottish League before retiring.

BEAUMONT, Dave

Defender

Born: Edinburgh, 10 December 1963.
Career: Dundee United 1978, Luton Town 1989, HIBERNIAN 1991.

■ Dave began his career with Dundee United in 1980 and rapidly progressed through the ranks. He helped Scotland win the Under-18 European Championship, was a Scotland Under-21 international, and represented Dundee United in the 1987 UEFA Cup Final. Interestingly, he scored his first ever United goal against Hibernian in 1985. He joined Luton Town after eight years on Tayside and helped his new club reach the 1989 League Cup Final. Alex Miller recruited him to the Hibernian squad in October 1991 and he was on the bench as Hibs won the Scottish League Cup Final weeks later. However, injury disrupted his Hibernian career and it is fair to say the Easter Road support never saw the best of him. In his four seasons in Edinburgh he was never able to manage more than 20-odd appearances in a season. Despite his career being a lengthy one he actually only played in just over 100 League games. Away from football he had a diploma in civil engineering.

BEEDIE, Stuart

Midfield

Born: Aberdeen, 16 August 1960.
Career: Aberdeen Sunnybank, Montrose 1978, St Johnstone 1981, Dundee United 1984, HIBERNIAN 1986, Dunfermline 1987, Dundee 1989, East Fife 1993, Montrose 1994.

■ A very solid midfielder, Stuart gave service to several clubs in a lengthy career. He started with Montrose and then moved to St Johnstone for £20,000 in 1981. He was an outstanding Saint, seldom absent and possessed of both flair and dependability. Stuart's consistency was rewarded with moves to Dundee United and then Hibs, neither of which really worked out. Indeed he played just nine games for Hibs (although he did score twice) and is perhaps best remembered around Easter Road for playing a major part in the infamous clash with Rangers at the start of the 1986–87 season. Rangers' new player-manager Graeme Souness was sent off at Easter Road for his assault on George McCluskey, an incident which had its roots in a challenge by Beedie on Souness. Beedie scored in that game and Hibs went on to claim a famous 2–1 victory. His spell with Hibs was followed by periods at Dunfermline, Dundee, East Fife and Montrose once more.

BELL, Dougie

Midfield

Born: Paisley, 5 September 1959.
Career: Cumbernauld United, St Mirren 1978, Aberdeen 1979, Rangers 1985, St Mirren (loan) 1986, HIBERNIAN 1987, Shrewsbury Town 1988, Hull City 1989, Birmingham City 1989, Partick Thistle 1991, Clyde 1993, Alloa 1995, Albion Rovers 1996.

■ Signed for £30,000 in January 1987, the former St Mirren, Aberdeen and Rangers midfielder was a cultured player who had made his name as part of Alex Ferguson's Aberdeen side. He was probably past his best when he joined Hibs, and he later served Shrewsbury Town and Hull City in England before a career in the lower reaches of the Scottish game. Small and compact, he was a thinking player ever busy with probing and searching passes. He was with Hibs for less than two seasons and scored on his debut against Falkirk in January 1987. Given that he had won both League and Scottish Cup honours while with Aberdeen, it was clear he was a class act but was perhaps one that came to Easter Road just a little too late to make a major impact.

BENJELLOUN, Abdessalam

Striker

Born: Morocco, 28 January 1985.
Career: WAF Fez (Morocco), Moghreb Fes (Morocco) 2004, HIBERNIAN 2006, Charleroi 2008.

■ Abdessalam was 21 when Tony Mowbray convinced him to join Hibs. Nicknamed 'Benji', he earned a special place in the Hibernian annals by scoring twice in the CIS Cup Final triumph over Kilmarnock in 2007. Tall, quick and with a good shot he was a refreshing talent to lure to the Scottish game. Benjelloun first caught the eye when playing for Morocco in the Under-21 World Championships in Holland. His Hibernian debut came in the 0–4 Scottish Cup semi-final defeat to Hearts and only then after a protracted transfer saga. His career had begun in Morocco with Second Division side WAF before he earned a move to First Division Moghreb Fes. Luring Benjelloun to Edinburgh was made easier, and more likely, by the presence of French-speaking players like Oumar Konde, Guillaume Beuzelin and Amadou Konte at Easter Road. By March 2008 Benji had earned his first call-up to the full Morocco international squad. As the 2008–09 season got underway he joined Charleroi in Belgium.

BEST, George

Winger

Born: Belfast, 22 May 1946.
Died: November 2005.
Career: Manchester United 1963, Dunstable Town 1974, Stockport County 1975, Cork Celtic 1976, Los Angeles Aztecs 1976, Fulham 1976, Fort Lauderdale Strikers 1978, HIBERNIAN 1979, San Jose Earthquakes 1980, Bournemouth 1983, Brisbane Lions 1983.

■ Born in Belfast in 1946, George Best was one of the greatest post-war European footballers. A left-winger of extraordinary skill, he was also one of the most famous personalities of the 'Beatles' era and sadly it was this exposure to the limelight that ultimately ended his football career prematurely. Capped 37 times by Northern Ireland, Best was part of Matt Busby's great Manchester United team that could boast talents such as Bobby Charlton and Denis Law. He won a European Cup medal in 1968, indeed he scored in the Final against Benfica. He was both European and English Footballer of the Year in 1968. However, he was not a dedicated professional and soon his fondness for the 'high life' caught up with him. After admirable patience on the part of Manchester United he was finally released from Old Trafford in 1974 and played with the likes of Fulham and Fort Lauderdale before Hibernian signed him in November 1979. His Hibs debut came against St Mirren at Paisley and the gate was hugely swelled. Hibs lost 2–1 but Best scored the Hibees' counter and a love affair was born. One week later over 20,000 turned up at Easter Road for an otherwise mundane match against Partick Thistle as he made his Edinburgh debut. His appearances were sporadic and Edinburgh was ablaze with rumours about Best's off-field antics. Hibs were patient with Best but he failed to apply himself and was soon on his way. Nevertheless, the feeling was that this was a marvellous cameo appearance and that no harm had been done although Hibs were relegated that season. With Manchester United Best played in 525 games and scored 210 times, of that total he contributed 11 goals in only 34 European ties. Best died in November 2005.

BEUZELIN, Guillaume

Midfield

Born: France, 14 April 1979.
Career: Le Havre, HIBERNIAN 2004, Coventry City 2008.

■ The 29-year-old midfielder left Hibs in the summer of 2008 when his contract expired. He had proved to be an extremely creative and influential midfielder at Easter Road. There was no doubt that when he played well then Hibernian appeared to have a greater tempo about their game. 'Boozy' (as he was rather unfortunately nicknamed) enjoyed his finest day as a Hibernian player in the 2007 Scottish League Cup Final as Hibs romped to a 5–1 Final triumph over Kilmarnock.

BLACK, Ian

Full-back

Born: 4 February 1960.
Career: Musselburgh Windsor, Hearts, HIBERNIAN 1980, East Fife 1980, Berwick Rangers 1980, Ormiston Primrose.

■ A left-back, Ian George Black was more successful in his spells at Hearts and Berwick Rangers than he was at Hibs. He joined the green half of Edinburgh in the summer of 1980 as the Easter Road club contemplated life in the First Division. Having played a handful of games for Hearts in that League it was hoped he would do well but he made only two outings for Hibs before moving to Berwick, via East Fife. His haul of just over 70 games in the senior ranks seemed a poor reward for a player who had been on the books of Celtic as a youngster.

BLACK, Jim

Centre-half

Born: Airdrie, 13 November 1943.
Career: Lochend Hearts, Airdrie 1962, HIBERNIAN 1969, Airdrie 1974, Stenhousemuir 1979.

■ A tall, dark-haired centre-half, Jim Black was commanding in the air and, while not the fastest player, fairly solid in the tackle. Arguably he first came to light when scoring an own goal against Hibs while an Airdrie player during the 1967–68 season, but it is doubtful if that lay behind his £30,000 transfer to Hibs in 1969. More probable is the display he gave at the heart of the Airdrie defence

when they knocked Hibs out of the Cup in January 1968. He made his Easter Road debut against Newcastle United in an August 1969 friendly and was able to hold his position in the team when Eddie Turnbull took over as a manager. All in all he proved a good buy for Hibernian and won a League Cup-winners' badge in 1972. Also a key performer in the two Dryburgh Cup wins over Celtic, there was a period when he seemed on the verge of international honours. He linked very well with John Blackley at the back and although not among the better known of the Turnbull side he was undoubtedly a key element. After eight seasons with Hibs he returned to Airdrie for five and then had three at Stenhousemuir in Larbert as his career wound down. In making just short of 700 senior outings in the Scottish game he proved that although his style was quiet and considered it was also effective.

BLACKLEY, John

Central-defender

Born: Falkirk, 12 May 1948.
Career: Gairdoch United, HIBERNIAN 1965, Newcastle United 1977, Preston North End 1979, Hamilton Accies 1981, HIBERNIAN 1983.

■ A wonderfully composed defender, John Henderson Blackley joined Hibs in 1964 from Gairdoch United and went on to have a great career with the club. He was part of the super 'Turnbull's Tornadoes' side and marshalled his defensive colleagues with assurance and no little style. He played in some truly memorable Hibernian matches including the 7–0 rout at Tynecastle on New Year's Day 1973 and the 6–1 European hammering of Sporting Lisbon. By the early-1970s he was easily one of Scotland's finest central-defenders and he graduated from League internationals to full internationals very quickly. Indeed, he played for Scotland in

John Blackley

the 1974 World Cup Finals in Germany. John made his Hibs bow in the 1967–68 season and as a new decade beckoned he was a first team regular. Throughout the early-1970s he was a bulwark in the Hibs defence, but for all his physical presence he was first and foremost a cultured and creative defender, never happier than when instigating an attack with a searching pass. Having said that he was rarely a goalscorer, but he did save one goal for a European tie with Swedish side Oesters Vaxjo. After amassing 424 appearances and collecting several Cup Final appearances, he was sold to Newcastle United for £100,000 in October 1977. He was highly appreciated at St James' Park before moving on to Preston and Hamilton (as player-manager eventually) before returning to Hibs and ultimately managing the club. He was responsible for some fine signings including an 18-year-old striker from East Fife by the name of Gordon Durie. Appointed Hibs boss in September 1984, he stayed until his resignation in the winter of 1986, arguably after having been expected to achieve too much too soon. John's love of football remained undiminished and he worked as a coach at Dundee United, St Johnstone, Plymouth and Sheffield Wednesday after leaving Easter Road. He represented Scotland at Under-23, League and full international level and in both playing for and managing Hibs is clearly one of the club's great success stories.

BLAIR, Jim

Forward

Born: Airdrie, 13 January 1947.
Career: Shotts Bon Accord, St Mirren 1967, HIBERNIAN 1970, St Mirren 1971, Norwich City 1972.

■ A centre-forward, Jim was signed from St Mirren in June 1970. He had bagged 18 goals for the Saints in the 1969–70 season and was a powerful six footer. What is more, he had been part-time at Paisley working as a chemical operator during the day. The expectation was that full-time football in Edinburgh would see him develop further. Sadly, he never lived up to his undoubted promise and went back to Saints in February 1971 having failed to settle. He played in 15 League games for Hibs and did score a few in the autumn of 1970, including two in a 3–2 win over Rangers at Easter Road. He had initially joined St Mirren in 1967 from Shotts Bon Accord and was also a one-time Scottish junior badminton champion!

BOCO, Jimmy

Defender

Born: Benin, 22 December 1983.
Career: RC Lens 1991, HIBERNIAN 1997.

■ Let us clarify one thing from the outset. Known as 'Jimmy Boco' to the Hibernian support, his real name was Jean-Marc Adjovi-Boco. It was Jim Duffy who brought Boco to Easter Road and in doing so he beat off competition from Kilmarnock and Motherwell. He had been a regular for over six seasons with RC Lens in the French top division and had over 200 French outings to his name. Signed at the start of the 1997–98 season, he made 29 appearances in that strange campaign, which started with a scintillating home win over Celtic but ended in relegation. Boco did not survive and played no part in the Alex McLeish revival of Hibs. After his playing days ended he played a key role in the Diambars Institute which sought to mix education with football and called upon the likes of Patrick Vieira and Bernard Lama to achieve a high profile. Based in Dakar, the move was a wonderful example of successful footballers putting something back into society.

BOGIE, Malcolm

Winger

Born: Edinburgh, 26 December 1939.
Career: Balgreen Rovers, HIBERNIAN 1956, Grimsby Town 1963, Aldershot 1964, Hawick Royal Albert 1967, Gala Fairydean 1970.

■ In 1955 Malcolm represented Scotland Schoolboys against England at Liverpool and this ensured a host of clubs chased his signature. Hibs convinced him to come to

Easter Road and the apprentice engineer finally made the move in 1956, signing from Balgreen Rovers. Two games in the 1958–59 season (his League debut was at home to Dunfermline in March 1959) when he was only 19 and one in the 1962–63 season was the sum of his Hibs League career. Although he tried his luck in England he played only three games for his two clubs south of the border and returned to settle in the Scottish borders. His full name was the rather impressive Malcolm Fisher McKenzie Bogie!

BOTTIGLIERI, Emilio

Midfield/defender

Born: Port Hardy, Canada, 13 April 1979.
Career: Metro Ford, HIBERNIAN 1997, Morton 2001.

■ This young Canadian player was signed in September 1997 from Metro Ford on what proved to be a prolonged loan deal and Emilio never quite made the impact hoped for. He enjoyed a rousing debut against Barnsley when the supporters, intrigued by his unusual surname, cheered his every move. However, such weakly-founded popularity could not propel him into the first team and he played a single game in Hibs' 1998–99 promotion run. Bottiglieri had a spell on loan with Albion Rovers then did likewise with Partick and East Fife before he joined Morton. He helped the Greenock club out of the Third Division and as he settled to life in the west of Scotland he clocked up his 100th League appearance.

BOYLE, George

Full-back

Career: Ballieston Juniors, HIBERNIAN 1952, Dumbarton 1959.

■ Signed as a right-back from Ballieston Juniors in 1949, George showed great patience while at Hibs. He was only 5ft 7in and 10st 7lbs but what he lacked in bulk he made up for with speed and tenacity. George's debut came in October 1954 away to Clyde and Hibs were

defeated 3–6. Between 1953 and 1959 he made a clutch of appearances and would probably have made more than 11 if competition was not quite so stiff. Hibs released him in April 1959, and although he fixed up with Dumbarton fairly swiftly he failed to settle there and by 1960 his senior career had ended with only 16 outings from his eight years in the game.

BRADLEY, Jimmy

Winger

Born: Greenock, 21 March 1927.
Career: Port Glasgow Rangers, HIBERNIAN 1948, Third Lanark 1951, Shrewsbury, Dumbarton, Gravesend.

■ Jimmy has perhaps the strangest Hibernian career of them all. When asked about his time at Easter Road he must answer 'I played in one game only, the Scottish League Cup Final!' An injury crisis on the eve of the 1950 clash with Motherwell saw Hibs bizarrely draft Jimmy in for a debut that must surely have been as nerve-wracking as it was sensational. Hibernian lost the game 0–3, Bradley was clearly overawed and before the season was out he had left to join Third Lanark. Later he would play in England with Shrewsbury and then back in Scotland with Dumbarton before moving to non-League English football with Gravesend.

BRAZIL, Ally

Defender

Born: Currie, 10 December 1958.
Career: Currie Hearts, HIBERNIAN 1976, Hamilton Accies 1986, Forfar Athletic 1987.

■ A cult hero among Hibernian fans, it would be fair to say that Brazil was not the most skilled footballer during his lengthy stay at Easter Road but was certainly one of the most reliable and popular. His approach to the game was of the no frills variety but he lacked nothing in effort or enthusiasm. Affectionately nicknamed 'Benny' (some said after the bumbling *Crossroads* TV character) he was tall, rangy and his cascading black locks and craggy features all served to make him instantly

recognizable. Manager Turnbull, it is alleged, was not sold on Brazil and it was the influence and persuasion of coach John Lambie that really helped Ally kick-start his career. Eddie Turnbull signed Brazil from Currie Hearts in December 1976 and by 1979 he had made sufficient progress to play in the Scottish Cup Final against Rangers. His debut had come against Aberdeen at Pittodrie in 1977. Ten years as a Hibee followed and although he had only a handful of goals he did score three against Celtic in a bizarre friendly. He was with Hamilton for the 1986–87 season but it was when he moved to Forfar that he found the perfect end to his career. He had five seasons in Angus and then was able to relax and watch his son carve out a career in the game too.

BREBNER, Grant

Midfield

Born: Edinburgh, 6 December 1977.
Career: Manchester United, HIBERNIAN (loan) 1998, Reading 1998, HIBERNIAN 1999, Dundee United 2004.

■ Born in 1977 in Edinburgh, Grant's midfield promise was such that he was capped 18 times by Scotland at Under-21 level. His

apprenticeship was spent with Manchester United but he initially joined Hibs when signed by Alex McLeish on loan at the tail end of the 1998 relegation season. Despite his finest efforts, and an excellent goal against Dundee United, he was unable to help Hibs stay in the Premier League and in the summer of 1998 elected to join Tommy Burns's Reading, with United receiving £300,000 in exchange. The 1998–99 season saw him in fine form for Reading and he scored 10 League goals but decided to return to Hibs, this time on a full-time basis, in the summer of 1999. Slipping into a midfield that could boast the likes of Latapy and Sauzee, Brebner added work-rate to an engine room that was rich in flair. Two moments best encapsulate his time at Hibs. A Scottish Cup hat-trick in a 3–2 win at Dundee United was memorable, and when he was sent off against Hearts in the first half of a fiery Easter Road clash few could have imagined that Hibs would win 1–0 (better still for Grant his red card was rescinded). In October 2000 Grant spent a period on loan to Stockport County in a bid to ensure first-team football. He retuned determined to regain his first-team spot and duly did this when Bobby Williamson took over from Alex McLeish. He joined Dundee United in 2004 and after two seasons on Tayside moved to Australia. He was caught up in a betting scandal in December 2008 when playing with Melbourne Victory.

BREMNER, Des

Defender

Born: Aberchirder, 7 September 1952.
Career: Deveronvale, HIBERNIAN 1972, Aston Villa 1979, Birmingham City 1984, Fulham 1989, Walsall 1990.

■ Desmond George Bremner joined Hibs from Highland League club Deveronvale in 1972. He came from good footballing stock, his uncles George and Hutton having played with Motherwell among others. Des went on to become one of the most versatile and determined performers at Easter Road and enjoyed a lengthy spell with the club before moving to Aston Villa. With Villa he scaled the heights, winning the European Cup and the

English Championship. Des made his Hibs debut against Dundee United in January 1973 and clocked up 11 outings in his first season. He was a vibrant midfield talent, whose powerful shooting always threatened goals, but equally he could be a studious full-back when needed. Thus, with versatility and skill in abundance he became one of the players tasked with taking Hibs beyond the 'Turnbull's Tornadoes' era. Capped by Scotland at Youth, Under-23, League and full international level he had boundless energy and enthusiasm. He made his Scotland debut against Switzerland in a 1–0 win, coming on for Kenny Dalglish. In total Des made 200 League appearances for Hibs and by the late-1970s his was one of the first names on the Hibernian team sheet. He moved to Aston Villa in September 1979 for an impressive £275,000. His career in England took in not only Villa, but also their great city rivals Birmingham. Unusually, he was held in high esteem by both halves of the Birmingham divide. After retiring from playing Des worked for the English PFA and settled in the English midlands. His brother Kevin was a notable player in Scottish Highland League circles.

BREWSTER, Craig

Striker

Born: Dundee, 13 December 1966.
Career: Forfar Athletic 1985, Raith Rovers 1991, Dundee United 1993, Ionikos 1996, HIBERNIAN 2001, Dunfermline 2002, Inverness Caledonian Thistle 2005, Dundee United 2006, Aberdeen 2006. Ross County 2009.

■ The ex-Forfar, Raith and Dundee United striker joined Hibs in July 2001 from Greek side Ionikos. He came with a considerable reputation for neat, clever, forward play and did not disappoint. At a time when Hibernian were blooding a number of youngsters his input was vital. While in Greece he had picked up many good habits including a realization that diet and lifestyle were key to a lengthy career. Alas, his stint with Hibs was cut short as the club slipped into a period of financial cut-backs and he was soon on his way to Dunfermline (he would return to torment

Hibs in the colours of the Pars). Craig had scored the winner in the 1994 Scottish Cup Final for Dundee United against Rangers and must surely have been close to being capped by Scotland. As it was he had enough presence and knowledge of the game to move into management when his playing days were over (he played his last senior game aged 41!) and both Inverness and Dundee United utilized his skills in this capacity. It is worth noting that he played over 500 senior games in Scotland alone with almost 150 League goals to his name.

BROGAN, John

Centre-forward

Born: Hamilton, 9 March 1954.
Career: Blantyre Celtic, Albion Rovers 1973, St Johnstone 1977, HIBERNIAN 1984, Ayr United (loan) 1984, Hamilton Accies 1985, Stirling Albion 1987.

■ John was a £15,000 capture from St Johnstone, where he had been their all-time top goalscorer. Hibs chased long and hard to land this marksman, indeed in 1980, when

Brogan briefly walked out on St Johnstone, Hibs offered £120,000 for his services and were astonished when this was rejected. When that deal collapsed Brogan returned to the fold at Saints and promptly scored seven goals in only nine games. Sadly, his eventual stay with Hibs was short and slightly disappointing, he played in only five League games and even a short loan spell to Ayr United could not kick-start a fruitless spell in Edinburgh. However, his confidence returned away from Easter Road and he later played with Hamilton and Stirling Albion before managing the latter. By the year 2002 he was manager of junior club East Kilbride Thistle.

BROWN, Alistair

Goalkeeper

Born: Irvine, 12 December 1985.
Career: HIBERNIAN 2002, Raith Rovers (loan) 2005.

■ A product of Hibernian's much vaunted youth system, Alistair joined Hibs straight from school and made good progression through the club's ranks. His debut came as a substitute in the 2004–05 season and he was quickly representing Scotland at Under-19 international level, but a 0–5 reversal to Austria dented his confidence somewhat. In 2005 he spent a period on loan with Raith Rovers, but the previous campaign had seen him play in all bar one of Hibs' 36 League fixtures. At 6ft 1in and with an athletic frame he appeared to have all the characteristics required to be a top class 'keeper.

BROWN, Jim

Defender

Born: Edinburgh, 11 August 1950.
Career: Salveson BC, Hearts 1967, HIBERNIAN 1979, Dunfermline 1981.

■ Jim had been a distinguished full-back for Hearts in the late-1960s and 1970s before moving to Hibernian in 1979. Solid and reliable, his claim to fame, however, was due to an event which occured outside of his time in Edinburgh. Jim was on the receiving end of a quite horrendous and sickening tackle by John Pelosi of St Johnstone (this when Brown was briefly at Dunfermline) which ended in a court case. Brown's career at Hibs got off to a fine start, when playing as a midfielder he scored two goals in his early outings, one against Manchester City in the Skol Cup at Tynecastle and one against St Mirren in an Anglo-Scottish Cup tie (the latter on his debut). He played with Hibs for two seasons, in the first of which Hibs were relegated and in the second promoted, so they were exciting years. As mentioned above he then moved to Dunfermline.

BROWN, Jim (2)

Midfield

Born: Musselburgh, 3 October 1953.
Career: Aston Villa 1969, Preston North End 1975, Ethnikos, Portsmouth 1980, HIBERNIAN (loan) 1980, Ghent 1981.

■ Signed initially on a one-month deal in 1980, Jim stayed for longer when it was clear Bertie Auld admired his midfield talents. His time at the club coincided with First Division football and he made 15 outings, scoring one goal. It was confusing that his spell at Easter Road should coincide with that of another Jim Brown (ex-Hearts). This particular Brown version played in Belgium with Ghent and in Greece with Ethnikos. However, he was better known for his spells in England with Preston North End and Aston Villa.

BROWN, John

Goalkeeper

Born: Portobello, 21 February 1915.
Career: Glenburn Rovers, Shawfield Juniors, Clyde 1934, HIBERNIAN 1942, Third Lanark (loan), Dundee 1948.

■ John was a former Scottish Schoolboy international who played for Hibs in the immediate post-war period. He made his Hibernian debut on 4 January 1947 against Morton, a game memorable for the fact that both Turnbull and Smith missed penalties for Hibs. He played in 11 games in the 1947–48 campaign but moved to Dundee in January

1948. By 1950 he was a physiotherapist with Dundee and seemed to have found his true home.

BROWN, John Thomas

Centre-half

Born: Edinburgh, 2 April 1935.
Career: Musselburgh Union, HIBERNIAN 1952, Third Lanark 1956, Tranmere 1961, Hartlepool 1962.

■ John played at centre-half in a rather sensational debut as Hibs lost 4–5 to Partick in December 1952. The likes of Hugh Howie and Pat Ward thwarted his first team ambitions, and when the 5ft 8in youngster spent the 1955–56 season on loan to Third Lanark and managed 23 outings it was clear he was not a bad player at all. Finally, in August 1956 he made his move to Cathkin permanent and he quickly took his tally of Scottish League games to 147. Later in his career he played in the lower reaches of the English game, converted to full-back and nabbed a handful of goals for Hartlepool. An electrician by trade he very nearly joined Motherwell before electing to sign up at Easter Road. While at Towerbank School he had played for Scotland Schoolboys.

BROWN, Scott

Midfield

Born: Dunfermline, 25 June 1985.
Career: Hibernian Youths, HIBERNIAN 2002, Celtic 2007.

■ Scott was perhaps the most notable product of John Park's excellent youth system in the late-1990s and early-2000s. Brown had it all, aggression, power, pace and an eye for goal. There were some who felt he had too much of the former and not enough of the latter. He could appear an extremely abrasive youngster but this masked a wonderful understanding of the game and a huge desire to play to the maximum in every match. He made his Hibernian debut late in the 2002–03 season and scored a glut of goals, including a lovely brace at Livingston. Hibs had him in their sights from around the age of 14 and carefully nurtured this precocious talent. In 2003 he scored in each and every Scotland Under-19 Championship fixture and his stock was rising rapidly. By 2004 he was a Scotland Under-21 international and a regular in the Hibernian first team, playing in the League Cup Final defeat against Livingston. It was clear that he would be a difficult talent to hang onto but Hibs did well to ensure that he at least stayed until a trophy was in the cabinet. Brown could have left for Charlton or Rangers in the run up to the March 2007 CIS Cup Final. As it was he stayed (Kevin Thomson left) and the reward was a thumping 5–1 Final victory over Kilmarnock. Although Rob Jones was the captain for the day he actually had Brown go up the Hampden stairs with him to collect the trophy, thus recognizing Scott's immense contribution in a few short years. In the summer of 2007 the inevitable move came and it is to Hibs' credit that they brought in a fee of £4.4 million from Celtic. He did not look out of place playing with Celtic in high-profile European ties or for Scotland on the international stage.

BROWN, Simon

Goalkeeper

Born: Chelmsford, 3 December 1976.
Career: Lincoln City 1997, Colchester United 1999, HIBERNIAN 2004, Brentford 2007, Darlington 2008.

■ Simon was a tall, powerful English goalkeeper who was rather error prone in his Easter Road career and famously fell out with John Collins. Standing at 6ft 2in and tipping the scales at just over 15st, Simon certainly had a presence between the sticks. He had been a regular at Colchester United when Tony Mowbray took him to Hibernian in 2004. A regular in his first season, he seemed set for a fairly decent Hibs career but was one of the ring-leaders in the player delegation that went behind John Collins's back to complain to chief executive Rod Petrie about Collins's methods. There could only ever be one winner from such an approach and Brown's days at Easter Road were numbered thereafter. He joined Terry Butcher's Brentford in the summer of 2007.

JOHN BROWNLIE — HERO

Full-back

Born: Caldercruix, 11 March 1952.
Career: HIBERNIAN 1966, Newcastle United 1978, Middlesbrough 1982, Hartlepool United 1984, Vasalunds, Berwick Rangers 1985, Blyth Spartans 1986.

■ A gifted full-back, John Brownlie was one of the stars of the Eddie Turnbull era. Speedy, tigerish in the tackle and creative going forward he was a permanent fixture in the Hibs team for nine years. Under-23 caps, full international caps, 211 League outings and, of course, a League Cup-winners' medal were suitable rewards for a player who was, above all else, classy. John was a provisional signing when he was 16 and finally joined when Bob Shankly called him up. He made his Hibs debut at Dunfermline in 1968. His attacking strengths quickly made him one of the best overlapping footballers in the Scottish game. By the early-1970s he was at the peak of his powers, highly sought after and hugely influential for Hibs. With Arthur Duncan patrolling the left-wing and Brownlie dominating the right-wing, Hibs had dangerous and exciting pace when attacking. A League Cup semi-final victory over Rangers at Hampden in November 1972 owed almost everything to his run and shot for the goal, and given that he had netted a brace against Airdrie in the quarter-finals he played a huge part in landing the Cup. Alas, just five days after Hibs had thrashed Hearts 7–0 in the League he broke his leg against East Fife and his season was over. So too was Hibs', and any hopes of adding the League title to the League Cup were gone. When Brownlie came back he was quickly back to his best but other clubs were hovering on the sidelines watching his recovery and waiting to pounce with an offer. They knew of course that Brownlie was made of good stuff. Proof of his talent had come when he played concurrently for the Under-23s and full international sides. Among those who loved watching Brownlie was actor Dougray Scott, a keen Hibs fan, who said of John: '...one of the most graceful players I've ever seen. He was quick, elegant, wonderful at bringing the ball from defence to attack, a great crosser and beautiful passer'. John finally left Easter Road in August 1978 to join Newcastle United in a deal that carried Ralph Callachan from Tyneside to Easter Road. He played 124 matches for the Magpies and was a hugely popular figure at St James' Park. John later played for Middlesbrough, Hartlepool, Berwick Rangers and Blyth Spartans. He was then manager at Cowdenbeath, East Stirling (1983–1998) and Arbroath, returning to East Stirling as caretaker manager in 2008. His nickname at Easter Road – 'Onions' – was apparently a reference to a particularly poor haircut in the late-1960s!

BROWN, Stephen

Midfield

Born: 21 October 1961.
Career: Tynecastle Boys Club, HIBERNIAN 1978, Whitehill Welfare.

■ Steve was signed as an 'S' form when only 15 and had gained Scotland Schools caps at both Under-15 and Under-18 levels. Yet his is a cautionary tale of promise not being realized. He made 18 outings for Hibs between 1978 and 1980 but seldom appeared to be a regular and ultimately left the club to join Whitehill Welfare and the ranks of non-League footballers.

BROWN, Willie

Forward

Career: Edinburgh Thistle, HIBERNIAN 1941, Airdrieonians 1948, Dunfermline 1954, Cowdenbeath 1954.

■ In a career that was stalled by World War Two, Willie made his Hibs debut some five years after signing in a League Cup quarter-final against Airdrie. The match finished 4–4 and clearly Airdrie liked what they saw. By March 1948 he was subject to a £5,000 bid which Hibs accepted having earlier tried to persuade Willie to join Barnsley. He was actually on loan to Arbroath at the time he left Hibs, and the former Leith Docks worker was just 25 when he departed. He enjoyed a lengthy spell at Broomfield before bringing the curtain down on his career in Fife. There was little shame in failing to cut the mustard at Hibs in the late-1940s as the club was collecting a fine array of forward talents.

BRUCE, Alexander T.

Forward

Career: HIBERNIAN, Ayr United 1949.

■ Alexander joined Hibs in the summer of 1948 as an amateur and his only outing came on 2 April 1949 when Hibs were beaten 2–0 at Paisley in a match made famous by one Bobby Johnstone making his Hibernian debut. That was Alex's single game as a Hibee. He joined Ayr United in October 1949 and scored two goals in three Second Division matches for the Honest Men before drifting from the public eye.

BRUCE, Willie H.

Goalkeeper

Born: Broxburn.
Career: Westerton Amatuers, HIBERNIAN 1948.

■ Willie was a pig-farmer who drifted into football almost by accident rather than by design. The club handbook said of Bruce: 'Works six and a half days a week and plays for Hibs the other half'! It was a bizarre arrangement and one which not surprisingly did not work out. He played against Raith Rovers in April 1951, then had outings against Hearts and Third Lanark at the start of the next season. However, with Tommy Younger and Jimmy Kerr on the scene his chances of making the grade at Easter Road were severely limited. He slipped rather quietly out of the spotlight and out of football.

BUCHANAN, Archie

Wing-half

Career: Edinburgh Thistle, HIBERNIAN 1945, St Mirren 1957, Cowdenbeath 1959.

■ Archie Buchanan was one of the great 'unsung' heroes of the post-war Hibernian side which won three Championships. A Hibee for over a decade when Hibs were arguably the best side in Scotland, he lent an enviable amount of energy and commitment to that team. At 6ft tall, but little over 11st, Archie was lithe and quick. Signed in 1943 from Edinburgh Thistle he rather handily lived round the corner from Easter Road and was a joiner by trade. Archie made his debut in wartime football as an inside-left. When football returned to normality in the 1946–47 season Archie was in the Hibs team from the start. Hibs' opening game was at home to Queen of the South and amazingly the Hibees won 9–1. Archie made it the perfect 'debut' by scoring in the rout. He started the season in quite scintillating form and had goals in the

opening three League Cup ties to boot. When Hibs won the 1948 title no player made more League appearances than Archie and he was an integral part of the 1951 and 1952 Championship-winning teams too. In all, Archie played 205 League games for Hibernian, which was no mean feat in an era when games were less frequent than today. In moving from an inside-forward to wing-half he proved his versatility. He had recovered from injuries such as a cartilage operation during his time in Edinburgh, proving his determination and athleticism. With 264 senior games in Scotland and his clutch of medals, he must be considered extremely unlucky not to have earned any representative honours. Arguably his leg break in 1954 hampered his international hopes.

BUCHANAN, John

Centre-forward

Born: Cumbernauld, 3 January 1935.
Career: Edinburgh Waverley, HIBERNIAN 1954, Raith Rovers 1961, Newport County 1961.

■ A red-head, Jock (as he was popularly known) started with Edinburgh Waverley before arriving at Hibs in 1954. This former pupil of David Kilpartick's School was an apprentice painter when Hibernian lured him to Easter Road and quickly impressed with his commitment. A scoring debut in a 2–1 win over Raith Rovers in October 1954 suggested good things to come, but the ultimate irony in Raith being his first victims came when he moved out of Easter Road to the Kirkcaldy-based club. For all he was with Hibernian for seven seasons he made only 13 outings, but a five-goal return was better than many players. By season 1961–62 he was a Rovers player but he would ultimately head to Wales and Newport to keep his senior career moving (with seven goals in 31 outings).

BURRIDGE, John

Goalkeeper

Born: Workington, 8 December 1951.
Career: Workington Town 1969, Blackpool 1971, Aston Villa 1975, Southend United (loan), Crystal Palace 1978, QPR 1980, Wolves 1982, Derby County (loan), Sheffield United 1984, Southampton 1987, Newcastle United 1989, HIBERNIAN 1991, Newcastle United 1993, Scarborough 1993, Lincoln City 1993, Aberdeen 1993, Dumbarton 1994, Falkirk 1994, Ayr United 1994, Manchester City 1995, Notts County 1995, Darlington 1995, Grimsby 1995, Northampton 1996, Queen of the South 1996, Scarborough 1996.

■ How to condense the career of one of the game's greatest nomads? Perhaps it is sufficient to dwell on his time at Easter Road and merely refer the reader to the list above to summarise his career. John joined Hibernian in 1991 when he was 39 years old. He was described in the match programme as a model professional and his tee-total, non-smoking lifestyle allied to a punishing fitness regime ensured he was able to make the most of his considerable experience (his career began in 1969). John played 65 League games for Hibs and starred in the League Cup Final over Dunfermline in 1991. Those who played with him recall a non-stop chatterbox who was unnervingly fit and not averse to the odd practical joke. Given his previous list of clubs there was no great expectation that he would be in Edinburgh for any significant length of time...and so it proved. For all his wanderlust he clocked up a staggering 700 appearances in the senior game.

BYRNE, Gordon

Defender

Born: Edinburgh, 30 December 1963.
Career: Salveson BC, HIBERNIAN 1980, Broxburn 1983.

■ A couple of substitute outings were the sum total of Gordon's time as a Hibee. His debut came against St Johnstone in December 1980 but he was unable to build upon the experience and left Hibs in the summer of 1983.

BYRNE, John

Inside-forward

Born: Glasgow, 20 May 1939.
Career: Pollok Juniors, Preston North End 1958, Hamilton, Queen of the South 1960, Tranmere 1961, HIBERNIAN 1962, Barnsley 1963, Peterborough 1965, Northampton 1967.

■ Recruited from Tranmere Rovers in June 1962, John was a left-sided player who could play either inside or outside-left. He got among the goals quite quickly for Hibs and had counters against St Mirren, Motherwell, Dundee and Queen of the South before October was out. He flitted in and out of the team thereafter and played in the infamous League Cup semi-final reversal against Morton at Ibrox in 1963, and shortly afterwards he was on his way to Barnsley. His Hibs career had brought five League goals in 23 starts. John played four games for Queen of the South and once for Hamilton prior to moving to Tranmere.

C

CAIG, Tony

Goalkeeper

Born: Whitehaven, 11 April 1974.
Career: Carlisle United 1992, Blackpool 1999, Charlton Athletic 2001, HIBERNIAN 2001, Newcastle United 2003, Barnsley (loan) 2004, Vancouver Whitecaps 2006, Gretna 2007.

■ Signed by Alex McLeish as back up to Nick Colgan, Tony found first team openings rather limited. When he did step into the breach he gave the impression of being a very solid and dependable goalkeeper. He started the 2002–03 season in possession of the number-one jersey but lost his place following the painful 1–5 thrashing Hibs endured at Hearts in the second game of the campaign. Although he made three more outings that season it was clear that he was no longer likely to oust Colgan. In January 2003 Tony moved to Newcastle United, and he would have short stints with Barnsley and Gretna before departing Britain to try his luck in Canada. That said, he was back with Gretna shortly before their demise.

CAIRNS, Jimmy

Left-back

Born: Bonnybridge.
Career: Dunipace Thistle, HIBERNIAN 1946, Third Lanark 1952, St Johnstone 1953.

■ It was from Dunipace Thistle in 1946 that Hibs recruited 5ft 11in Jimmy. He was making solid progress when he broke his leg in 1949 and this badly hampered his career. By the time he had regained full fitness Hibs were on their way to the 1950–51 title and Jimmy was on his way to Third Lanark in January 1952. His Hibernian career had brought 55 appearances. Jimmy had made his Hibernian debut against Falkirk at Easter Road in March 1948, a Championship-winning season for the club. He was then a regular in the second half of the 1948–49 season taking over from the redoubtable Davie Shaw. It is fair to say that Jimmy was a 'hard' character; evidenced by the fact that on the occasion in

which he broke his leg he actually completed the game against Rangers. Given that he tried to play on after breaking a jaw against Queen's Park Strollers a few years earlier he was something of an 'iron man'.

CALDWELL, Gary

Central-defender

Born: Stirling, 12 April 1982.
Career: Newcastle United, HIBERNIAN (loan) 2002, Coventry City (loan), Derby County (loan), HIBERNIAN 2003, Celtic 2006.

■ Lured to Leith by Donald Park while Franck Sauzee was in charge of Hibernian, Gary stayed for the tail end of the 2001–02 season in a loan deal from Newcastle United. During that stay he played well enough to play for Scotland against France and Nigeria. However, there was little chance of Hibernian being able to offer him comparable or suitable terms when Newcastle United, from whom he was on loan, offered him an attractive contract. So back to Tyneside he went after 11 very useful outings. Nevertheless, Newcastle were unable to find a regular first-team spot for Gary and so he had various loan spells when he returned to Tyneside from Easter Road. However, in 2003 Hibernian and Bobby Williamson, in a firm statement of intent, signed Gary permanently. Caldwell himself was delighted with the move and said at the time: 'I have made no secret of the fact that I love it at Easter Road, I've always said that should the opportunity arise to return here I would jump at it.' He was able to score five times in 88 matches before he joined Celtic – sadly on a free transfer. It was ironic that he should sign for Celtic, given that he had been with their Boys Club as a schoolboy. His departure from Hibs was controversial in that some sections of the Hibernian fans questioned his ability to play at Easter Road when it was common knowledge that he would be moving to Celtic at the end of the season (he signed a pre-contract agreement in January 2006 but elected to stay at Hibs until the end of the season). But Caldwell was nothing if not professional and gave Hibs sterling service before his move to Glasgow.

CALLACHAN, Ralph

Left-midfield

Born: Edinburgh, 29 April 1955.
Career: Heart of Midlothian 1971, Newcastle United 1977, HIBERNIAN 1978, Morton 1986, Meadowbank 1986, Berwick Rangers 1988.

■ This slim, left-sided midfielder made over 500 senior appearances and represented both Hearts and Hibernian in Scottish Cup Finals. A cultured player, he had both excellent close control and good vision. When he ticked so too did most of the teams he played in. His career followed fairly common Edinburgh roots. From Tynecastle Boys Club he went to Hearts and between 1974 and 1977 he was a first-team regular. In February 1977 he joined Newcastle United but he returned to the capital with Hibernian in August 1978. His move to Easter Road saw popular full-back John Brownlie head for Newcastle as part of a swap deal. This could have proved awkward for Callachan but his composed style of football quickly won over any doubters. In August 1979 he scored one of the great Easter Road goals when slaloming through the Dundee defence before rounding

the 'keeper to net. He had a single game for Morton in the 1986–87 season before settling with Meadowbank and then Berwick Rangers. Off the field Ralph was a great friend of Jackie McNamara and they ran a public house together.

CAMERON, Alex

Centre-half

Born: Leith, 5 October 1943.
Career: St Bernards, HIBERNIAN 1961, Oldham Athletic 1964.

■ Alexander Ramsey Cameron was snapped up from St Bernards 'A' in July of 1961. However, despite a couple of runs in the team (he played a dozen games in 1962–63 and three the next season) he was never able to fully establish his first-team credentials. A move to Oldham in May 1964 saw him converted into a right-back and he made 15 appearances for the Latics in that position.

CAMERON, Ian

Midfield

Born: Glasgow, 24 August 1966.
Career: St Mirren 1983, Aberdeen 1989, Partick Thistle 1992, HIBERNIAN 1996, Raith Rovers 1997, Clyde 1998, Clydebank 1999, Partick Thistle 2000, Airdrie 2001.

■ Ian made his League debut for St Mirren in 1983 and won a Scottish Cup medal in 1987. He moved to Aberdeen two years later for £300,000 and almost instantly added a League Cup-winners' badge. He joined Partick in the early-1990s and helped the Glasgow club stay in the Premier League. He became a Hibernian player in August 1996 but played only 17 League games as a Hibee (and eight of those as a substitute) before moving to Raith Rovers in July 1997. Thereafter his career saw stints in the lower leagues with a variety of clubs, two of whom sadly folded. Perhaps the most productive of those was while with Ian McCall at Clydebank and that certainly played a factor in his joining Airdrie in 2001 following the collapse of the Steve Archibald rescue package and the appointment of Ian McCall as

Diamonds manager. With well over 400 senior games in Scotland Ian was a vastly experienced and very competent footballer.

CAMPBELL, Colin

Centre-forward

Born: Benbecula, 1 December 1956.
Career: Hutcheson Vale BC, Dundee, HIBERNIAN 1978, Dundee United 1980, Airdrie 1981, Meadowbank Thistle 1983.

■ Colin was a 5ft 11in centre-forward who joined Hibs in August 1978. He made his debut ironically enough in the Highlands – against Inverness Thistle – and was a strong and direct leader. His first League outing was in a 3–2 win at Motherwell and with a considerable sense of occasion he reserved his first goal for the Edinburgh derby of March 1979 when Hibs and Hearts drew 1–1. Although he started out with that traditional Hibernian nursery of Hutcheson Vale, it was Dundee who had initially offered him terms. However, he failed to take to life at Dens Park and left without

having made a senior appearance, also leaving in order to study at Edinburgh University. Lured away from academia, he played one of his best games for Hibernian in the 1979 Scottish Cup Final against Rangers, coming very close to landing the Cup for Hibs. Nevertheless, by the 1981–82 season he was leading the Airdrie attack against Hibs.

CAMPBELL, John

Left-half

Career: Musselburgh Union, HIBERNIAN 1953, Merchiston Thistle, Raith Rovers 1957.

■ A left-half who came to Hibs from Musselburgh Union in 1953, John played just two games for Hibs. Both came at the end of the 1953–54 season, his debut in a 3–0 win over Aberdeen at Easter Road (when Willie Ormond scored twice) and his last game just a week later in a 2–2 draw at home to Rangers. A bricklayer by trade, he had attended Craiglockhart and Tynecastle schools as a youngster and as a youth was with Slateford Athletic before making the switch up to Musselburgh Union. From Hibs he went back to juvenile football with Merchiston Thistle but Raith Rovers lured back to the senior ranks in June 1957.

CAMPBELL, Ross

Forward

Born: Galashiels, 3 July 1987.
Career: HIBERNIAN 2004.

■ Ross came through the Hibernian youth system and was offered a full-time contract in 2004. He caught the eye when he scored a last-minute winner in a friendly against Middlesbrough in July 2007 but thereafter found first-team openings somewhat limited, and as the 2008–09 season got into full swing he was very much on the fringes of the first team.

CANNING, Martin

Defender

Born: Glasgow, 3 December 1981.
Career: Clydebank, Ross County 1999, Gretna 2005, HIBERNIAN 2008.

■ Martin was signed by Mixu Paatelainen on transfer deadline day February 2008 following his release from Gretna who were sliding towards administration. Martin was 26 years old when he joined Hibs on a 15-month deal. Although hampered by an ankle injury while at Gretna, he was nevertheless their record signing at £60,000 and the Borderers had high hopes of him. He made a solid debut at Falkirk when Hibs won 2–0 there in February 2008. Standing at 6ft 2in it was always likely that he would make a useful central-defender.

CARROLL, Pat

Outside-left

Born: Bridge of Allan, 23 October 1957.
Career: Sauchie BC, HIBERNIAN 1974, Raith Rovers 1979, Falkirk 1982, Bo'ness United 1983.

■ Raised in Tullibody, 5ft 7in winger Pat joined Hibs as a 16-year-old in 1974. He was an 'S' form signing and was recruited on the strength of having given a wonderful display for

Scotland Schools against their English counterparts at Wembley. His first outing as a Hibee came in the 1974–75 season as Hibs defeated Dundee United 3–1 at Tannadice. Although he made sporadic first-team outings over the next five seasons, he was unable to command a regular starting spot and moved to Raith Rovers in 1980. He spent four seasons at Kirkcaldy before ending his senior career with Falkirk.

CARSON, Tom

Goalkeeper

Born: Alexandria, 26 March 1959.
Career: Vale of Leven, Dumbarton 1979, Dundee 1984, HIBERNIAN (loan) 1987, Partick Thistle 1987, Queen of the South (loan) 1987, Dunfermline (loan) 1987, Raith Rovers 1992.

■ Tom joined Hibs on loan from Dundee in 1987 in a goalkeeping emergency and played in just a couple of games. A solid 'keeper, he enjoyed a lengthy career in the Scottish game which began in season 1979–80 and did not end in a playing sense until 1993–94. There was a degree of success in his career and he experienced promotion with Dumbarton, Dundee and Raith Rovers. He also won the Challenge Cup with Dundee in 1990. Much of his career centred on the Vale of Leven area. He started out with the junior football club there and maintained strong links with Dumbarton throughout his career. Indeed, by 2001 Tom was putting his considerable experience to good use as manager of Dumbarton at their new 'Rock' stadium but he resigned in May 2002.

CAUGHEY, Mark

Centre-forward

Born: Belfast, 27 August 1960.
Career: Linfield, HIBERNIAN 1986, Burnley (loan) 1987, Hamilton 1987, Motherwell 1987, Ards 1988, Bangor City.

■ Mark was part of the initial Northern Ireland squad for the Mexico 1986 World Cup Finals. Indeed, he was with the squad in America when Hibs chairman Kenny Waugh flew over to secure his signature. Alas, in 14 games as a Hibee he failed to find the net once. He then went on loan briefly to Burnley before joining Hamilton Accies where he was much more successful, indeed in the 1987–88 season he scored 10 First Division goals for the Lanarkshire club. He had a brief stint back in the Premier Division with Motherwell but again drew a blank. Later he returned to Northern Ireland to continue his career and he was last heard of working as an officer in the Royal Ulster Constabulary.

CHARNLEY, Jim 'Chic'

Midfield

Born: Glasgow, 11 June 1963.
Career: St Mirren 1982, Ayr United 1984, Pollok Juniors 1986, Clydebank 1987, Hamilton Accies 1988, Partick Thistle 1989, St Mirren 1991, Bolton Wanderers (loan) 1992, Djurgården 1992, Partick Thistle 1993, Dumbarton 1995, Dundee 1996, HIBERNIAN 1997, Clydebank (loan) 1998, Partick Thistle 1998, Kirkintilloch Rob Roby 2001, Partick Thistle 2002.

■ Mere words can hardly do service to the character that was 'Chic' Charnley. Cheeky, irrepressible, talented and flawed…Charnley was a complex character, who came to Hibernian during the Jim Duffy era and was harnessed as well as could be expected. One of the great nomads of the Scottish game, Jim was as well-loved by supporters as he was feared by officialdom. Very gifted, he was also extremely voluble and seldom away from trouble or controversy. His sendings off were frequent and rarely boring! Listing his clubs is in itself a major task, but few would disagree that he brought flair and vibrancy to any club he served. His was a natural brand of talent and it was welded to a sharp temper and a willingness to speak his mind which often brought him into conflict with authority. Nevertheless, he brightened up the scene at Easter Road. Chic scored one of the all-time great Hibs goals at the start of the 1997–98 season when he scored in the opening League game against Celtic. It was the first match of the season, he was 40 yards or so out, and scored with an audacious lob moreover, Hibs

Jim Charnley

won 2–1…quite a memory. He could not sustain such heroics and his work-rate was never really ideal in the modern game. Yet for all his lack of reliability it has to be said he played in over 300 senior games and netted over 50 goals…not a bad haul by any midfield standards. Chic was a noted Celtic fan and had even 'guested' for them in a testimonial match at Manchester United.

CHISHOLM, Gordon

Defender

Born: Glasgow, 8 April 1960.
Career: Sunderland 1978, HIBERNIAN 1985, Dundee 1987, Partick Thistle 1992.

■ Gordon enjoyed an excellent apprenticeship with Sunderland which culminated in a League Cup Final appearance in 1985. By one of football's strange quirks he then turned out for Hibernian in the Scottish equivalent in the same calendar year. Signed from Sunderland for £60,000, Gordon had played over 200 appearances for the Roker Park club, but he managed just a couple of seasons with Hibs before moving to Dundee. He cut out a steady career coaching in Scotland, starting out with Partick Thistle as an assistant and progressing via Clydebank (who folded) to Ross County and then Queen of the South. He finally became a manager in his own right in Dumfries and steered them to the 2008 Scottish Cup Final.

CHISHOLM, Ross

Full-back

Born: Irvine, 4 January 1988.
Career: HIBERNIAN 2004.

■ Another product of Hibernian's successful youth system, Ross made his debut in April 2007 at St Mirren and was signed on a two-year contract a few days later while still only 19. The man who signed Chisholm was John Collins and he said of the promising youngster: 'He came in at full-back and looked as if he had been playing that position for 10 years. Spraying the ball about with great composure he did everything I expected of him.'

CLARK, Andrew

Midfield

Born: Glasgow, 31 March 1963.
Career: HIBERNIAN 1980.

■ During the 1980–81 season Hibernian's sole aim was to achieve promotion from the First Division. They did so with some ease but used a huge number of players in the course of what was at times a stressful season. Clark made his only competitive Hibernian appearance in a second leg League Cup tie against little Alloa Athletic, when Hibs had won the first leg tie and the second leg was a mere formality. He came on as a replacement for a notable Hibee in Peter Cormack. Less than 2,500 paid to watch this low key game.

CLARK, Willie

Full-back

Born: Cockenzie, 27 September 1918.
Died: 28 December 2008.
Career: Bonnyrigg Rose, HIBERNIAN 1939, St Johnstone 1953.

■ Signed in 1939 from Bonnyrigg Rose, Willie made his senior bow for Hibs in a 0–0 draw at Hamilton Accies in January 1947. The task of establishing himself at Easter Road was a daunting one, for Hibs had both Hugh Howie and Davie Shaw vying for full-back berths with Jock Govan. But Willie stuck to the task diligently and was making good progress when he suffered a broken nose and bad leg injury in quick succession. He did, however, come back and played in one of the most memorable Easter Road matches. When Hibs beat Celtic 4–1 in February 1950 the match was noted for two things, firstly Edie Turnbull scored all four Hibs goals (three of them were penalties) and secondly Clark played most of the game in goal, having taken over from Tommy Younger when the score was only 1–1. Remarkably, that was Clark's only appearance of the season! His best run in the first team came in the 1952–53 campaign when he played in 13 consecutive League games, and it was in that season that he scored his only senior goal (in a 5–1 win over Clyde). In early-July 1953 he moved to St Johnstone in the Scottish B League and made

32 appearances for the Perth club before being freed in April 1955.

COLGAN, Nick

Goalkeeper

Born: Drogheda, Ireland, 19 September 1973.
Career: Chelsea 1992, Bournemouth 1998, HIBERNIAN 1999, Barnsley 2004, Sunderland 2008.

■ An Irish goalkeeper, Nick was signed by Alex McLeish and joined Hibs on the eve of their return to the Premier League in the wake of Bryan Gunn's serious injury. Born in Drogheda, he worked hard to win over a rather sceptical Hibs support. Week by week he improved and his shot-stopping in the 2002–03 season finally cemented his place in the list of excellent Hibernian goalkeepers, indeed it was sufficient to earn him a place in the Republic of Ireland squad. Signed from Bournemouth, after a top-class apprenticeship at Chelsea, Nick made his debut in a CIS tie at Clyde in August 1999. As well as having served Ireland at Under-21 level Nick played with Brentford and Reading on loan. A very approachable player off the field, Nick had an ability to relate to the fans. Occasionally he displayed a wonderful temper that would see him hoof the ball clean out of Easter Road in a rage, most notably against Hearts when he conceded a last-minute penalty to Ricardo Fuller. He was sent off in the aftermath and this gave his rival Tony Caig a run in Bobby Williamson's side. He later returned to England and played with Barnsley, and, surprisingly as a veteran, Sunderland.

COLLINS, Derek

Full-back

Born: Glasgow, 15 April 1969.
Career: Renfrew Waverley, Morton 1987, HIBERNIAN 1998, Partick Thistle (loan) 2000, Morton 2001, Gretna 2005.

■ With well over 600 senior games to his name it is clear that Derek Collins was one of the fittest players of his generation. Seldom troubled by injury he established a reputation as a solid and dependable full-back whose ability to overlap was a decided asset. Derek joined Morton in 1987 from Renfrew Waverley and spent over a decade with the Greenock club before Alex McLeish signed him for Hibernian. Ostensibly a full-back, he could also play in midfield and he quickly grabbed a quite sensational goal for Hibs in a Scottish Cup tie against Dunfermline. He contributed solidly to the First Division promotion campaign and the

subsequent Premier League season. A short loan spell at Partick and a stint in Cyprus with Sliema Wanderers preceded a return to Morton. The money that flowed into Gretna via Miles Brookson saw Derek move to the borders and he helped them win the Scottish Third Division and then the Second in quick succession. But Greenock and Cappielow Park was Derek's spiritual home and he was back at Morton in 2008 as manager Davie Irons's right-hand man.

COLLINS, John

Left-midfield

Born: Galashiels, 31 January 1984.
Career: Hutcheson Vale BC, HIBERNIAN 1984, Celtic 1990, Monaco 1996, Everton 1998, Fulham 2000.

■ One of the truly great Hibernian post-war players, John Angus Paul Collins joined Hibs as a youngster from Hutchison Vale Boys Club. A native of Galashiels, he quickly revealed himself to be a talented and stylish left-sided midfielder. His debut came when aged just 16 in a pre-season match against Manchester City, and when he made his League bow he was only 17. Capped by Scotland at youth level he rapidly moved through the grades and won a clutch of Under-21 caps while at Easter Road. A League Cup Final appearance in 1985 was followed by the Scottish Young Player of the Year award in 1988 and there were times when he was by far the silkiest player on the books at Hibs. With his cultured left foot and dedication to improving his physique he was the perfect young professional, and Hibernian benefited greatly from his input. He earned his first Scotland cap while at Hibs (making a scoring debut against Saudi Arabia). His subsequent move to Celtic in 1990 for £990,000 was an early example of a transfer tribunal being required to settle a fee. It was also somewhat ironic that Hibs collected the League Cup within a year of John's move to Glasgow. It was his move to Monaco in 1996 that perhaps turned Collins from a very good player into an exceptional one. In France he picked up very good habits both in terms of diet and physical

preparation. These were aspects of lifestyle that he would carry into his international and managerial career. His Scotland career ran from 1988 to 1999 and provided him with 12 goals from 58 caps. In 2006 John returned to Easter Road as manager, a surprise appointment to replace Tony Mowbray who had left to take over at West Bromwich Albion. Six months into his managerial career (Hibs was his first post) he guided the club to a famous League Cup Final win over Kilmarnock. However, all was not well in the Hibernian camp and a delegation of players went to club chairman Rod Petrie to complain about Collins's methods. Claim and counter-claim came to the fore, but it would be difficult to imagine that Collins's methods were

ROBERT COMBE — HERO

Wing-half/inside-forward
Born: Edinburgh.
Career: Inveresk Thistle, HIBERNIAN 1941, Dumbarton 1957.

■ Robert 'Bobby' Combe was an integral part of the hugely successful Hibernian team of the immediate post-war era. There are many who concede that mention of the 'Famous Five' is harsh on Bobby for he was every bit as influential as the five forwards who grabbed the headlines. An incredibly versatile player, Bobby succeeded in whatever position Hibs chose to field him over an impressive 16-year career. He was able to boast of having played in every position except in goal. Signed in 1941 by Willie McCartney when only 17 years old, he was the epitome of the old head on young shoulders and scored on his debut against Hearts at Tynecastle. It was to be a famous game in Hibs' history for also making his debut that day was Gordon Smith. Shortly afterwards Combe made his own little piece of history as he managed to bag four in the sensational 8–1 demolition of Rangers. Indeed, in season 1941–42 he scored an astonishing 27 goals, a remarkable haul for an inside-forward who had a liking for playing deep. His position in the Hibernian attack was lost when the club decided he should be fielded as a midfield enforcer, and they compensated him financially (to the tune of £2 per week) to make up for the harm this did to his international prospects as an inside-forward. Bobby was capped three times in 1948 – against England, Belgium and Switzerland – and added two League caps in the following year. He was fondly remembered at international level and this brought him a further Scottish League cap in 1954. Combe's lengthy career allowed him to talk of there being two 'Famous Fives'. While acknowledging that Smith, Johnstone, Reilly, Turnbull and Ormond were the prime recipients of the label, he was adamant the forward line of Gordon Smith, Leslie Johnstone, Alex Linwood, Eddie Turnbull and Willie Ormond was equally worthy of praise. Bobby stayed with Hibs until retiring at the end of the 1956–57 season. He won three League championship medals and at one stage was club captain. In 1959 he spent a short time in charge of Dumbarton, even donning the Sons jersey in an emergency. When he retired from football he worked with Scottish Gas in their marketing department.

anything other than those of a player who had played at the very highest level and expected high standards from his charges. In December 2007 he resigned 14 months into the job saying he had taken Hibs as far as he could. He returned to football management in December with Belgian club Sporting Charleroi.

CONNOLLY, John

Forward

Born: Barrhead, 13 June 1950.
Career: Glasgow United, St Johnstone, Everton 1972, Birmingham City 1976, Newcastle United 1978, HIBERNIAN 1980, Gateshead 1982.

■ A superb young inside-forward with St Johnstone and then Everton, John came to Hibernian in the twilight of his career. He stayed for 15 months and played a key role in Hibs' First Division promotion in 1981. In all, his 49 outings brought eight goals which was no mean return for a veteran forward who liked to play tucked in behind a traditional centre-forward. John won Scotland Under-23 caps while with Saints (whom he joined from Glasgow United) before leaving for Everton in a £70,000 deal in March 1972. The Merseysiders beat off stiff challenges from Rangers and Aberdeen for Connolly's services. It is interesting to note that it was former Hibernian legend Willie Ormond who sold Connolly to Everton. Several years later John's name came to prominence in the Scottish game when as a manager he rekindled the fortunes of Queen of the South. He was Second Division Manager of the Year in 2002.

CONROY, Mike

Centre-forward

Born: Johnstone, 31 July 1957.
Career: Johnstone Burgh, Celtic 1978, HIBERNIAN 1982, Blackpool 1984, Wrexham 1986, Orient 1987, Cork City 1989.

■ Between 1982 and 1984 Mike played in 31 matches for Hibernian and grabbed two goals. The first of those two was a neat finish against Kilmarnock in a 2–0 win at Rugby Park. Mike scored a couple of League Cup goals and a League goal in the 1983–84 season before moving on to Blackpool in August 1984. He later played with both Wrexham and Leyton Orient.

COOPER, Neil

Utility

Born: Aberdeen, 12 August 1959.
Career: Aberdeen 1974, Barnsley 1980, Grimsby Town 1982, St Mirren 1983, HIBERNIAN 1989, Aberdeen 1991.

■ A composed and fairly constructive central-defender, Neil joined Hibs in August 1989 from St Mirren for £30,000. His initial impact was to lend a degree of composure to the Hibernian defence. He eventually lost out to the central defensive pairing of Gordon Hunter and Tommy McIntyre and returned to Aberdeen (his first senior club) for £20,000 in September 1991. Neil was born in Aberdeen in 1959 and had started his career at Pittodrie. Very much a fringe player there, he joined Barnsley in January 1980 and played at Oakwell and Grimsby Town before moving to St Mirren. A Scottish Cup winner at Paisley, he was a regular in their defence. Keen on coaching, Neil later managed Forfar Athletic.

COUSIN, Allan

Inside-forward

Career: Alloa YMCA, Dundee 1955, HIBERNIAN 1965, Falkirk 1969.

PETER CORMACK   HERO

Inside-forward

Born: Edinburgh, 17 July 1946.
Career: Tynecastle Athletic, HIBERNIAN 1962, Nottingham Forest 1970, Liverpool 1972, Bristol City 1976, HIBERNIAN 1980, Partick Thistle 1982.

■ Peter joined Hibs as a 16-year-old straight from schoolboy football and stayed with Hibs for eight years making an inside-forward role his own. Skilful, energetic and creative, he thoroughly endeared himself to the Hibs faithful so much so that he returned to Easter Road for a second spell. Fiercely competitive, he fell foul of several referees (he was sent off four times as a Hibee) and was always capable of brightening up the dullest afternoon. Peter Barr Cormack, to give him his full Sunday name, made his Hibs debut against Airdrie at Broomfield in November 1962 and scored. As a 17-year-old he netted for Hibs against the mighty Real Madrid – arguably the most famous football team in the world. He could turn his hand to goalkeeping and twice (against St Mirren and Hearts) deputised for the injured Willie Wilson. He gained Under-23 caps while a Hibee and scored in a 3–1 victory over England in 1967 (Pat Stanton was also in the victorious Scottish side). Among his many highlights was a hat-trick at Aberdeen in a 6–2 Hibernian triumph.

He moved to Nottingham Forest for £80,000 in 1970 (having made 294 outings for Hibs) but it was a transfer to Liverpool that really 'made' his reputation. He joined just as Liverpool were emerging as one of Britain's greatest-ever club sides and thrived under the managerial spell of Bill Shankly. In all, Peter won two Championships, two UEFA Cup medals and an FA Cup badge in his time on Merseyside. He then moved to Bristol City, where in an Anglo-Scottish Cup tie against Hibs he contrived to get sent off. Eddie Turnbull then brought him back to Hibs. A short stay followed before he spent three years managing Partick Thistle, two years in Cyprus, three back coaching at Hibs then another two in Cyprus. He later managed Morton in 2001 and combined that role with running a painting and decorating business in Edinburgh, but his most bizarre appointment had come at Cowdenbeath where he was only in charge for a matter of days.

■ Signed by Bob Shankly, who had been his manager at Dundee when the Dens Parkers won the League in 1962, Cousin was a thinking player who combined goalscoring with great teamwork. He cost Hibernian £15,500 and could have made his debut against Dundee but for the fact that Hibs had just beaten Hamilton Accies 11–1 away from home and were thus reluctant to change a winning team. As it was, Hibs lost 3–4 to Dundee and Cousin stepped out against Stirling Albion the following week. Capped by Scotland at Under-23 and League international level he was unfortunate not to earn a full cap in what was a distinguished career and one that was fitted around being a school-master. He had been Dundee's Player of the Year just five months prior to his switch to Easter Road and totalled 141 goals for Dundee in 379 matches. Alan joined Dundee in 1955 and broke into their team late in the 1955–56 term. By the 1957–58 season he was Dundee's top marksman with 15 goals in only 31 starts. He scored against Hibs in December 1958 and netted four goals at Hibernian's expense in the very next season. Between 1957 and 1962 he was a regular, always returning double-figures to the 'goals for' column. He was in the Dundee team that lost the 1964 Scottish Cup Final and had played in the Dens Park big European nights. He was a part-time player with Hibs, teaching in an Alloa school, but still displayed enough class to be a valuable team member. He scored two goals in 89 League games for Hibs and then played just a handful of matches for Falkirk, but his overall total of 105 Scottish League goals from just under 400 matches shows his true worth.

COWAN, Steve

Centre-forward

Born: Glasgow, 17 February 1963.
Career: St Mirren, Aberdeen 1979, HIBERNIAN 1985, Motherwell 1987, Albion Rovers 1990, Portadown 1990.

■ Steve was something of a protégé of Alex Ferguson's who never quite made the huge impact he seemed capable of. Raised in East Kilbride, he starred with Claremont High

School and was an 'S' form signing for St Mirren. When Ferguson moved to Aberdeen he returned to take Cowan with him and the youngster gradually entered the fray at Pittodrie. Nevertheless, in a side dominated by quality forwards he struggled to impose himself and joined Hibs when the chance occurred in 1985. He settled quickly at Easter Road and had 19 League goals in the 1985–86 season, and what is more he had helped the club reach the League Cup Final. He joined Motherwell in October 1987 but did not have quite the same explosive start there. From the Premier League and Motherwell it was into the basement League and Albion Rovers. As his career wound down he commuted to Ireland to play with Portadown.

CRAIG, Tommy

Midfield

Born: Glasgow, 21 November 1950.
Career: Banks o'Dee, Aberdeen, Sheffield Wednesday 1969, Newcastle United 1974, Aston Villa 1978, Swansea 1978, Carlisle United 1982, HIBERNIAN 1984.

■ Small, red-headed, fiery Tommy was an excellent little player who had guile, passion and skill in his game. He won several Scotland Under-21 caps and one full international cap.

He made his Aberdeen debut in 1967 and when he was sold to Sheffield Wednesday in 1969 he became the first teenager to be sold for a six-figure sum. Signed by Hibernian in the winter of 1984 from Carlisle United, Tommy was a midfield schemer who had in all fairness probably played his best football at the likes of Sheffield Wednesday and Newcastle United before joining Hibernian. Certainly he had captained Newcastle in a League Cup Final. He would fit in 11 games for the Hibees and gave a calm, assured performance on his debut, which came in a derby against Hearts. But his main role was to act as assistant to John Blackley the then Hibs boss. When John Collins was appointed Hibernian manager it was Tommy Craig that he recruited as his right-hand man. By this stage Craig had served a number of clubs in a back-room capacity.

CRAWFORD, Stevie

Striker

Born: Dunfermline, 9 January 1974.
Career: Rosyth Recreation, Raith Rovers 1992, Millwall 1996, HIBERNIAN 1997, Dunfermline 1999, Plymouth Argyle 2004, Dundee United 2005, Aberdeen 2005, Dunfermline 2006, East Fife 2008.

■ A lithe, intricate forward, Stevie began his career with Rosyth Recreation and served notice of his talent when scoring on his debut for Raith Rovers in the Fife derby against Dunfermline. He won promotions, scored in a League Cup Final and won his first Scotland cap with Raith before joining Millwall. Millwall were bossed by Jimmy Nicholl at the time and the genial Irishman had been Crawford's boss for most of his career at Raith Rovers. Although a prolific marksman for the London side, he soon found himself to be an asset in a side that was financially strapped. He duly signed for Hibs for £400,000 in 1997. His goals in the First Division campaign were vital to the club's promotion and his speedy play and clever distribution made him a very popular player at the club. He was top scorer in the promotion campaign. He moved to Dunfermline in 1999 and proved a most able striker for the Pars, indeed he was First Division Player of the Year in 2000 thus repeating the feat he achieved in 1995 when at Raith Rovers. He was a Scottish

Cup Finalist with both Dunfermline and Dundee United and spent a brief spell with Aberdeen before returning to Fife.

CROPLEY, Alex

Midfield

Born: Aldershot, 16 January 1951.
Career: Edina Hibs, HIBERNIAN 1967, Arsenal 1974, Aston Villa 1976, Newcastle United (loan) 1980, Toronto (US League), Portsmouth 1981.

■ Born in Aldershot in January 1951, 5ft 8in Alex James Cropley was one of the key elements of the famous 'Turnbull's Tornadoes' side. A gifted, slight and crafty inside-forward he burst into the team in the 1968–69 season and by the early-1970s was a vital part of the Hibernian side. Alex made his debut against St Mirren in March 1969 and for a couple of seasons flitted in and out of the first team from the sidelines. He served notice of his talent on the opening day of the 1971 season when he scored against Hearts in a 2–0 win at Tynecastle and he repeated his goalscoring exploits some two years later when he scored in the 7–0 massacre. Clearly he enjoyed the derby games for he also scored twice when Hibernian beat Hearts 3–1 in January 1974. When he left Hibs to join Arsenal in December 1974 for £150,000 he had played 118 League games and scored 27 goals. Highlights of Alex's Easter Road career include winning a League Cup badge and playing in a Scottish Cup Final. His debut for Arsenal was quite odd in that it came at Carlisle United, the nearest English League ground to Scotland! Sadly, he was injured in scoring against the same opponents a few weeks later and this hindered his Highbury career. After 34 games for the Gunners he joined Aston Villa in 1976 and went on to play in over 70 matches for them, winning a League Cup badge in the process. Capped by Scotland at Under-23 and full level (two caps) Alex returned briefly to Hibernian when he was 31 following a stint in Canada with Toronto Blizzard and then a short spell at Portsmouth. After retiring he ran a pub that bore his name and later worked in the taxi industry in Edinburgh.

CUTHBERT, Ian

Outside-right
Career: Edina Hibs, HIBERNIAN 1960.

■ Ian was registered with Hibs as an amateur on 5 July 1960. He then signed professional terms on 9 January 1961. Season 1961–62 saw him make his only outing for the club and he was given a free transfer at the end of the 1962–63 campaign.

CUTHBERTSON, Johnny

Centre-forward

Career: Craigmark Juniors, HIBERNIAN 1939, Third Lanark 1949, Stenhousemuir 1953.

■ A 1939 signing from Ayrshire junior club Craigmark, 'Cubby' become a Hibernian hero with his dashing forward play. Although his career was badly hampered by the Second World War he gave notice of his talents during that period, particularly in season 1940–41 when he had 27 League goals in the same number of matches. His impressive haul included five in the 7–1 defeat of Falkirk and four in a 5–2 win over Queen's Park. When peace-time football returned he burst into the team in the 1946–47 season and bagged five goals in only nine League starts, and the following season he had ten goals in only nine starts! The high point of his three-season career at Easter Road was scoring the opening goal in the 1947 Scottish Cup Final against Aberdeen, which was timed at just 30 seconds. Alas, Hibs lost that Final. He had more joy with a late goal in the 1947–48 season, scoring in the final minute of a 1–0 win over Rangers that gave Hibs a new record gate at that time of 53,000. Capped by the Scottish League against their English counterparts in 1948, he moved to Third Lanark in July 1949. While he scored frequently for Thirds he was more prolific at Stenhousemuir where he had 22 goals in the 1954–55 season. After hanging up his boots in April 1957 he worked as a civil servant, completing his service in Wetherby.

D

DACQUIN, Frederic
Midfield

Born: Bordeaux, France, 23 September 1978.
Career: Paris St Germain, HIBERNIAN 2002, Rouen 2003, Dunfermline 2006, Dundee 2007.

■ A clever young French midfielder, Frederic made his Hibernian bow in a 2–2 draw at Dundee in April 2002. He struggled to gain a regular start at Hibs and returned to France with Rouen. However, clearly he had enjoyed his taste of Scottish football and he was back in January 2006 with Dunfermline. From Fife Freddie moved to Dundee, and in March 2008 he scored the only goal when Dundee beat Dunfermline 1–0 at East End Park.

DALGLISH, Paul
Forward

Born: Glasgow, 18 February 1977.
Career: Celtic 1995, Liverpool 1996, Newcastle United 1997, Norwich City 1999, Blackpool 2002, Linfield 2003, Modena 2004, Livingston 2005, HIBERNIAN 2006, Houston Dynamos 2007, Kilmarnock 2008.

■ The son of Scotland legend Kenny Dalglish, Paul had the unenviable task of trying to emulate one of the greatest players to grace the European, let alone Scottish, game. He was on the books of the likes of Celtic, Liverpool, Newcastle and Norwich without any real success. He then tried his luck away from these shores playing with Linfield and Modena. When he joined Livingston in the 2005–06 season he made a genuine impact playing in almost half of Livi's games and scoring his first goal against Hearts. The January transfer window saw Hibs step in and the slightly built but clever Dalglish made his bow at Rangers. Despite a goal against Kilmarnock, Paul was unable to settle with Hibs and he was off on his travels soon afterwards. He did, however, come back to Scotland with Kilmarnock in 2008 following a spell in America with Houston Dynamos. He had a clutch of Under-21 caps from his days at Newcastle and Norwich City.

D'ARCY, Tommy
Centre-forward

Born: Edinburgh, 22 June 1932.
Career: Edinburgh Waverley, Armadale Thistle, HIBERNIAN 1952, Bournemouth (loan) 1954, Southend 1956, Queen of the South 1958, Stranraer 1959.

■ A centre-forward, Tommy was signed in 1952 from Armadale Thistle where he had earned Scottish Junior caps. His progress at Easter Road was rapid. His big chance came at the start of the 1953–54 season when Lawrie Reilly was in dispute with Hibs and not playing. D'Arcy scored against Falkirk in two 1953 League Cup ties and had a hat-trick in the quarter-final thrashing of Third Lanark (8–0 on aggregate). But five League Cup goals were not added to in the League and when Reilly returned D'Arcy slipped down the pecking order and was overtaken by the likes of Mulkerrin, Moran and Thomson as deputies. D'Arcy gradually realised his future lay elsewhere and in September 1954 moved to Bournemouth on loan. Alas, he did not fit in their either and returned to Hibs only to move to Southend in the summer of 1956. As his career wound down he had a spell with Queen of the South and then a more productive stint with Stranraer where he was among the goals for a season.

DAVIDSON, Kenny
Midfield/winger

Born: 14 February 1952.
Career: Loanhead Mayflower, HIBERNIAN 1970, Dunfermline 1974, Meadowbank 1975.

■ Signed in August 1970, Kenny had to overcome a compound leg-fracture to make his mark with Hibernian. A talented winger, his debut was memorable in that it came in a Fairs Cup tie against Malmö. His first goals came early in the 1970–71 season when he bagged a brace against St Mirren. He had another two in a Scottish Cup win over Forfar and was an established part of the first-team pool by the end of that season with four goals in 11 League matches. However, he managed only a handful of games the following season and as a left-winger lost out to the more experienced Arthur Duncan. From Hibs it was on to Fife with Dunfermline and then back to Edinburgh with Meadowbank Thistle

DAVIN, Joe

Inside-forward/full-back

Born: Dumbarton, 13 February 1942.
Career: Edinburgh Thistle, HIBERNIAN 1959, Ipswich Town 1963, Greenock Morton 1966, Dumbarton 1967.

■ Joseph James Davin, a Scottish Schoolboy international, played in a handful of matches for Hibs between 1959 and 1963 without ever being a regular. It is a measure of how embryonic the European competition was at this time, for while Joe struggled for League outings he was a regular in European ties! His official Hibs debut came in the penultimate match of the 1959–60 season when he turned out at Ayr United in a 2–1 defeat for Hibs. However, earlier in the same season he had played in the floodlit friendly against the British Army. He moved to Ipswich in July 1963 and went on to make 77 outings in two seasons for the Suffolk club. As his career progressed he switched from inside-forward duties to playing at full-back and it was in that position that he served both Morton and Dumbarton.

DAVIS, Joe

Left-back

Born: Glasgow, 22 May 1941.
Career: Shettleston Juniors, Third Lanark 1961, HIBERNIAN 1964, Carlisle United 1969.

■ Joe signed from Third Lanark in November 1964 and it is doubtful if Hibs have had a more prolific goalscorer in defence. He netted his first goal for Hibs in a League Cup tie against Alloa in September 1965 and by August 1967 had 31 goals to his name! The bulk of his goals came from the penalty spot, indeed at one stage he converted 29 out of 34 spot kicks (sadly of his misses two came in vital derbies against

Hearts). In short, Davis was remarkably consistent and he is credited with an astonishing run of 273 consecutive games for Hibernian (he was ever present in 1965–66, 1966–67, 1967–68 and 1968–69). He was a League Cup Finalist with Hibs in the 1968–69 season but in December 1969 he made the short trip over Hadrian's Wall to sign for Carlisle United. He did not score for the Cumbrians which rather suggests that they had another penalty taker.

DEITRICH, Klaus

Central-defender

Born: Austria, 26 June 1974.
Career: Casino Salzburg, Grazer AK, HIBERNIAN 1998, Carinthia, Dynamo Dresden, FC Magdeburg, Dresdner, St Mirren 2002, Lask Linz.

■ A former Austrian Under-21 international, Klaus joined Hibs when the club were in the First Division under Alex McLeish. He played only one competitive match for Hibs, a shock 2–0 defeat at Love Street against St Mirren. Ironically he did return to Scotland in the 2002–03 season and appeared in one First Division match for St Mirren. Alas, that game ended in an ignominious 4–0 defeat at home against Inverness and Klaus never again pulled on a Saints shirt.

DE LA CRUZ, Ulises

Wing-back

*Born: Bolivar, Ecuador, 8 February 1974.
Career: Aucas, Deportivo Universatari Quito 1997, HIBERNIAN 2001, Aston Villa 2002, Reading 2006.*

■ Ulises came to Scotland as an Ecuadorian international (he had over 50 caps), when Hibernian made him their record signing in the summer of 2001 at £700,000. He quickly made a huge impact with his surging runs and clever use of the ball. His golden day came in the Hibernian–Hearts derby at Easter Road in October 2001 when he scored both Hibs' goals in a 2–1 win, including a quite stunning first-minute opener. Those two goals were his only

counters for the club and in the summer of 2002 he played with some style for Ecuador in the Japan & Korea World Cup Finals and was arguably that nation's finest player. His form was sufficient to earn him a £1.5 million transfer to Aston Villa in July 2002 and he later played with Steve Coppell's Reading in the FA Premiership.

DEMPSIE, Allan Henry

Defender

Born: Bellshill, 5 November 1982.
Career: HIBERNIAN 1999, Elgin City 2003, Ayr United 2008.

■ Allan broke into the first team during Bobby Williamson's reign but was only able to muster six outings in two campaigns before moving on. He made his debut as a substitute in a 4–0 win at Motherwell in April 2002 and started in the final two games of the campaign against Dundee and St Johnstone. His travels took him to Elgin City where he established himself as a useful left-back in the Third Division. His elder brother Mark also played for Hibs and they were at the club together.

DEMPSIE, Mark

Defender

Born: Bellshill, 19 October 1980.
Career: HIBERNIAN, St Mirren 2003, Dumbarton 2005.

■ A central-defender, Mark made his debut in 1999 against St Mirren. Given that Hibs won the match despite playing much of it with 10 men it was an impressive bow. Mark had been linked with Hibs from the age of nine when Martin Ferguson lured him to the club as a schoolboy signing. It was Jim Duffy who signed him officially as a professional and by that stage the club had high hopes for the Lanarkshire youngster. Sadly, he was plagued by injury and this hampered his progress. He also had the misfortune to play at the heart of the defence that lost 5–1 to Hearts at Tynecastle Park in 2002. He never really recovered from the humbling at Hearts and was off to St Mirren to ply his trade in the First Division. In the 2002–03 season he was one of 36 players the Paisley club used, Andy Dow and Klaus Dietrich being other ex-Hibees at St Mirren that season.

DENNIS, Shaun

Centre-half

Born: Kirkcaldy, 20 December 1969.
Career: Lochgelly Albert, Raith Rovers 1988, HIBERNIAN 1997, Raith Rovers 2001.

■ A towering central-defender, Shaun had been a mining apprentice when Raith Rovers offered him an escape into football. He seized it with both hands and gave Rovers seven years' excellent service before moving to Hibs in January 1997. But it would be fair to say that Shaun is essentially associated with Raith and his journeys away from Kirkcaldy were never as passionate as his times at Rovers. By the early-1990s he was a regular at Stark's Park and he helped Raith win promotion and the Scottish League Cup in a memorable time for the club. He joined Jim Duffy's Hibs for £200,000 in the 1996–97 season but was missing for much of the following campaign when Hibernian slipped to relegation. His First Division experience was extremely useful when Hibs battered their way out of that League and Shaun chipped in with three goals in a campaign that hardly wavered. In February 2001, having slipped from favour at Easter Road, he returned to Raith and First Division football (following a trial period with Swindon Town), and there was a short stint with Brechin City in 2004 but he was soon back at Raith. With 422 games in the Scottish Leagues it is clear that Shaun was both respected and reliable.

DOBBIE, Stephen

Centre-forward

Born: Glasgow, 5 December 1982.
Career: Rangers 1999, HIBERNIAN 2003, St Johnstone 2005, Dumbarton (loan), Queen of the South 2006.

■ A prolific young marksman in the Rangers reserves, Stephen came to Hibernian with a considerable amount of promise. When he scored in the thrilling League Cup win over Rangers it seemed he was destined to be a Hibs star, and two earlier goals in a friendly against Sunderland had been equally spectacular. Alas, he appeared to be overweight and never quite stamped his authority on Hibs. A move to St Johnstone saw him begin to rebuild his career and a prolific spell on loan to Dumbarton furthered his options. He then moved to Queen of the South and was a frequent marksman in Dumfries scoring in the Scottish Cup run that took them to the Final in 2008.

DOCHERTY, Peter

Midfield

Born: Edinburgh, 3 October 1962.
Career: Tynecastle BC, HIBERNIAN 1979.

■ Sadly, Peter's career must be filed under the 'one game wonder' heading. It was his misfortune to find himself at Easter Road in the 1979–80 relegation season. He was a substitute in the final game of that season, which, rather fittingly, Hibs lost 1–0 at home to Partick Thistle.

DODS, Darren

Centre-half

Born: Edinburgh, 7 June 1975.
Career: Hutcheson Vale BC, HIBERNIAN 1992, St Johnstone 1998, Inverness CT 2004, Dundee United 2007.

■ Born in Edinburgh in 1975, Darren joined the Hibees in August 1992 from Hutcheson

Vale BC. After impressing in the youth system, and helping the club win the BP Youth Cup, he made his full debut in May 1995 against Kilmarnock and in the following two seasons edged his way further into the first team picture. Despite winning five Scotland Under-21 caps and displaying enormous enthusiasm and will to win he could never quite make himself an automatic selection. With that in mind he moved on to St Johnstone in the summer of 1998 and while a regular at Saints he tasted relegation in 2002. After a couple of seasons in the First Division he headed north to help Inverness' Premier League quest.

DONALD, Graeme

Midfield

Born: Stirling, 23 September 1978.
Career: Gairdoch United, HIBERNIAN 1991, Stirling Albion 1998, Stenhousemuir 2001.

■ A very versatile youngster, Graeme Still Donald joined Hibs in 1991 and was soon breaking into the first team. In his first season he scored three goals in just five games and a promising career beckoned. Unfortunately he was not quite able to build on that start. What went wrong is quite hard to identify. He gained Scotland Under-21 caps in 1992 and made over 30 outings for Hibs but was never really an automatic selection. He later moved on to Stirling Albion and Stenhousemuir.

DONALDSON, Ally

Goalkeeper

Career: Tynecastle BC, Dundee 1964, Falkirk 1972, Dundee 1976, HIBERNIAN 1981, Dundee 1981, Raith Rovers 1980.

■ Ally was a quality goalkeeper of many clubs. His stint at Hibs was a short-term fix during an injury crisis and his Easter Road career was limited to all six League Cup matches at the start of the 1981–82 season. Ultimately Donaldson was better known for his two stints with Dundee and a spell at Falkirk which brought over 100 appearances. Ally made over 300 outings for Dundee and was in their side that won the League Cup Final.

DONALDSON, Clayton

Forward

Born: Bradford, 7 February 1984.
Career: Hull City 2002, Harrogate Town 2002, Scarborough 2003, Halifax 2004, York City 2005, HIBERNIAN 2007, Crewe Alexandra 2008.

■ Clayton signed on a 'Bosman' transfer from York City where he had grabbed 42 goals in 86 matches. His Hibernian career was initially productive; including as it did a hat-trick against Kilmarnock. With a touch of the bizarre he scored his first goal against Falkirk and then contrived to get himself sent off. Sadly, he struggled to make any impression during Mixu Paatelainen's reign and left for Crewe having failed to build on his good start at Easter Road.

DOUMBE, Mathias Kouo-

Defender

Born: France, 28 October 1979.
Career: Paris St Germaine, HIBERNIAN 2001, Plymouth Argyle 2004.

■ It was under the reign of Bobby Williamson that young Mathias came to prominence at Easter Road. After a fairly nervous start he began to impose himself on the team and he even netted against Celtic as he added attacking prowess to his undoubted defensive flair. When he followed Williamson to Plymouth in 2004 there was a fair deal of regret in the Easter Road stands for here was a player with a sound temperament and an athletic physique who looked as if he could have been a mainstay of the Hibernian side for some time to come. Hibernian supreme Rod Petrie had tried his level best to secure Doumbe long-term, noting that: 'We offered him a three-year deal which, in the current climate, represents a long-term deal offering a high level of security.'

DOW, Andy

Midfield

Born: Dundee, 7 February 1973.
Career: Dundee 1990, Chelsea 1993, HIBERNIAN 1996, Aberdeen 1998, Motherwell 2001, St Mirren 2002, Arbroath 2003, Raith Rovers 2004.

■ Signed from Chelsea for £125,000, Dow, an industrious and busy player, made an instant

Andy Dow

ARTHUR DUNCAN — HERO

Left-winger/wing-back
Born: Hamilton, 5 December 1947.
Career: Falkirk High, Partick Thistle 1965, HIBERNIAN 1970, Meadowbank 1984.

■ Nicknamed 'Nijinksi', after the famous racehorse, Arthur Duncan was one of the great speed merchants of his era. Supremely fit he proved to be a wonderful signing for Hibs and played with the club for 14 years. No Hibernian player can boast of having made more appearances. Add his previous five seasons with Partick and the three he squeezed in at Meadowbank and it is clear to see why he was so popular in his career.

Arthur joined Partick straight from school and made his Thistle debut with a story to recall. Alex Hamilton of Dundee was his direct opponent and proceeded to hand the young Duncan a complimentary stand ticket with the advice 'use this son because you won't get a kick of the ball this afternoon!' Fortunately, Arthur was not put off by this gamesmanship and made sufficient progress to convince Hibs boss Willie McFarlane to sign him.

At just £35,000 he proved to be a genuine bargain. Arthur came to Hibs on 17 January 1970 and wowed fans up and down the country with his sprinting, trickery and effective crossing. Not surprisingly, the fully committed and non-stop Arthur quickly won over the Hibs support. He played in many memorable matches but had the misfortune to score the own goal when Hibs lost the Scottish Cup Final replay to Rangers in 1979. Arthur would win the League Cup while at Hibs, and he also had Drybrough Cup and League Cup Final appearances. A competent international, he had his first League international cap in September 1967 when he was still with Partick, and he added an Under-23 cap in 1971. By 1975 he was winning the first of his six full Scotland caps. All of his six caps came in a 114-day period when Willie Ormond, formerly an Easter Road outside-left himself, was in charge of the international side. Awarded a testimonial match by Hibernian, Duncan is Hibs' all time top appearance maker. His career in the senior game shows the following:

- League: 577 appearances (plus 23 as sub) – 106 goals *(Hibernian League record 448 games – 73 goals)*.
- League Cup: 107 appearances (plus seven as sub) – 25 goals.
- Scottish Cup: 56 appearances (plus two as sub) – eight goals.
- Europe and others: 40 appearances (plus two as sub) – eight goals.

Arthur Duncan's career at Hibs ended when he broke a collar bone in an East of Scotland Shield match against Meadowbank Thistle. Hibs were so enraged by the injury that they declined to treat the tournament as a fitting stage for first-team players thereafter and the competition slipped into terminal decline. After concluding his wonderful career at Easter Road Arthur played with Meadowbank before becoming a full-time chiropodist, a profession he had pursued throughout his Hibs career.

impact. A former Scotland Under-21 cap, Andy had both pace and strength, key assets for a full-back in the modern game. Prior to joining Hibs he had played with Dundee and Bradford City. He left Hibs in 1998 after two and half years in Edinburgh to join his former boss Alex Miller at Aberdeen. Stints with Motherwell and St Mirren were also squeezed in before his senior career ended. He retained an interest in the game after retiring and had a spell as assistant manager at Dundee North End. He was made redundant by Motherwell when the club went into administration in April 2002.

DUCHART, Alex

Outside-left

Born: Falkirk, 3 May 1933.
Career: Petershill Juniors, HIBERNIAN 1951, Third Lanark (loan) 1955, Southend United 1956, East Fife 1957, Dumbarton 1959, Falkirk 1960, Brechin City 1964.

■ Recruited from the ranks of Glasgow junior football, Alex played three matches in the 1953–54 season. He was not able to establish himself in a position that Willie Ormond dominated, and although a loan spell at Third Lanark in the 1955–56 season yielded six goals in 19 matches he left Hibs to join Southend United in England. In June 1957 he joined East Fife, and although he could not help them stay in the top League he was a prolific marksman in the Second Division with 22 goals in 32 matches. This earned him a move to Dumbarton and after two seasons there he joined Falkirk and helped them achieve promotion. Nicknamed 'The Duke' by the Brockville faithful, he was freed in 1963 and went to non-League football in England but in 1964 was back north with Brechin City.

DUNCAN, Bobby

Defender

Born: 27 April 1945.
Career: Bonnyrigg Rose, HIBERNIAN 1961, East Fife 1971.

■ Consider the statistics. A senior player for 13 seasons and a goalscorer in just one match…a European tie! It was in November 1967 that Hibs famously beat Napoli 5–0, and Bobby got the opening goal. He had come to Hibernian as an inside-forward and in truth took a few seasons to break into the first team. However, by the mid-1960s he was a regular. He then began to fall from favour as the decade ended, particularly following a leg-break suffered against Celtic in 1968. In July 1971 he moved to East Fife where he had three solid seasons.

DURIE, Gordon

Forward

Born: Paisley, 6 December 1965.
Career: Hill of Beath, East Fife 1981, HIBERNIAN 1984, Chelsea 1986, Tottenham Hotspur 1991, Rangers 1993, Heart of Midlothian 2000.

■ A magnificent striker, Gordon joined Hibs from East Fife and proved to be John Blackley's finest signing for the club. Powerful, direct, strong in the air and an astute user of the ball he fitted well into Hibernian's team. He started his senior career in midfield with East Fife but in season 1983–84 scored 16 goals to help the Bayview club win the Second Division. In nine First Division matches he scored seven goals and this convinced Hibs to sign him. He had eight goals for Hibs in his first campaign and six the following season. As news of his burgeoning talent spread he was sold in May 1986 to Chelsea for £381,000, a record fee at the time for both clubs. It was a great pity that he left when he did for he was far from the finished article. As it was Chelsea, Tottenham and Rangers benefited hugely from his array of talents. His 17 goals in 47 matches for Hibs were laced with examples of the talents he would later exploit to the full.

E

EASTON, Jim

Centre-half

Career: Drumchapel Amateurs, HIBERNIAN 1959, Dundee 1964, Queen of the South 1971.

■ A centre-half, James Howatson Easton was signed from Drumchapel Amateurs in 1959. By season 1960–61 he was an integral part of the Hibernian defence. In December 1963 he was in the Scotland Under-23 side that played Wales. Sadly, his window of opportunity only lasted a couple of seasons and he was sold to Dundee in October 1964. He had six very solid seasons at Dens Park before winding down his career at Queen of the South in the early-1970s. Jim was a League Cup semi-finalist with both Hibs and Dundee and a European semi-finalist with the same two clubs, but alas he was not able to manage a Final appearance of any note.

EDGE, Roland

Full-back

Born: Gillingham, 25 November 1978.
Career: Gillingham 1997, HIBERNIAN 2003, Hull City 2004, Folkestone 2006, Maidstone United 2008.

■ A Bobby Williamson signing, Roland had energy and enthusiasm aplenty but failed to win over a critical Hibs support. He was allowed to return to English football after one fairly low key season at Easter Road. It would be fair to point out that he lost much of his career to injury. Speed and a willingness to get stuck in were his key attributes but it was felt that his positional sense was not all that it could have been. From Edinburgh he moved back to the south-east of England where he was clearly most at home.

EDWARDS, Alex

Winger

Born: Dunfermline, 14 March 1946.
Career: Dunfermline Athletic 1961, HIBERNIAN 1972, Arbroath 1978.

■ The wonderfully passionate and fiery Alex Edwards joined Dunfermline when he was 15 and made his debut against Hibernian having just turned 16 five days earlier. He excelled with the Pars, winning a Scottish Cup medal (against Hearts), featuring in several European matches and attracting interest from several big English clubs. Here was a little man with a big heart and a real footballing brain. Hibs signed Alex when he was 24, after no fewer than 12 seasons at Dunfermline. They picked up a real bargain at £13,000, especially considering Leeds United boss Don Revie had tried to secure the player's services a little over a year earlier for considerably more. Any questions about Edwards's longevity or temperament were answered by his staying at Hibs for the best part of 10 seasons. Under Turnbull Edwards thrived and won a League Cup-winners' medal and Dryburgh Cup badges. This was hardly surprising as he had been capped by Scotland at Amateur, Under-18, Under-21 and League levels. Indeed, it is probably fair to say that only the presence of Celtic's Jimmy Johnstone and Willie Henderson of Rangers prevented him gaining a full cap. Aged 32 Alex finally left Hibs and joined Arbroath briefly before retiring from the game. Known for his spicy temper, Alex was nevertheless one of the key men in Turnbull's fine side of the early to mid-1970s. He played in almost 400 Scottish League fixtures, and one solitary Under-23 cap was scant reward for such a talented footballer.

ELLIOT, David

Winger/wing-back

Born: Glasgow, 13 November 1969.
Career: Celtic 1987, Partick Thistle 1990, St Mirren 1991, Falkirk 1995, HIBERNIAN 1997, Partick Thistle 1999.

■ David began his senior career with Celtic but like many youngsters there struggled to gain regular football. He moved to Partick Thistle, then St Mirren and Falkirk, and acquired a solid reputation as a good journeyman

EVANS, Gareth

Forward
Born: Coventry, 14 January 1967.
Career: Rotherham United, HIBERNIAN 1988, Partick Thistle 1996, Airdrie 1998, Alloa Athletic 2000.

■ Gareth John Evans was the kind of busy forward that fans and fellow players could greatly admire. Never one to shirk a tackle, Evans was the perfect foil to more skilled colleagues and proved extremely popular at Easter Road. Signed in February 1988 from Rotherham United, Gareth made the conversion from English Third Division football to the Scottish Premier League in a gradual rather than instant fashion. He scored on his debut against Dundee but took time to settle and at one stage was keen to return to England. So keen indeed that he welcomed loan spells with Stoke City and Northampton Town. A Hibernian League Cup winner in 1991, Gareth's confidence seemed to soar thereafter and with his electric pace and busy manner he was a handful for defences. After leaving Hibs he played with Partick Thistle, Airdrie and Alloa. He even contrived to get himself sent off against Hibs while with Airdrie! By 2008 he was helping Hibernian with their youth system.

footballer. It was Jim Duffy who took 5ft 9in David to Hibs in January 1997 and he featured fairly regularly until Alex McLeish arrived. Although he played sporadically under Alex his Easter Road career was drawing to a close and he played only eight games in the promotion-winning season before moving on. His final club was Partick Thistle but injuries were beginning to impact his career.

F

FALCONER, Duncan

Inside-forward

Career: Edinburgh Norton, HIBERNIAN 1959.

■ Signed from Edinburgh Norton in 1959, this strong inside-forward was just under 6ft and able to use his physique to good advantage. Nevertheless, he made a slow start to his Hibs career. In the 1959–60 season he made his breakthrough into the first team but 10 games produced no goals. Such a return ensured that he only played in five League fixtures of the next campaign, but quite surprisingly he topped the Hibernian scoring charts in the 1961–62 season, grabbing 12 League goals. It proved a false dawn. Over the next couple of seasons he barely managed to add to that total, although he did enjoy hitting the winner in a Fairs Cup tie against Utrecht. Not surprisingly, his Hibs career somewhat fizzled out and in April 1964 he was granted a free transfer. After playing with Hibernian he emigrated to Australia but returned to join the police force in Tunbridge Wells, Kent.

FARM, George

Goalkeeper

Born: Slateford, 13 July 1924.
Career: Armadale Thistle, HIBERNIAN 1946, Blackpool 1948, Queen of the South 1960.

■ George Neil Farm was one of Scotland's finest post-war goalkeepers, and that he also proved himself to be a sound manager merely added to his solid reputation. However, from a Hibernian perspective the feeling is that he was a great talent that slipped through the club's fingers. Born in Slateford in 1924, he joined Hibernian from Armadale Thistle and played in seven matches in the League-winning side of 1947–48. When George joined Hibs he found that Jimmy Kerr and John Brown were vying for the position of goalkeeper. The more experienced Kerr, who had been with Hibs since before the war, was the man in possession. But when both were ruled out injured in the Championship-winning season of 1947–48 George had his chance. He made his Hibs debut away to Third Lanark in February 1948 and played well in a 4–1 win. From here until the end of the season he held his place and Hibs won all bar the last, and meaningless, League fixture against Dundee. What is more, Hibernian advanced to the Scottish Cup semi-final only to unluckily lose 1–0 to Rangers at Hampden Park. At the start of the 1948–49 season, as Hibs sought to defend their title, Farm found that Kerr had been reinstated as goalkeeper and thus asked away. His brief, but quality-laden, showings ensured that there were a clutch of clubs interested, and in September 1948 Farm headed for the bright lights of Blackpool. The seaside club were a leading light in the English game and paid Hibs £2,700 for Farm, an impressive total for a man who had yet to reach double figures in his career. Joining Blackpool when he did meant that Farm featured in what became the legendary 'Matthews FA Cup Final' when the great English winger starred in a thrilling 4–3 Cup Final triumph over Bolton Wanderers. Farm flourished at Blackpool, even scoring a goal in one game, and kept goal for Scotland 10 times, most notably at Wembley in a 4–1 defeat. As a Blackpool regular he made a staggering 462 appearances between 1948 and 1958. In 1958 Blackpool pulled off a shrewd piece of business when they sold Farm for £3,000 (£300 more than they had paid for him!). But Farm proved a sound acquisition for Queens and became player-manager and then sole manager in a career in Dumfries that ran from 1958 to 1964. Later he would spend three years in charge of Raith Rovers. But it was his stint in control of Dunfermline between 1967 and 1970 that caught the eye and in 1968 he steered them to the Scottish Cup Final and a

3–1 win over Hearts. When his playing career ended he worked at Radio Forth and then with the Lighthouse Service. Sadly he died in July 2004.

FARMER, Jim

Full-back

Career: Stonehouse Violet, HIBERNIAN 1978.

■ A full-back, Jim joined Hibs in June 1978 from Lanarkshire Junior club Stonehouse Violet. As this was the club that had given Scottish football Tom Forsyth there were high hopes of Jim. The lad who hailed from the Stenhouse district of Edinburgh made his Hibernian debut as a substitute in the final game of the 1978–79 season against Rangers at Easter Road which Hibs won 2–1. The following season ended in relegation from the Premier League and Jim played in the opening match of the season – also against Rangers – and at Partick Thistle in September. Hibs lost both games and Jim was freed shortly after relegation was confirmed.

FARRELL, David

Midfield

Born: Glasgow, 29 October 1969.
Career: Oxford United, HIBERNIAN 1988, Partick Thistle 1996, Airdrie 1997, Stranraer 2001, Albion Rovers 2003.

■ David was signed as a 19-year-old in December 1988 from Oxford United. A gritty midfielder, he stayed at Hibernian for a few years and was something of a mainstay in the side of 1993–94. That was fortuitous timing as Hibernian reached the League Cup Final in October and David played his part that day. A Scotland Under-18 cap, he made his Hibs debut against Aberdeen in 1990 but rather flitted in and out of the team before moving to Partick Thistle, by which time he had amassed 110 League outings in his six years at Easter Road. He later played with Airdrie when Hibernian were in the First Division.

FELLINGER, David

Midfield

Born: Edinburgh, 6 June 1969.
Career: Hutchison Vale BC, HIBERNIAN 1985, Cowdenbeath 1994.

■ David was signed as a 16-year-old by John Blackley from Hutcheson Vale BC, despite the attentions of Hearts, Dundee United and East Fife. He made his debut in the 1988–89 season against Aberdeen in a League Cup tie. Over the following two seasons the Edinburgh-born forward began to increase his presence in the first team but a complicated leg-break in 1992 virtually ended his Hibs career. In October 1994 he moved to Cowdenbeath after proving himself in the non-League ranks with Craigroyston.

FENWICK, Paul

Centre-half

Born: Canada, 25 August 1969.
Career: Birmingham City, Dunfermline 1995, St Mirren 1995, Greenock Morton 1998, Raith Rovers 2000, HIBERNIAN 2000.

■ A tall, quite elegant centre-half, Paul enjoyed what could perhaps be described as an effective career; albeit one that ended strangely. After a faltering start at Dunfermline he made his big breakthrough at First Division St Mirren where a series of commanding performances caught the eye. He moved to Morton in 1998 when the Greenock club was under the rather unorthodox and controversial chairmanship of Hugh Scott. Fenwick, like many others, fell out with Scott and at one point was almost lost to the game, but he managed a few outings at Raith Rovers and then Alex McLeish made him a Hibernian player. For three seasons he was a mainstay of the Hibs defence, playing in the Scottish Cup Final and generally performing admirably. In the 2001–02 season he even popped in three goals. But when cash became tight at Easter Road he refused to budge wage-wise and sat out his career on the sidelines with two entire seasons of non-activity (thus saving the club from paying appearance money). The big Canadian international won a Gold Cup medal in 1999 and also turned out for Canada against Scotland at Easter Road!

FINDLAY, Billy

Midfield

Born: Kilmarnock, 29 August 1970.
Career: Kilmarnock BC, HIBERNIAN 1987, Kilmarnock 1995, Ayr United 1998, Queen of the South 1999, Sligo Rovers, Kilwinning Rangers, Maybole Juniors.

■ William McCall Findlay was in essence an Ayrshire boy and this was reflected in his career. Born in Kilmarnock, Billy joined Hibs from Killie Boys Club and in truth made more of a name for himself when returning to Kilmarnock than he had with Hibs. Like several Hibs players at that time who showed promise he was a Scotland Under-21 international. When Billy moved to Kilmarnock, it was in a swap-deal for Andy Millen. From Killie it was on to Ayr United where he earned local fame when he scored a vital goal for them that saved their First Division status at the expense of Partick Thistle in a 'do-or-die' clash at Firhill.

FINNEGAN, Willie

Inside-forward

Career: Bo'ness Cadera, HIBERNIAN 1937, Dunfermline 1950.

■ Recruited in April 1937 from Bo'ness, William Jordan Finnegan had led the Scottish Junior team against their Irish counterparts. It was a considerable coup for Hibernian to secure his services for Finnegan had also trialled with East Fife earlier in the season and scored a hat-trick. His career was badly disrupted by the war, however, he did play in 18 matches in the first full season following World War Two. He had eight games the very next season but was slipping from the picture as the 1950s approached. Nevertheless, his career as a Hibee had seen a League Championship, Scottish Cup Final and semi-final appearances, and a League Cup semi-final outing. In the match programme for the latter he was described thus: '…has made a big contribution to the style which has won the Easter Road team so much renown. Not much of Willie, but awful guid!' In June 1950 he made the short trip to Dunfermline, who were then in the Second Division.

FLAVELL, Bobby

Full-back

Born: Berwick, 7 March 1956.
Career: Burnley 1973, Halifax Town 1976, Chesterfield 1978, Barnsley 1979, Halifax Town, Västar Haninge (Sweden), HIBERNIAN 1981, Motherwell 1982, Dundee United 1983, Berwick Rangers 1983.

■ Not to be confused with the Hearts player of the same name and earlier vintage. This Flavell (Robert William in full) had played with Bonnyrigg Boys Club before embarking on a fairly nomadic career in northern England. Hibernian boss Bertie Auld signed Flavell in the summer of 1981 from Swedish football (Västar Haninge). A regular in the 1981–82 season, he netted at Ibrox in a 1–1 draw. But he played just four games in the very next season before moving to Motherwell in the deal that brought Willie Irvine to Easter Road. The nomad in Bobby could not be suppressed and he had two clubs after Motherwell before ending his senior career. His Scottish League career had yielded just under 100 games and, rather surprisingly, 10 goals.

FLEMING, Rikki

Centre-half

Career: Benburb Juniors, Rangers 1966, Kilwinning Rangers, Ayr United 1968, HIBERNIAN 1978, Berwick Rangers 1979.

■ Signed from Ayr United in 1978 for £10,000, Rikki had once been on the books of Rangers. He was a commanding centre-back for the Honest Men, spending a decade at Somerset Park and being an integral part of Ally MacLeod's excellent team of the early-1970s that reached the unprecedented heights of a Scottish Cup semi-final and Premier League survival. Remarkably injury-free, he was an ever present in several seasons at Ayr. He never quite hit it off with Hibs, however, and his stay was a surprisingly short one. Rikki played just a dozen games in the 1978–79 campaign before he was off. His debut came against Dundee United at Tannadice, and away from football he retained an interest in pursuing his trade as a boilermaker. By the start of the 1979–80 season Rikki had joined Berwick Rangers and his Scottish League cap against their English counterparts of 1974 was but a distant memory. Nevertheless, with over 300 Scottish League matches under his belt and a further 54 League Cup ties his was clearly a lengthy career.

FLETCHER, Steven

Striker

Born: Shrewsbury, 26 March 1987.
Career: HIBERNIAN 2003.

■ A product of Hibernian's fruitful youth system, Fletcher was one of the most exciting young strikers in the Scottish game by 2009. Purposeful, intelligent and deceptively slight, he helped Hibs get over a period that had seen talented youngsters like Brown, Whittaker, Thomson and Riordan all leave for pastures new. He made his Hibs debut in 2004 and with two goals in Hibernian's 2007 Scottish League Cup Final win over Kilmarnock he cemented his role at Easter Road. Hibs, ever aware of transfer values, ensured he would be their next big profit when they convinced him in December of that year to sign a contract tying him to Leith in theory until 2013. Perhaps a bit slight for a target man, he nevertheless was able to make good use of his sense of position and strong finishing. When Mixu Paatelainen added Colin Nish to the Hibs squad he gave Fletcher the perfect physical foil. Four goals in four Under-21 internationals catapulted him into the Scotland full team and he made his debut against Croatia in March 2008...on his 21st birthday. He had given notice of his talents by being voted Scotland's Young Player of the month in August 2007.

FOX, Desmond

Inside-forward

Career: Armadale Thistle, HIBERNIAN 1955, Raith Rovers 1961.

■ A centre-forward, despite standing at only 5ft 5in, Desmond saw his early Hibernian career disrupted by national service. He was stationed at one point in Cyprus but when posted to Dover he made the most of the situation by playing for Dover Town. He had joined Hibs in 1955 from Armadale Thistle. From that point until 1961 he was to play in 32 League fixtures which brought him eight goals. His first goal for the club, however, came in a sectional League Cup tie against Dunfermline Athletic. In February 1960 he joined the Pars' great rivals – Raith Rovers – where he scored 11 goals in 25 League games.

FRANKS, Mike

Goalkeeper

Born: Alberta, 27 April 1977.
Career: Vancouver 86s (Canada), PSV Eindhoven (Holland), HIBERNIAN 2000. Vancouver Whitcaps.

■ A 6ft 5in goalkeeper, Mike joined Hibernian in the autumn of 2000 and made a quite dramatic debut. He came on for Nick Colgan in a 0–0 draw with Celtic when the Irishman sustained an injury. A quick save and he settled to the task. Mike had been raised in Edmonton, Canada, and his football career had taken him from Vancouver 86s to PSV Eindhoven. Capped by the Canadian Under-23 Olympic team he played just one more game for Hibernian (the match against Motherwell that followed the Celtic game) before moving on.

FRASER, John

Wing-half

Career: Edinburgh Thistle, HIBERNIAN 1954.

■ When John joined Hibernian in August 1954 from Edinburgh Thistle there was considerable difficulty working out which was his best position. Listed as an outside-right, he filled three forward positions in his first season. And what a first season it was too with three goals in just four outings! A native of Portabello, John was initially on national service when he came to Easter Road. However, when he broke into the first team he did so in style. His three goals in that first season included two against Stirling Albion and the winner in a 2–1 win over Celtic.

Signed by Hugh Shaw, few could have imagined that John would be part and parcel of the Hibs scene for some 25 years. Given that his first task was to replace the wonderful Gordon Smith it would have been easy for John to give up but he gradually established himself as a Hibernian favourite, albeit in defence. In season 1956–57 he scored nine times in just 20 starts and had the considerable pleasure of scoring one of the goals in a Ne'erday 2–0 win at Tynecastle. Measuring 5ft 9in and bristling with enthusiasm, John did what many players have since done and moved from the forward line to a position further back. There he could use his uncanny knack of spotting danger before it reached crisis point and offer assistance to younger players further forward. His goals tended to come in fits and starts and in 1961 he scored twice in a Fairs Cup tie against Belensies. At one stage in his career John was Hibs' captain, and that seems a fitting accolade for a very faithful player who made just under 200 League appearances for the club. John brought the curtain down on his playing days with a short coaching spell at Stenhousemuir then returned to Hibs working as a coach under Shankly, MacFarlane and finally Turnbull.

FRASER, Robert

Wing-half

Born: Glasgow, 23 January 1917.
Career: HIBERNIAN 1946, Newcastle United 1947.

■ Robert played in five League games and one League Cup match during the 1946–47 season as normal football resumed after the war. His debut came on 21 August at home to Clyde and he helped Hibs to a 1–0 win. It was their fourth consecutive win and all appeared rosy. But on 30 November he played in a 1–0 win at St Mirren which proved to be his final game in Hibs colours. In January 1947 Robert joined Newcastle United where he played 26 games as a centre-half. His senior career ended in 1948.

FRYE, John

Outside-right

Born: Ardrossan, 27 July 1933.
Career: Ardrossan Winton Rovers, HIBERNIAN 1954, St Mirren 1960, Sheffield Wednesday 1961, Tranmere Rovers 1961, Queen of the South 1962, Hamilton 1963, Stranraer 1966.

■ Rather unfortunate with injuries and illness while at Easter Road, John had scored in prestigious floodlit matches against Tottenham and Wolves before his career was halted in its tracks as he suffered ligament damage in a match against St Mirren. His Easter Road impetus was lost and in a supreme irony he was sold to St Mirren in March 1960. He had joined Hibs as an outside-right from Ardrossan Winton Rovers in 1955 and scored his first League goal in 1957 against Queen's Park at Hampden Park; although in 20 League outings that was his only goal. He struggled at Paisley and down south but he was more influential in the colours of his later clubs. His son Derek was a professional (and noted scorer) with Stranraer, Dundee United, Ayr United and Clyde.

FULTON, Mark

Centre-half

Born: Johnstone, 16 September 1959.
Career: Johnstone Burgh, St Mirren 1977, HIBERNIAN 1985, Hamilton 1987.

■ A towering centre-half, Mark was born in Johnstone in 1959 and he played with the local Burgh junior side until 1977 when he joined St Mirren. He was outstanding at the heart of the Paisley defence, collecting five Under-21 caps, until Hibs came calling. Joining Hibs for the 1985–86 season he made 30 Premier League appearances that season and also played in a League Cup Final. However, he only played nine games in the following season before moving to Hamilton Accies. He gave up football quite early in order to pursue a career in the police force.

FYFE, Graham

Forward

Born: Glasgow, 18 August 1951.
Career: Ashfield Juniors, Rangers 1968, HIBERNIAN 1976, Dumbarton 1977.

■ There is a whiff of controversy, and the taste of a bygone era, when looking at the career of Graham Fyfe. In 1976 Hibs swapped the gifted Ian Munro for two fringe Rangers players. Ally Scott was one and 25-year-old Graham Fyfe was the other. Fyfe had been a player who promised much at Ibrox but never quite established himself despite playing in almost 100 matches. There were those who cited Rangers' then anti-Catholic policy as having played a part – Fyfe apparently being linked with a Catholic girl. This may be a rumour with no substance but it certainly had a wide audience at the time. At Hibernian he could not quite impress himself upon the team and he flitted into the squad briefly in the 1976–77 season. This was doubly disappointing for as a Rangers player he had constantly menaced Hibernian and scored several goals against them. He played less than a dozen games as a Hibee and was singularly unimpressive. He fared a little better at First Division Dumbarton but the impression is that his was a career that promised much and delivered little.

GALLACHER, Michael

Wing-half

Career: Alloa Athletic, HIBERNIAN 1947, Ayr United 1954.

■ Three times a League Cup semi-finalist with Hibs, Michael Gallagher was more grateful than most for Hibernian's 1952 League title triumph as it gave him the medal he craved. But the 1951–52 campaign was by far Michael's best and the remainder of his nine seasons at Easter Road saw him very much as a fringe player and he was essentially a squad player. He went to Ayr United in October 1954 along with Jock Govan (a deal which cost Ayr around £3,000), not long after being capped by Eire against Luxembourg in a 1954 World Cup qualifying tie. Gallacher made a great success of his move to Ayrshire. He played in 76 League matches for United including all of those required for Ayr to win promotion in 1955–56. Unfortunately, he was injured the following season and in the summer of 1957 was granted a free transfer and moved to Weymouth. After retiring from playing he emigrated to America and ran a bar in Chicago until his death on 3 January 1984.

GATHUESSI, Thierry

Right-back

Born: Cameroon, 17 April 1982.
Career: Montpellier 2001, Cannes 2005, FC Sete 2006, HIBERNIAN 2007.

■ An Cameroon international, with six caps, Thierry joined Hibs as a 25-year-old. This clever right-back found himself at the centre of a storm in March 2008 when he was the victim of an awful tackle by Rangers' Nacho Novo. The Rangers man was sent-off but in an amazingly undignified aftermath Walter Smith and Mixu Paatelainen clashed with the Rangers boss being sent to the stand in disgrace. Gathuessi joined Inverness on loan in January 2008.

GIBSON, Davie

Centre-forward

Born: Winchburgh, 23 September 1938.
Career: Livingston United, HIBERNIAN 1956, Leicester City 1962, Aston Villa 1970, Exeter City 1972.

■ National Service duties disrupted the early Hibernian career of this powerful centre-forward who went on to win seven Scotland caps, alas all after he had left Easter Road. Signed from Livingston United in 1956 he was a clever player who used the ball very well and as his career progressed he proved a useful

finisher too. After making 41 League appearances between 1956 and 1962 his enthusiasm for Easter Road drained away and he was sold to Leicester City in January 1962. He had only scored eight goals for Hibs in that time but he proved a most effective striker for City and bagged 41 goals in 280 League matches for the Foxes. Perhaps the peak of his achievements with the Foxes was playing in the 1969 FA Cup Final. In the early-1960s matches between an Edinburgh Select and English opposition were a traditional curtain raiser to the season in Edinburgh and in one of those matches Dave Gibson scored a hat-trick but still ended on the losing side. Burnley won the game 7–4 and two of their players netted hat-tricks!

GLASS, Stephen

Winger/wing-back

Born: 23 May 1976.
Career: Crombie Sports, Aberdeen 1994, Newcastle United 1998, Watford 2001, HIBERNIAN 2004, Dunfermline Athletic 2006.

■ A 5ft 9in winger, Stephen was a boy-star at Aberdeen and when he went to Newcastle United great things were expected. Four seasons as a Don had brought well over 100 appearances and he was a fixture in Scotland's Under-21 side. He did play as a substitute for Newcastle in the 1999 FA Cup Final against Manchester United but never quite made the breakthrough expected and had two seasons at Watford (which included a magnificent televised FA Cup goal) before joining Hibs. He featured under Alex McLeish's regime but was less successful thereafter and was allowed to joined Dunfermline in 2006. In truth, injury had severely hampered his Easter Road career.

GORAM, Andy

Goalkeeper

Born: Bury, 13 April 1964.
Career: West Bromwich Albion, Oldham Athletic 1980, HIBERNIAN 1987, Rangers 1991, Notts County 1998, Sheffield United 1998, Motherwell 2001, Manchester United 2001, Coventry City 2002, Oldham Athletic 2002, Queen of the South 2003, Elgin City 2005.

■ If the game truly yearns for characters then Andy Goram can be said to have fulfilled that longing. Arguably the finest post-war goalkeeper to represent Scotland, he was the son of former Hibs 'keeper Lew Goram (who never played a first team game for Hibs but did play on loan for Leith Athletic). From humble beginnings with Oldham Athletic (and

selection for three England Under-21 squads) Andy moved to Hibs for a club-record fee of £325,000 in October 1987. He was an instant success at Easter Road and in 1988 earned a special niche for himself by scoring from a goal-kick against Morton. By 1990 he was in the Scotland squad travelling to Italy for the World Cup Finals, but alas a year later he was sold to Rangers for £1 million. He was an outstanding 'keeper for the Glasgow club too and won many, many honours while there. He represented Scotland at cricket but was occasionally attracting newspaper headlines for the wrong reasons. In 1998 he was axed by

Rangers and after stints with Sheffield United and Notts County he joined Motherwell as John Boyle sought to make the Lanarkshire club 'the third force' in Scottish football. In 2001 he sensationally played for Manchester United when the English Champions had an injury crisis. Flamboyant, controversial and a wonderful shot-stopper he was always an entertaining figure. As late as 2002 he was still playing first-team football, despite his second debut for Oldham ending in a 7–1 defeat! By 2003 he had joined Queen of the South and had won the Challenge Cup while there. The appointment of former Rangers teammate John Brown as manager of Clyde early in 2008 saw Andy join their coaching staff.

GORDON, Alan

Forward

Born: Edinburgh, 14 May 1944.
Career: Edinburgh Athletic, Hearts 1961, Durban United (South Africa) 1967, Hearts 1968, Dundee United 1969, HIBERNIAN 1972, Dundee 1974.

■ Hibernian fans savoured the all too brief contribution of Alan Gordon at Easter Road. With 51 League goals, a League Cup-winners' badge, and no fewer than five Hibs hat-tricks to his name, his was a short but sweet Hibs career. When you consider that Alan also managed to play with distinction for both Dundee clubs and Hearts too it is clear he is well known beyond the confines of Easter Road. After all, how many players can claim to have played for all four Edinburgh and Dundee clubs? Born in 1944, Alan started his senior career with Hearts in 1961 and he soon proved himself an efficient goalscorer. He first came to Hibs' attention in season 1964–65 when he scored twice for Hearts in a 5–3 win at Easter Road. In that season, when Hearts narrowly failed to land the title, he scored 23 times. He went to South Africa in 1967 but was back with Hearts within a year. He joined Dundee United for £8,000 in 1969 and spent three years on Tayside until Eddie Turnbull persuaded him to join Hibs. It cost Hibs £12,000 to secure his talents but what a bargain that was. He was a Scottish Cup runner-up in 1972 (scoring Hibs' goal in the Final) and a League Cup winner months later. Alan scored twice in the New Year massacre of Hearts; his second effort striking both posts before crossing the line to make it 7–0. An elegant striker and an educated man off the field, he was every bit the cultured footballer. His easy and controlled style was pleasing on the eye and the Edwards, O'Rourke, Gordon, Cropley and Duncan forward line relied on him more than many appreciated. His impact was such that many Hibernian supporters are surprised to learn that Alan Gordon was only with Hibs for two years before moving to Dundee. He joined the Dens Park outfit in 1974 for £1,000 more than Hibs had paid and retired in 1976.

GOTTSKALKSSON, Olafur

Goalkeeper

Born: Keflavik, Iceland, 12 March 1968.
Career: Akranes 1988, FC Reykjavik 1990, Keflavik 1994, HIBERNIAN 1997, Brentford 2000, Grindavik 2003, Keflavik 2004, Torquay United 2004.

■ The handsome frame of Ole Gottskalksson frequently sent the pulses of female Hibernian fans racing, but all too often his errors sent even more into despair. Ole was an Icelandic goalkeeper who unfortunately carried much of the blame when Hibernian were relegated in 1998. Nevertheless, he was still with the club when the First Division campaign that followed got underway and he played in each and every League fixture as Hibs roared to promotion. Signed as a 29-year-old in July 1997 he had nine Icelandic caps and had been the substitute goalkeeper for his nation no fewer than 30 times. Tall (he was 6ft 3in), athletic and a thoroughly nice man he was well liked by the Hibs support but had an alarming tendency to make crucial mistakes at the wrong time. Prior to playing in Edinburgh he had been with Akranes, FC Reykjavik and Keflavik in Iceland. He moved from Hibernian to Brentford.

GOVAN, Jock

Full-back

Born: Larkhall, 16 January 1923.
Career: Larkhall Thistle, HIBERNIAN 1942, Ayr United 1954.

■ Jock Govan was a talented full-back who enjoyed a 13-year career at Easter Road and played 163 League games for the Hibees. He experienced the thrill of Scottish and League Cup Finals and was part of the side that won three League titles. Jock collected six Scotland caps and as well as playing for the Scottish League he was on the prestigious tour to North America with the SFA. Never a goalscorer, he went his entire League career without bagging a single goal. In October 1954 Jock left Hibs with Michael Gallacher to join Ayr United and was immediately made club captain. The fee for both players was reckoned to be in the region of £3,000 but Jock was freed by United at the end of the 1954–55 season having made a disappointing impact. Indeed, the local paper was less than complimentary in noting that Jock arrived at Somerset Park 'carrying too much bulk'. One interesting footnote to Jock's career is that in April 1948 Scotland played

England and Hibernian contributed both full-backs to the Scotland XI with Govan partnering Davie Shaw.

GRAHAM, Johnny

Inside-forward

Born: 8 January 1945.
Career: Strathclyde Juniors, Third Lanark 1962, Dundee United 1964, Falkirk 1965, HIBERNIAN 1969, Ayr United 1971, Falkirk 1976.

■ A rumbustious forward, John Ramsay Graham was as physical and combative a player as you could wish to see. He had an interesting career that took in a flurry of clubs including the now defunct Third Lanark. It was Falkirk's relegation in 1969 that precipitated his move to Hibs. Just a handful of games into the 1969–70 campaign (in November) he opted to play top-flight football once more. But when he decided he would not be living in Edinburgh his chances of a lengthy Hibernian career were greatly reduced. Yet with 10 goals in his first season he was scoring a goal every other game and proving his worth. With Hibernian he was full-time for the first time in his career, and his aggressive forward play made him a big favourite. His endeavour was rewarded with a Scottish League Cap against England at Coventry. Eased out of Hibernian he joined Ally MacLeod's Ayr United (in September 1971) and became a great favourite there too, scoring 62 League goals before bringing the curtain down on his career with a move back to Falkirk. Johnny was almost as keen on sailing as he was football and he embarked upon some fairly epic journeys when his career ended. He also ran a successful engineering business, while his son played with – and captained – Queen's Park.

GRANT, Brian

Midfield

Born: Bannockburn, 19 June 1964.
Career: Fallin Violet, Stirling Albion 1982, Aberdeen 1984, HIBERNIAN 1996, Dundee 1998, Stirling Albion 1999.

■ Twice a League Cup winner and once a Scottish Cup victor with Aberdeen, Brian Grant enjoyed a lengthy career in the Granite City that brought him a testimonial for 13 seasons' service. He joined Hibernian halfway through the 1996–97 season when Hibs needed the play-offs to survive, one year later he was tasting relegation. It was a pity that he arrived at a time when the club was in the doldrums for at his peak he had been a wonderfully energetic and purposeful midfielder. Hibs fans knew him well, in September 1988 he scored a Skol Cup quarter-final winner for the Dons against Hibs at Easter Road. But the clock could not be turned back and two short stints with Dundee and Stirling ended what had been a very consistent career.

GRANT, Colin

Centre-forward

Born: 21 July 1944.
Career: Linlithgow Rose, HIBERNIAN 1965, Linlithgow Rose, Peterhead 1974, Chelmsford City.

■ Two cartilage operations in 1968 severely hampered Colin's progress at Easter Road. Between 1965 and 1970 he played just over a dozen League games in a Hibernian jersey. Eventually, battered and bruised, he reverted to the junior ranks and then he moved north and took the opportunity to join the then Highland League side Peterhead. He became better known after his playing career was over when he fronted the Peterhead bid to join the SFL.

GRANT, John

Full-back

Born: Edinburgh, 1931.
Career: Colinton Mains United, Merchiston Thistle, HIBERNIAN 1949, Raith Rovers 1964.

■ The Hibernian handbook described John as 'a stylish inside-forward or wing-half'. That was in 1954 and by that stage Grant was growing impatient to make his Hibernian debut. He joined Hibs in 1949 from

Merchiston Thistle but two years of national service and completion of his joiner's apprenticeship had seriously stalled his career. When he did finally make the breakthrough at Easter Road he found playing at full-back more rewarding than striving for a wing-half spot. Others agreed and between 1958 and 1961 he made six appearances for the Scottish League and earned two full Scotland caps. In the decade following on from his 1954 debut John made 225 League appearances for Hibs. Interestingly, he scored two League goals in his Hibs career; the first a penalty in a 3–2 win at East Fife in December 1958 and the second in his final season as a Hibee during a 4–1 win over St Johnstone. He was a Cup Finalist with Hibernian in 1958. In September 1964 he joined Raith Rovers but he played for only a year before retiring from the game in April 1965.

GRANT, Johnny

Winger

Career: Ardeer Thistle, Kilwinning Rangers, HIBERNIAN 1963, Ayr United 1965.

■ Johnny played just a single season for Hibs, and unfortunately for club historians it coincided with the final season of the career

of John Grant. But whereas John senior was a defender, young Johnny was a winger. He played 14 League games and scored one goal in the 1963–64 season. Johnny had been raised in Govan, Glasgow, and started his career with the influential Harmony Row Youth Club. From there he moved on to Queen's Park, Ardeer Thistle and Kilwinning Rangers and it was from the latter that Hibernian signed him. After his short stint at Easter Road he moved to Ayr United in the 1965 close-season. Alas, his career at Ayr was short-lived too and when freed at the end of the 1966–67 season he emigrated to South Africa and played with Durban United.

GRAY, Damon

Striker

Born: South Shields, 11 July 1988.
Career: HIBERNIAN 2007, Partick Thistle (loan) 2008.

■ Damon made a scoring debut for Hibernian at the tail end of the 2006–07 season. He played against Aberdeen in a 2–2 draw at Pittodrie, a match in which Hibs had two players sent off. Later in the same campaign he turned out against both Killie and Hearts but it was a loan move to Partick Thistle in January 2008 that really caught the eye. Allowed to turn out for Thistle in a Scottish Cup tie at Rangers (when Hibernian were knocked out by the Ibrox club) the 19-year-old promptly scored in a shock 1–1 draw. He was back on loan with Thistle when the 2008 season got underway with the Glasgow club desperate to sign him permanently.

GRAY, Eddie

Inside-forward

Born: Bellshill, 19 October 1954.
Career: Kirkintilloch Rob Roy, HIBERNIAN 1952, Third Lanark (loan), Yeovil Town, Barrow 1957, Accrington Stanley 1959, Stirling Albion 1960, Forfar Athletic 1960, Albion Rovers 1961.

■ An inside-forward, Gray was a small player (measuring just 5ft 6in) but was full of energy and desire. His Easter Road career was bizarre to say the least. 'Out of the blue' in season 1953–54 he was plucked from the reserves and handed a starting jersey for the Scottish League Cup semi-final against East Fife. It was a strange selection by any standards and a quiet performance did not help as Hibs surprisingly lost 3–2. Not surprisingly, Gray's career stalled and he did not play first-team football again until picked for a League game in the 1956–57 League season. He had spent a brief period on loan to Third Lanark while a Hibee (four goals in just nine games) and had been capped by Scotland at Schoolboy and Youth international level. From Hibs he moved around a fair bit, at one point playing with Forfar to some effect.

GROF, David

Goalkeeper

Born: Hungary, 17 April 1989.
Career: HIBERNIAN 2008.

■ Young David Grof had a baptism of fire in the Hibs goal. He came on for an injured Andy McNeil in a League Cup tie against Morton in 2008. Hibs had battled back from 2–0 down but Grof conceded a goal in extra-time that reflected badly on him and saw the club lose 3–4. It was a painful exit for manager Mixu Paatelainen and one that cost the club financially.

GUGGI, Peter

Midfield

Born: 25 September 1967.
Career: Grazer AK, LASK Linz, Vfb Modling, Admira Wacker, HIBERNIAN 1998, DSV Leoben (Austria), Wiener Sportsklub Weinstrom.

■ Hibernian manager Alex McLeish loved to dabble in the transfer market. Some of his signings brought long-term benefit to Hibs, while others only short-term. Guggi's transfer fell into the latter category. A clever little midfielder, he was signed as a free agent in August 1998 and made his debut against Hamilton Accies in a League Cup tie. He showed neat touches and was soon popping in the odd goal, Ayr United being early victims. However, he fell out of favour not long after

arriving and left rather quietly within a matter of months. Somewhat laid-back he appeared to have taken rather too well to the nightlife on offer in Edinburgh.

GUNN, Bryan

Goalkeeper

Born: Thurso, 22 December 1963.
Career: Aberdeen, Norwich City 1986, HIBERNIAN 1998.

■ Signed from Norwich City by Alex McLeish, Bryan Gunn's signing represented Hibs' desperate bid to stay in the Premier League. He was a vastly experienced 'keeper having played several times for Scotland and had served at Aberdeen alongside Alex McLeish before moving to Norwich City. Alas, for all Gunn's undoubted experience he was unable to keep Hibs in the top flight. Worse was to follow when he was injured in a freakish training ground accident and his career was virtually over thereafter. He returned to East Anglia to take up a goalkeepers coaching course. Bryan had been understudy to Jim Leighton at Aberdeen until moving to Norwich City for £100,000 in 1986.

GUNNING, James

Outside-right

Born: Helensburgh, 25 June 1929.
Career: Wolverhampton Wanderers, Forres Mechanics, HIBERNIAN 1946, Manchester City 1950, Barrow 1954.

■ Poor Jimmy Gunning; a single game for Hibs – the first of the 1950–51 title stroll when the League flag was won by a clear 10 points. And that single game…a 6–0 thrashing of Falkirk at home; what more could he have done? Of course, the problem was he was an outside-right and that was the position held by the mighty Gordon Smith. He took perhaps the only course of action available and sought a transfer. Thus he moved to Manchester City in November 1950 and made 13 outings for the Maine Road club before bringing the curtain down on his senior career with Barrow.

H

HALL, Alex

Full-back

Born: Kirknewton, 6 November 1908.
Career: Wallyford Bluebell, Dunfermline 1928, Sunderland 1929, HIBERNIAN 1945.

■ Alexander Webster Hall joined Hibernian ostensibly as a coach during the Second World War. Although born in Scotland he had made his name, and considerable reputation, with Sunderland. He played over 200 matches for the Roker Park side and won both the English Championship and the FA Cup. He only played three senior matches for Hibs: there were two outings in the League Cup during October 1946 and he had a single League game on 4 January 1947 in a 1–1 draw at Easter Road with Morton. When he left Hibernian he settled in the Scottish borders and by 1948 he joined the committee of Kelso United in the East of Scotland League.

HAMILL, Hugh

Inside-forward

Born: 15 February 1959.
Career: Dumbarton 1978, HIBERNIAN 1980, Dunfermline 1981, Queen of the South 1983, Partick Thistle 1984, Vale of Leven Juniors 1985.

■ Hugh was with the club in the early-1980s, but saw his career badly hampered by a leg break. He played a handful of games in the 1980–81 season when Hibernian found themselves in the First Division. It was not a great time to be at the club for although they quite easily won promotion there was a lack of stability at Easter Road, evidenced by the use of 30 players in the League campaign alone. Hugh made his debut in a 3–0 home win over Berwick Rangers but was injured a few weeks later as Hibs won 3–1 at Ayr United. In May 1981 Hibs allowed him to move to Dunfermline and a couple of season later he was a regular in Fife. Nevertheless, when he quit the senior ranks in 1985 he had barely managed 100 senior appearances.

HAMILTON, Brian

Midfield

Born: Paisley, 5 August 1967.
Career: Pollok United BC, St Mirren 1985, HIBERNIAN 1989, Hearts 1995, Falkirk 1996, Clydebank 2000, Partick Thistle 2000.

■ A talented left-sided midfielder, Brian made his mark with St Mirren helping them to the Scottish Cup in 1987. Capped four times by Scotland at Under-21 level (initially while a Saint and latterly while a Hibee), he joined Hibernian in July 1989 and within a couple of years had added a League Cup-winners' medal. Consistent, skilled and possessed of a very good temperament he was very popular with his fellow professionals who to a man declared him 'a player's player'. Alas, in a two-club city the sure way to damage your popularity on the terraces is to switch allegiances and Brian made the move to Hearts in January 1995. It is foolish that this should have led to his verbal abuse by Hibs fans thereafter. Brian had given the club nothing but sterling service and in a business world had simply made a move that better provided for his family. He was a solid player and quietly effective with it.

HAMILTON, Donald

Goalkeeper

Career: Armadale Thistle, HIBERNIAN 1953, Falkirk 1955, Dunfermline 1956, Stranraer 1957, Alloa Athletic 1958, Albion Rovers 1958.

■ Although only 5ft 9in tall Donald was a competent goalkeeper who unfortunately found himself at the club when good goalkeepers abounded. He played in 17 League games during the 1953–54 season, but with only five outings in the next season he was granted a free transfer in April 1955. He moved to Falkirk but was just one year there before slipping down to the lower reaches of the game. His Hibernian debut speaks volumes of a bygone era. It came against East Fife at home in November 1953 and prior to the game he received telegrams from Tommy Younger (whom he was replacing) and Third Lanark's 'keeper Robertson.

HAMILTON, Johnny

Midfield

Born: Glasgow, 10 July 1949.
Career: Cumbernauld United, HIBERNIAN 1967, Rangers 1973, Millwall 1978, St Johnstone 1978, Blantyre Celtic 1980, Forth Wanderers 1983.

■ Signed as an 18-year-old from Cumbernauld Juniors by Bob Shankly, Hamilton was a clever midfielder whose left-footed skills were delightful and incisive. It was always going to be a difficult task to hold on to such a 'natural' talent and Hibs are to be congratulated for holding him as long as they did. Between 1969 and 1973 Johnny made 58 League appearances for Hibs. In due course this rather stocky player moved on to Rangers where he won two League Cup medals and played in a Scottish Cup triumph against Hearts. Although he enjoyed some success at Ibrox, he did not wholly fit in with Jock Wallace's work ethic. He later played with Millwall and St Johnstone.

HAMILTON, Willie

Midfield

Born: Airdrie, 16 February 1938.
Career: Drumpellier Amateurs, Sheffield United 1956, Middlesbrough 1961, Hearts 1962, HIBERNIAN 1963, Ross County, Hamilton Accies 1971.

■ Willie was one of the most enigmatic performers ever to pull on a Hibs jersey. Hamilton could be sublime, a near genius, but like so many genius footballers he was essentially a flawed character. A lack of dedication and a fondness for the good life were ultimately his undoing. There were games where he dominated the scene magnificently, arguably never more so than in a friendly against the mighty Real Madrid at Easter Road as he inspired Hibs to a 2–0 win. He was capped once by Scotland while at Hibs, guided the club to a Summer Cup triumph and had won the League Cup as a Hearts player, but

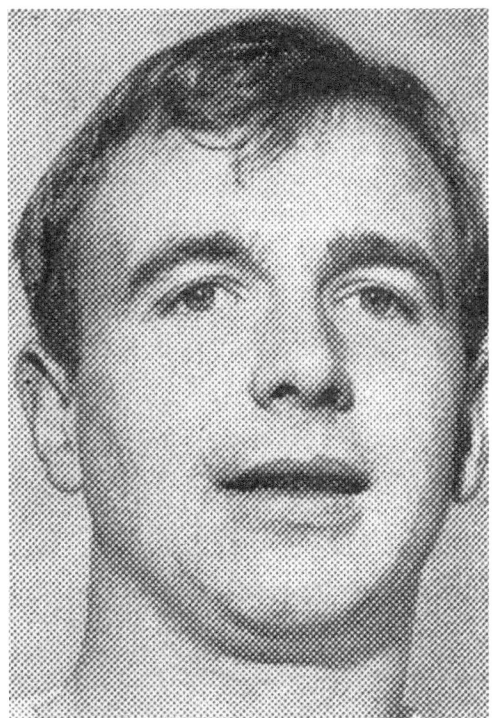

overall he failed to take the honours his immense skills deserved. Willie also turned out for Sheffield United, Middlesbrough and Aston Villa. He died tragically young and is remembered fondly as a rare and natural talent. It is worth recalling that the great Jock Stein, not one given to excessive praise, said of Hamilton that he was one of the most naturally gifted players he ever managed.

HANLON, Paul

Left-back

Born: 20 January 1990.
Career: HIBERNIAN 2008, St Johnstone (loan) 2009.

■ Paul made his debut in January 2008 against Inverness in a Scottish Cup tie, and thanks to a Shiels hat-trick Hibernian romped home 3–0. Paul was standing in at left-back because David Murphy was on the verge of his move to Birmingham and Lewis Stevenson was injured. He was just 17 when he made his bow in what was Mixu Paatelainen's first game in charge. The arrival of Abdel Zarabi, an Algerian international, temporarily put Paul's first-team ambitions on hold but when Zarabi bought out his contract Hanlon was able to return to first XI duties and he duly grabbed his first goal for Hibs in the August 2008 home win over Falkirk. He captained the Scotland Under-19 side in 2008.

HARPER, Kevin

Winger

Born: Oldham, 15 January 1976.
Career: Hutchison Vale BC, HIBERNIAN 1982, Derby County 1998, Walsall (loan), Portsmouth 1999, Norwich City (loan), Leicester City (loan), Stoke City 2005, Dunfermline Athletic 2008.

■ A clever little winger, Kevin joined Hibs in 1992 as an apprentice and was promptly capped at Youth, Under-21 and 'B' international level. Tricky, direct and useful around goal he became a firm Hibs favourite very quickly. It was an Under-21 hat-trick that finally propelled Kevin Harper from the local to the national stage. In 1995 he scored a threesome against Finland – one with his right, one with his left and a header neatly proving his versatility. His Easter Road career might well be remembered for one goal in particular…against Hearts. When Hibs slipped into the First Division it was clear he would be looking to move on and in September 1998 he joined Derby County. Kevin was back in Scotland by 2008 playing with Dunfermline and in March of that year he scored a hat-trick at Stirling Albion to show he had lost none of his verve or sense of purpose.

HARRIS, Colin

Forward

Born: Sanquhar, 22 February 1961.
Career: Exit Thistle, Raith Rovers 1979, Dundee

Kevin Harper

JOE HARPER — HERO

Centre-forward
Born: Greenock, 11 January 1948.
Career: Larkfield BC, Greenock Morton 1963, Huddersfield 1967, Greenock Morton 1968, Aberdeen 1969, Everton 1972, HIBERNIAN 1974, Aberdeen 1976, Peterhead 1981, Keith 1982.

■ A small, barrel-chested striker, Joe was one of the finest goal-grabbers of his era. He started his career with Morton in the mid-1960s and then, following a glut of goals, moved to Huddersfield Town. Failing to settle he returned to Morton and did so well that Aberdeen snapped him up. He instantly won a Scottish Cup-winners' badge while with the Dons (scoring in the 1970 Final against Celtic) then moved to Everton in a lucrative transfer that cost the Merseyside club £180,000. It is important to note that it was Eddie Turnbull who was Aberdeen manager when Harper was recruited from Morton. The Dons were keen to bring him back from Goodison when Hibs pipped them. This was largely on the back of Tom Hart's sheer determination and financial muscle to land a player that he considered to be one of the finest Scottish marksmen of his era. Harper cost £120,000 – a figure that represented a record sum for a player going from England to Scotland. Debut day came on 9 February in a 0–0 draw at Falkirk and in the little that remained of the season he scored nine League goals. But there was a problem for the likeable Harper. His inclusion in the side appeared to be at the exclusion of Jim O'Rourke, and despite Harper being clearly a better finisher he could not win over a section of the Hibs support who were 'O'Rourke fans'. Despite this situation Harper had many highs in his Hibernian career, short as it was. He scored their first-ever Premier League goal when Hibs beat Hearts 1–0 and scored all five in a 5–0 win over Nijmegen (he also hit the post in that game!). Harper's first full season as a Hibee brought 12 League goals; three less than O'Rourke managed at St Johnstone, and with O'Rourke scoring in both League meetings between the clubs Harper's position was made even more awkward. This was despite a stunning performance on the biggest stage of all – Hampden Park. In the 1974 League Cup Final Harper had the unusual distinction of scoring a hat-trick and still managing to end up on the losing side as Hibs went down to Celtic 3–6. As football historian Bob Crampsey remarked: 'no man ever played better in a losing cause'. A less happy occasion came in October 1975 at Celtic Park as Joe and Des Bremner scored in what would have been a 2–0 win but for the referee abandoning it with around five minutes left due to fog. Joe had not only scored but appeared to be the target of a mini-field invasion by Celtic fans from the notorious 'Jungle'. He left Hibs in 1976 to rejoin Aberdeen (Hibs almost got Davie Robb in exchange) and went to become a real Dons legend. This was hardly surprising as he was already a huge hit with the Dons fans and his departure had been universally bemoaned on the Pittodrie terraces. Prior to going to Everton he had scored 33 goals in 34 games during the 1971–72 season and won the European Bronze Boot – included in that total were three goals against Hibs. In his first season back at Aberdeen he helped them land the League Cup and by 1980–81 he was the deserved recipient of a testimonial from the Pittodrie club. After his senior playing career ended he played briefly in the Highland League before returning to the West of Scotland and renewing his association with Morton. At both Morton and Aberdeen Joe is viewed as one of their all-time greats and he would surely have won more than four international caps were it not for his involvement in the infamous 'Copenhagen incident'.

1984, HIBERNIAN 1985, Raith Rovers 1986, Hamilton Accies 1988, Cowdenbeath 1993, Clydebank 1993, Meadowbank 1995, Queen of the South 1995.

■ Between 1984 and 1986, Colin made 26 outings in a Hibs jersey one of which was in the 1986 League Cup Final against Aberdeen. This was to prove just a fraction of what was by any standards a lengthy football career. From joining Raith Rovers in 1979 until turning out for Queen of the South in 1996 Colin enjoyed a longevity few players achieve. He proved a slightly nomadic player as his career path suggests. He was most successful at Hamilton where he scored a winner in the B&Q Cup Final, picked up another winners' badge 12 months later and won a First Division Championship badge. Occasionally Colin could play in goal and he did so on more than one occasion for Accies.

HARROWER, Jim

Centre-forward

Born: Alva, 18 August 1935.
Career: Bo'ness United, HIBERNIAN 1954, Liverpool 1958, Newcastle United 1961, Falkirk 1962, St Johnstone 1963, Albion Rovers 1965, Alloa Athletic 1966.

■ Jimmy was a prolific marksman in junior football with Sauchie, Kilsyth Rangers and Bo'ness United. It was from the latter that Hibs signed him and he broke into the Hibs first team in season 1955–56. Half a dozen goalless outings in his first season gave way to a handful in the following two campaigns but in January 1958 his form was sufficiently good to tempt Liverpool to sign him. He was with Liverpool from 1957 to 1960 and scored 21 goals in 96 League matches. From Liverpool he moved to Newcastle United, where he played just five games, then Falkirk. He later played with St Johnstone and at one stage in his Perth career threatened legal action against the SFA when handed a 28-day suspension. Capped once by Scotland at Under-23 level he was the archetypal inside-forward; a raider who could both create and take chances.

HARTLEY, Paul

Winger/midfield

Born: Glasgow, 19 October 1976.

Career: Mill United BC, Hamilton 1994, Millwall 1996, Raith Rovers 1997, HIBERNIAN 1998, St Johnstone 2000, Hearts 2003, Celtic 2007.

■ Signed by Alex McLeish from Raith Rovers for £200,000, Paul helped in the push to promotion from the First Division in 1999. However, he never quite made the same impression when Hibs played in the Premier League and he was allowed to leave and join St Johnstone. He had in fact been a Hibernian 'S' form but joined Hamilton on a YTS programme and made his debut for Accies when only 17. He spent three years with Accies but never once played at Douglas Park, as throughout his time with the Lanarkshire club they sought a new ground. Jimmy Nicholl bought him for Millwall (one of four Scots signed on the same day!) but Paul did not settle in London and followed Nicholl back to Scotland with Raith Rovers. There was consternation when he joined Hearts and this was magnified when he scored a hat-trick against Hibernian in the Scottish Cup semi-final of 2006. His star was on the rise at this point and he was capped several times by Scotland and earned a move to Celtic in January 2007 for £1.4 million.

HARVEY, Graham

Forward

Born: Musselburgh, 23 April 1961.
Career: Ormiston Primrose, HIBERNIAN 1983, Dundee 1985, Airdrie 1989, Livingston 1995.

■ A debut goalscorer for Hibs (in a home win over Morton in February 1983), Graham was nevertheless a slow starter in his Hibernian career (he managed just three goals in over 30 matches). The feeling was that he was a little too light for the role Hibs envisaged, and he was allowed to join Dundee in January 1985. Graham had more success at Dundee and Airdrie after leaving Easter Road. Indeed, his career return of 83 goals from just under 300 League matches was a very respectable total.

HAZEL, John

Midfield

Born: 30 November 1952.
Career: Dunipace Juniors, HIBERNIAN 1969, Morton 1974, East Stirling 1977, Alloa Athletic 1979.

■ Between 1970 and 1974, John was a fringe player at Easter Road. An incisive and direct player, he scored memorably against Hearts in a 2–1 Scottish Cup win at Tynecastle in 1971 but was always on the edges of breaking through permanently. Arguably his finest hour was playing in the team that landed the Dryburgh Cup in 1972. In and out of the side, his challenge was to try and earn a place in the Edwards, O'Rourke, Gordon, Cropley and Duncan forward-line. However, John had a pedigree that suggested he would do so, having been capped by the Scottish Professional Youth team. His breakthrough in the Hibs team came in the 1970–71 campaign, but by the 1973–74 season it was clear to Eddie Turnbull that John was not going to make the grade at Easter Road. He later played with Morton where he wore the number-nine jersey.

HENDERSON, Martin

Centre-forward

Born: Kirkcaldy, 3 May 1956.
Career: Rangers 1973, HIBERNIAN (loan) 1977, Philadelphia Furies 1978, Leicester City 1978, Chesterfield 1981, Port Vale 1983.

■ In early 1978 Hibs went to Rangers to secure the services of gangly striker Martin Henderson. A straight, no frills centre-forward, Henderson had bagged his share of goals at Rangers but in truth never looked likely to create his own quota at Hibs. His spell as a Hibee was a three-month loan arrangement, and he later played in the United States and with Leicester City in England. The sum total of Martin's Hibs career is half a dozen matches. It is interesting to note that when Rangers won the League in 1976 (Martin's breakthrough season in their first team) he recorded double figures in the 'goals for' column yet never scored a League goal in Scotland again. He enjoyed greater success in terms of goals when he played at Leicester and Chesterfield.

HENDRY, Ian
Inside-forward

Born: Glasgow, 19 October 1959.
Career: Eastercraigs, Aston Villa 1977, Hereford 1979, Cambridge United 1981, HIBERNIAN 1981.

■ A tragic debutant, Ian suffered a compound fracture just 20 seconds into his debut at Berwick in January 1981. Signed as a 21-year-old from Cambridge United he would make only two appearances for Hibs in his short career and in August 1982 he returned to England.

HENRY, Fabrice
Midfield

Born: Paris, France, 13 February 1968.
Career: Sochaux 1982, Marseille 1995, Toulouse 1996, Toledo 1996, Basel 1997, HIBERNIAN 1999.

■ A thoughtful French midfielder, Fabrice's career began in 1982 with Sochaux. He stayed there for 11 years and gained French Under-21 recognition. He joined Marseille for one year before moving to Toulouse then in June 1996 moved to Spain with Toledo, before sampling Switzerland with Basle. Fabrice joined Hibs in the summer of 1999 and made his debut in the opening League fixture that summer against Motherwell, a thrilling game that ended 2–2. Thereafter he was used rather sparingly before being released, having failed to fulfil the expectations placed on his experienced shoulders.

HERRIOT, Jim
Goalkeeper

Born: Airdrie, 20 November 1939.
Career: Douglasdale, Dunfermline 1958, Birmingham City 1965, Mansfield Town 1970, Durban City 1971, HIBERNIAN 1971, St Mirren 1973, Partick Thistle 1975, Morton 1975, Dunfermline 1976, Morton 1978.

■ A very capable 'keeper, Jim won the League Cup and Dryburgh Cup with Hibernian and played in the 1965 Scottish Cup Final for Dunfermline. His award of eight Scotland caps and several Under-23 awards proved his ability. His senior career lasted 17 seasons. Sold by Dunfermline to Birmingham City in May 1965 at the same time as Jackie Sinclair went to Leicester, he played in 200 matches for the Brummies before moving to Mansfield Town. He joined Hibs in 1971 from Durban City, a South African side, after Hibernian had endured a nightmare tour of the north of England in which young 'keeper Eddie Pryde had struggled to prove he was ready for League action. Jim was influential in helping Hibs, lending experience to a defence that was beginning to gel and combined youthful energy with natural skill. He was also the last line of defence in the 1972 Scottish Cup Final which Hibs lost 6–1 to Celtic. His name lives on in literary circles, having been 'used' by the author of the famous veterinary books set in the Yorkshire Dales. Many Scottish football fans remember him as the goalkeeper who blackened the skin under his eyes to counter any glare.

HIGGINS, Anthony 'Tony'
Forward/midfield

Born: Glasgow, 3 June 1954.
Career: Kilsyth St Patrick's BC, HIBERNIAN 1972, Partick Thistle 1980, Morton 1982, Stranraer 1982.

■ A big, bustling midfielder who could also play up front, Tony joined Hibs in July 1972. He made his debut soon afterwards in a League Cup tie against Aberdeen and became one of Eddie Turnbull's favourite players, but for all that he was used rather sparingly. His career at Hibs brought 23 goals in 104 League fixtures. In March 1980 Higgins moved to Partick Thistle and he later formed a formidable partnership with Andy Ritchie at Morton. An entertaining speaker, with a wicked sense of humour and wonderful impersonations, Tony worked as a Player's Union Representative before taking his panache onto the football after-dinner speakers' circuit.

HIGGINS, Hugh

Wing-half

Career: Bonnybridge Juniors, Tranent, HIBERNIAN 1956, Third Lanark (loan) 1957, Dunfermline 1958, Falkirk 1959, East Stirling 1960.

■ A useful junior with Bonnybridge and Tranent, Hibs had to beat off competition from Celtic and Sunderland to secure this talented youngster. His debut came in a 3–3 draw with Spurs in 1956. Replacing the injured Gordon Smith he stunned all and sundry by scoring the final Hibs goal. Alas, such a promising start was not to signal a lengthy career in green and white. Hugh went

to Third Lanark on loan in December 1957 before making a permanent move to Dunfermline in November 1958. He actually played only 10 matches as a Hibee.

HIGGINS, John

Full-back

Born: Kilmarnock, 27 January 1933.
Career: Dalry Thistle, HIBERNIAN 1952, St Mirren 1957, Swindon Town 1959.

■ Between 1954 and 1956 John Wilson Higgins made a dozen outings as a Hibee. At 5ft 8in he was not particularly big for a defender, and Hibs freed him in April 1957. He had one solid season at St Mirren (even scoring in a League Cup tie) before moving to Wiltshire to try his luck with Swindon Town.

HIGGINS, Laurie

Outside-left

Career: Edinburgh Thistle, Bo'ness United, HIBERNIAN 1949, Aberdeen 1953, Dundee United 1954.

■ Although signed in 1949, Laurie had to be patient in waiting for his debut; like many young players of his era national service requirements meant he was unavailable for a couple of years. A jeweller by trade, he finally made his bow on 11 April 1951 at Clyde. Historians of Hibernian will know that that was the evening Hibs clinched the 1951 League title. Young Lawrie performed admirably in a 4–0 win. It is perhaps surprising that this was his only outing as a Hibee! He joined Aberdeen in 1953, failed to play in any matches and moved to Dundee United.

HILLAND, Paul

Defender

Born: Edinburgh, 28 July 1983.
Career: HIBERNIAN 2001, Cowdenbeath (loan), Berwick Rangers, 2004, Queen of the South 2004, Clyde 2005, Raith Rovers (loan) 2005, Irvine Meadow 2008.

■ Paul began his senior career with Hibs and went on loan to Cowdenbeath with Derek Riordan. But whereas the loan move was the making of Riordan, things didn't work out so well for Hilland and he moved on to a number of smaller Scottish clubs over the course of his career. His work commitments outside football made being a part-time player extremely difficult. At one point he contemplated life in Australia but by 2008 he was performing well in Scottish Junior football.

HOGG, Chris

Centre-half

Born: Middlesbrough, 12 March 1985.
Career: York City 2000, Ipswich Town 2001, Boston (loan) 2003, HIBERNIAN 2005.

■ Recruited for free in the January 2005 transfer window, Chris developed into a powerful centre-half. His partnership with Rob Jones was a key part of Hibernian's success at Hampden Park in the League Cup Final. He had captained England at Under-16 level and his spell at Ipswich had provided him with a wonderful apprenticeship.

HOGG, Davie

Outside-right

Born: 23 August 1946.
Career: Tynecastle BC, HIBERNIAN 1963, Dundee United 1968, Dumbarton 1969, Berwick 1970, Ballieston Juniors 1971, Durban 1973.

■ Davie joined Hibs as a 17-year-old in late-1963 but quickly gave up full-time football in order to work part time in insurance. It was hardly surprising as he had shown an academic bent at Holy Cross Academy which led to him being offered a chance to study languages at Edinburgh University. Given a free transfer in 1968, he moved to Dundee United and thereafter he combined playing at lower levels and abroad with his education and subsequent career.

HOLSGROVE, Paul

Midfield

Born: Wellington, 26 August 1969.
Career: Aldershot 1987, Wokingham 1991, Luton Town 1991, Heracles (South Africa), Millwall 1992, Reading 1994, Grimsby (loan) 1997, Crewe 1997, Stoke City 1998, Brighton 1998,

HIBERNIAN 1998, Airdrie (loan) 1999, Darlington 2000, Hayes 2001.

■ During Alex McLeish's reign a number of players enjoyed brief cameo appearances for Hibs. Paul Holsgrove was one such player. Signed for a rather surprising £110,000 on the eve of the 1998–99 First Division campaign he flitted in and out of the Hibernian midfield without ever imposing himself fully. Perhaps Paul can be accurately described as a 'journeyman' player having played with a raft of smaller English clubs, and with the notable exception of Hibs he rarely generated a transfer fee.

HOUCHEN, Keith

Centre-forward

Born: Middlesbrough, 25 July 1960.
Career: Chesterfield 1977, Hartlepool 1978, Orient 1982, York City 1984, Scunthorpe 1986, Coventry City 1986, HIBERNIAN 1989, Port Vale 1991, Hartlepool 1993.

■ Keith's senior career was relatively anonymous until the summer of 1987 when he sprung to national attention by scoring with a wonderful diving header in the 1987 FA Cup Final against Tottenham Hotspur which Coventry won 3–2. He joined Hibs in a blaze of publicity on the back of a £100,000 transfer fee just four years later, and cemented his good reputation with a goal against Hearts within 25 minutes of his debut. Big and strong, his was a physical approach to the game and as well as netting a decent amount of goals (11 in 57 League games) his presence allowed others around him to flourish. Hibernian, in a smart piece of business, were able to recoup their money on Keith when he went to Port Vale in August 1991 for £100,000 – a move which made his total transfer fees a whopping £476,000.

HOWIE, Hugh

Full-back

Born: Glasgow, 14 February 1924.
Career: Newton Juniors, HIBERNIAN 1943.

■ The cold statistics show that Hugh Howie played in 139 League matches for Hibs without scoring a single goal. It is, therefore, a surprise to learn that Hugh is remembered for not one, but two goals he scored in his career. One was a legendary Scottish Cup semi-final winner and the other was an international debut goal! Hugh was something of a utility player and far more skilful than many observers realised. He started his football with Hallside Juveniles then moved on to Newton Juniors and it was from there that Hibs signed him in 1943. He played in two League games in the 1942–43 season, and throughout the wartime campaigns he made sporadic outings. The first official season after the cessation of hostilities was the 1946–47 campaign and Hugh played in 29 of Hibs' 30 League matches. Starting out an out-and-out right-back he ended the season playing either centre-half or right-half. His input was significant and his efforts helped the club reach the Scottish Cup Final and the League Cup semi-final. A tall man (he measured just under the 6ft mark), he was a lithe 11st 12lb and could move with surprising speed. However, there was precious little need for that speed when he scored his famous counter in the March 1947 Scottish Cup semi-final against Motherwell. That goal has become one of the most talked about goals in Hibernian's rich history. The 1946–47 season attracted huge crowds as the game returned to normality after the war years. Hibernian battled through to the semi-final stage of the national Cup only to come up against a resolute Motherwell. In the era before penalty shoot-outs it was decided to play the game to a finish. It was 1–1 after 90 minutes had elapsed and thus the game went into a 'golden goal' period which would not end until one side scored. Ultimately, the match lasted an astonishing 142 minutes until Howie scored in spectacular fashion by returning a long punt upfield by the Motherwell goalkeeper Johnston back over his head and into the net. In September 1948 he was badly injured playing against Aberdeen at Pittodrie and when he was allowed out of hospital the club sent him to Switzerland to recuperate. Given that this was in March 1949 the severity of his injury is clear. But recover he did and he was ever present in the 1951–52 title-winning side, and Hugh also played a peripheral role in the other two championship-winning sides. Capped once by Scotland, against Wales in the 1948–49 season, he made it a memorable occasion by scoring another unlikely goal. Remarkably, although Howie did not feature in the next Scotland game, Hibs still supplied both full-backs. It was a measure of the strength of pool Hibs had that Jock Govan neatly slipped in to partner Davie Shaw. After retiring from the game Hugh took up journalism and he was occupied in that capacity until he tragically lost his life in a motor accident in January 1958.

HUGGINS, Dave

Goalkeeper

Born: Edinburgh, 2 February 1962.
Career: Tynecastle BC, HIBERNIAN 1978, East Fife 1981, Arniston Rangers 1981, Cowdenbeath 1983.

■ Dave joined Hibernian straight from Tynecastle Boys Club. He made his goalkeeping debut against Morton in April 1980 and as a Scottish schoolboy cap was expected to show up well. However, he managed only three games in that season and his Hibernian career ended soon afterwards. In May 1981 he joined East Fife but he was able to make only a single appearance there, and despite being linked with Cowdenbeath he actually played the remainder of his football in the junior ranks with non-League Arniston Rangers. Nevertheless, he can at least reflect on a career that fortunately took place in 1979–80. It may have been the season that saw Hibs relegated to the First Division, but it did boast the presence (at times!) of George Best.

HUGHES, John

Centre-half

Born: Edinburgh, 19 September 1964.
Career: Arbroath, Newtongrange Star, Berwick Rangers, Swansea 1989, Falkirk 1990, Celtic 1995, HIBERNIAN 1996, Ayr United, Falkirk 2002.

■ Something of an enigma, Hughes was a larger than life player who defended with his heart and soul, was vocal in his play and by dint of his large frame was seldom missed. He was a noted prankster in the dressing room and training ground, so how then to square his transformation after playing into a wholehearted manager who was both thoughtful and also committed to playing silky, passing football? John Hughes was actually aged 23 when he finally made it into the ranks of professional football, joining Berwick after an abortive spell with Arbroath and having reverted to junior football with Newtongrange Star. From Berwick, Hughes, who was nicknamed 'Yogi', moved to Wales with Swansea. Jim Jefferies signed Hughes for Falkirk and the big centre-half never looked back. He won two First Division Championships with the Bairns and was a 'man mountain' of a captain. From Falkirk it was on to Celtic in a £250,000 deal. A Leith-bred youngster, John was happy at Celtic but maintains he was delighted when Hibernian stepped in to sign him. Quickly made club captain, he was the type of 'hero figure' that the Hibernian support was able to establish a huge rapport with. John helped Hibs battle out of the First Division but as father time crept on was allowed to leave and join Ayr United. Remarkably, he was in the Ayr side that dumped Hibs from the League Cup in the 2002 semi-final. He returned to Falkirk initially as player-coach but then ultimately as manager, and he was First Division Manager of the Year in 2005. Falkirk then established themselves in the Premier Division and in 2008 were within an ace of making the top-six split.

HUGHES, Pat

Centre-half

Born: Coatbridge, 28 February 1945.
Career: Whitburn Juniors, HIBERNIAN 1954, St Mirren, Darlington 1965.

■ A tall, left-sided player who despite never being one of the 'big' names at Easter Road made 68 League appearances in his eight years at the club. He broke into the first team in the 1956–57 season and made a dozen outings as Hibernian achieved mid-table anonymity.

When his career ended the club had hardly progressed; indeed in 1963 they only just avoided the drop. In April 1964 Pat was given a free transfer.

HUNTER, Gordon

Centre-half

Born: Wallyford, 3 May 1967.
Career: Musselburgh Windsor, HIBERNIAN 1983, Dundee 1998, Cowdenbeath 1998, Hamilton Accies 1999.

■ Gordon had a strange start to his Hibs career. Bertie Auld signed him in 1983 and 24 hours later Auld was sacked! Fortunately, the subsequent manager Pat Stanton kept Hunter on and 13 years of loyal service followed. A wonderfully perceptive centre-half, he was also noted for his fairness in his desire to win. Picking highlights from such a lengthy career is never easy but a few do stand out. In August 1994 Gordon entered Hibernian history when he ended the nightmare run of 22 consecutive games against Hearts without victory. He scored the only goal of a derby game at Tynecastle in the 62nd minute of the game at the Gorgie Road end, and the press photograph of Gordon leaping to the crowd to celebrate is an enduring image. To this day Gordon has mixed feelings about that goal: '…it was embarrassing that it took so long to end that miserable run and if someone else could have scored a derby winner in half the time I would have been happier'. Gordon, who was not the tallest of centre-backs, was the lynchpin in Alex Miller's defence and won a League Cup-winners' medal in 1991 against Dunfermline Athletic. Hibs, having beaten Rangers 1–0 at Hampden in an epic semi-final, had understandably high hopes for the Final but it was no foregone conclusion and Gordon played with his customary concentration to ensure the trophy came back to Easter Road. It was doubly satisfying for Gordon as he had been an 18-year-old in the Hibernian side beaten by Aberdeen in the 1985 League Cup Final. Remarkably he played in three Finals, the last one being the 1993 match against Rangers at Celtic Park which Hibs lost 1–2. After 13 years' service he was granted a testimonial in September 1996 and Coventry City provided the opposition. He was sent-off twice in his Hibernian career; coincidentally both occasions while in direct opposition to Mark Hateley of Rangers. Gordon made 339 outings in League matches alone for Hibs before moving to Australian side Canberra Cosmos, and although he returned to Scotland he was

unable to resurrect his career – despite a five-day spell with Cowdenbeath! Only Arthur Duncan, Pat Stanton, Willie Ormond, Eddie Turnbull and Gordon Rae were able to better Hunter's 339 appearances for the club.

HUNTER, Willie

Winger

Born: Edinburgh, 14 February 1940.
Career: Edinburgh Norton, Motherwell 1957, Detriot Cougars 1967, HIBERNIAN 1968.

■ Despite being raised in Abbeyhill, it was as one of Motherwell's excellent 'Ancell Babes' side that Willie had made his name. How unfortunate that Willie did not join Hibernian until 1968 for as a youth for he was a keen Hibs fan. Nevertheless, he made light of his late arrival and gave some inspired performances in 1969. His debut came in February against Clyde and he nabbed his first goal for the club against Morton. In truth his role was helping to bring on the younger players around him but perhaps Willie had arrived too late to make a real impact for he soon drifted from the picture. He travelled to South Africa to end his playing career and was then assistant manager at Portsmouth to his former 'Well teammate Ian St John. He later managed Queen of the South and Inverness Thistle in his own right.

HURTADO, Eduardo

Centre-forward

Born: Ecuador, 8 August 1974.
Career: Colo Colo (Chile), Los Angeles Galaxy, New England Revolution, Liga Deportivo Universitario (Ecuador), St Gallen, HIBERNIAN 2001.

■ An Ecuadorian centre-forward, it appears that Eduardo (or 'The Tank' as he was nicknamed) was past his best when he joined Hibs. Alex McLeish signed him as Hibs had made a faltering start to the 2001–02 season but sadly the big centre-forward was unable to reverse things. He stood at 6ft 3in and weighed over 14st but the important statistic was that he had scored 43 goals in 71 international outings for Ecuador. Ulises De La Cruz, the Hibs full-back, was a welcoming teammate for Eduardo. Hurtado was arguably seen as a direct replacement for Mixu Paatelainen who had moved to Strasbourg and Craig Brewster who was out injured. Ultimately, Hurtado proved slow and cumbersome and other than goals against St Johnstone and Stranraer did little to impress. He was released when Bobby Williamson took over from Franck Sauzee.

HUTCHINSON, Bobby

Forward

Born: Glasgow, 19 June 1953.
Career: Aberdeen Lads' Club, Montrose 1972, Dundee 1974, HIBERNIAN 1977, Wigan Athletic 1980, Tranmere Rovers 1981, Mansfield Town 1982, Tranmere Rovers 1984, Bristol City 1984, Walsall 1987, Blackpool (loan) 1987, Carlisle United 1988.

■ Four times a Cup semi-finalist and one time a beaten finalist, Bobby was quite an unlucky player. He joined Hibs in November 1977 from Dundee in the deal that took the hugely popular Erich Schaedler to Dens Park. This was a considerable handicap for any player and it was clear that Bobby would have to justify his presence pretty swiftly. He was a forward with an eye for goal and made his Hibs debut against Partick Thistle at Easter Road in November 1977. He hit a bit of a purple patch in late 1978, scoring in three consecutive League games and overall he bagged 13 goals in 68 League matches. That, however, was never going to be enough to dispel the memories of Schaedler and thus Bobby moved on. His career took him to England where he crammed in an impressive number of low-level clubs, scoring goals for almost all of them, most notably Bristol City.

Eduardo Hurtado

I

IRVINE, Willie (1)

Centre-forward

Born: Stirling, 28 December 1963.

Career: Dunipace Juniors, Stirling Albion 1982, HIBERNIAN 1986, Dunfermline 1987, Meadowbank Thistle 1990, Berwick Rangers 1992, Alloa Athletic 1996, Stenhousemuir 2001.

■ With well over 500 senior appearances in the Scottish game (and 199 League goals) there is no doubting the longevity of Willie Irvine's career. Willie started out with Stirling Albion in 1982, joining them from Dunipace Juniors. He was a noted striker for them and scored five times in the famous 20–0 Scottish Cup demolition of Selkirk in 1984. Indeed, he scored 25 goals that season and 20 the next which was sufficient to lure Hibs to buy him for £35,000 in June 1986. His career at Easter Road saw him make a quite stunning start. He had a goal in a friendly against Seville and then two days later bagged a hat-trick against Chelsea. But such a prolific rate proved impossible to maintain and he scored twice in six games over the remainder of the season with both goals coming in a 3–2 win over Clydebank. It was, however, a time when Hibs were not scoring enough goals generally and Willie was not to stay long. From Easter Road his career carried him to Dunfermline, FR Vidar (Norway), Airdrie, Meadowbank and Berwick Rangers before he settled with Alloa Athletic. He proved himself an able marksman for the Wasps but it was his unwilling part in a siege at Glenochil Prison that catapulted his name into the national newspapers. He emerged unscathed from that hostage incident and continued to give Alloa excellent service into the early 2000s.

IRVINE, Willie (2)

Centre-forward

Born: Whitburn, 26 May 1956.

Career: Dunipace Juniors, Celtic 1972, Fauldhouse United, Alloa Athletic 1977, Motherwell 1979, HIBERNIAN 1982, Falkirk 1986.

■ Another Willie Irvine, and another who started his career with Dunipace Juniors and played with both Alloa and Hibernian! Best known for the striking partnership he forged with Steve Cowan, Irvine was a quick striker whose approach to the game was direct and pacy. Willie began his senior career with Celtic, signing for Jock Stein's club as a 16-year-old. He was farmed out to Whitburn Juniors before being called up to Celtic Park. Competition was inevitably keen at Parkhead and he was freed in 1977 having failed to reach the first team. He then went from junior football to Alloa Athletic, bagged 29 goals in a season and in 1979 Motherwell snapped him up for £25,000. Given that he had already netted 13 goals for Alloa that term there were understandably high hopes for him. Scoring on his debut against Dundee United he quickly revealed himself to be a lightening quick and direct poacher. In the Steelmen's promotion-winning team of 1981–82 he was their top scorer with 21 goals. However, like manager Davie Hay, he was to leave in the shadow of that triumph, electing to move to Hibernian. While at Hibs he was slow off the mark. In the 1982–83 campaign he mustered only four League goals, but he was the second top scorer in the Premier League during the following 1983–84 campaign. His haul of 19 goals was such that Aberdeen tabled a sizeable bid to lure him north…to no avail. Willie was nicknamed 'Noddy' by virtue of his unusual running style and if he had a fault it was perhaps that he was exceedingly left-sided. He spent a period on loan to Falkirk at the tail end of the 1985–86 season before joining Ayr United.

JACK, Mathias

Midfield/defender

Born: Leipzig, 15 February 1969.
Career: Stahl Brandenburg, VFL Odenburgh 1991, Rot Weiss Essen 1993, VFI Bochum 1995, Fortuna Dusseldorf 1997, HIBERNIAN 1999, Grindavik (Iceland) 2003, SV Meppen 2006.

■ Mathias was a powerful German-born defender who could also occupy the holding midfield berth. He joined Hibernian in July 1999 and provided much needed muscle to a Hibernian side that was increasingly earning respect for its flair. A rather combative player his name found its way into referees' notebooks with alarming frequency. However, without his energy the likes of O'Neill, Latapy and Sauzee might have found it harder to flourish. There was an odd 'tail-piece' to his Hibs career. He was out of contract in Edinburgh in the summer of 2002 and spent a brief time looking for a club before Bobby Williamson offered him a single year 'extension'. Legend has it that Williamson spotted Jack out running near Arthur's Seat and was so impressed by his 'get up and go' that he offered him terms. However, he played very few games in the 2002–03 season. Mathias was enigmatic in that his 'growling' persona on the pitch was offset by a lovely friendly manner off the field that made him a pleasure to chat to.

JACKSON, Chris

Midfield

Born: Edinburgh, 29 October 1973.
Career: Salveson BC, HIBERNIAN 1991, Stirling Albion 1998, Cowdenbeath 1999, Clydebank 1999, Montrose 2000, East Fife 2000, Stenhousemuir 2001, Brechin 2002, Arbroath 2005.

■ Flame-haired midfielder Christopher Robert Jackson was part of the Easter Road scene for most of the 1990s, but he had the misfortune to arrive too late to impact on the League Cup win in 1991 and to leave before the promotion success of 1999. Nevertheless, he did make his mark and scored early in his career against Hearts at Tynecastle. He was never quite able to grab an automatic spot and eventually moved on to Stirling Albion. Chris then had the pleasure of coming back to haunt Hibs, scoring the winner in a replay as Albion knocked the Hibees out of the Scottish Cup in season 1998–99. From Stirling his career took on an almost 'blink and you miss it' series of stays at several smaller clubs.

JACKSON, Darren

Midfield/forward

Born: Edinburgh, 25 July 1966.
Career: Broxburn Athletic, Meadowbank 1985, Newcastle United 1986, Dundee United 1988, HIBERNIAN 1992, Celtic 1997, Hearts 1999, Livingston 2001, St Johnstone 2001, Clydebank 2002.

■ One of the more extrovert players in recent football, Jackson had a natural ability that encompassed not just playing but also upsetting referees and opposition supporters. Yet when he concentrated on the game he was a wonderfully talented player capable of moments of sublime ability. A proven goalscorer, he initially served Meadowbank Thistle, Newcastle United and Dundee United and played for the latter in the epic 1991 Scottish Cup Final against Motherwell (which United lost 3–4 despite a Jackson goal). When moving from Newcastle to Dundee United he cost £200,000 and this was indication of the latent talent that lurked beneath a rather spiky exterior. It was on Tyneside that he had formed a lasting friendship with Paul 'Gazza' Gascoigne that saw the bold Jackson feature in the centre spread of *Hello* magazine when Gazza got married. Darren joined Hibernian in the summer of 1992 and scored 13 goals in his first League season as a Hibee. Indeed, he remained a frequent marksman for Hibs over the next five seasons and must have caused consternation when he scored the winner for Hibs in the 1993 League Cup semi-final against his former Dundee United employers. In all he scored 50 goals in 172 League matches and was rarely missing from first-team action due to his super fitness. While at Hibs he won both Scotland B and Scotland full international caps. Darren spent more time with Hibernian than any of his other eight senior clubs, which is measure in itself of how much he enjoyed Easter Road. He moved to Celtic in the close season of 1997 for £1.5 million which was a good return for Hibernian, but his time at Parkhead was blighted by a serious illness which required a brain operation to rectify. Later Darren played for Hearts and Livingston and his performances against Hibs always seemed to carry a little extra spice.

JAMES, Craig

Full-back

Born: Middlesbrough, 15 November 1982.
Career: Sunderland, HIBERNIAN (loan) 2002, Port Vale 2003, Darlington 2006, Livingston 2007.

■ An astute signing for Hibs, this lithe and quick full-back added much to the Hibernian scene in his short stay during the 2002–03 campaign. He played in over 20 matches for the club and scored twice, including a strike in the never to be forgotten 4–4 draw with Hearts at Tynecastle. Alas, Hibernian were unable to secure his services on a long-term deal and he returned to Sunderland.

JAMIESON, Willie

Centre-forward/centre-half

Born: Barnsley, 27 April 1963.
Career: Edina Hibs, HIBERNIAN 1979, Hamilton Accies 1985, Dundee 1990, Partick Thistle 1992, Hearts 1994, Ayr United 1995.

■ A tall and powerful youngster, Willie broke into the Hibs side in the early-1980s and provided a glut of goals. The fact that he was comfortable at either centre-half or centre-forward enhanced his prospects no end. He won a First Division Championship badge at Easter Road in 1981 but was rather surprisingly allowed to leave on a free transfer some four years later. His Easter Road career had run from 1980 to 1985 and brought 27 goals from 117 League matches. John Lambie signed him for Hamilton and what an astute move that proved; Willie helping Accies to two First Division titles. He joined Dundee in 1990 and won a Centenary Cup medal at Fir Park that year before adding another First Division badge two years later. His career thereafter carried him to Partick Thistle, Hearts and Ayr United. He was with the Honest Men when they landed the 1997 Second Division Championship and in the summer of 1998 joined Partick Thistle as assistant manager.

JEAN, Earl

Midfield

Born: St Lucia, 9 October 1971.
Career: Leca FC 1993, FC Felgueiras 1995, Ipswich Town 1996, Rotherham United 1997, Plymouth Argyle 1998, HIBERNIAN 2000, W Connection 2000.

■ Signed in the 1999–2000 season, Earl made just five outings as a substitute and failed to make the impression hoped for. He hailed from the Caribbean island of St Lucia and joined Hibs with a solid reputation having picked up 68 international caps and having served clubs in Portugal (Olieveirense, Lecca and Selgoireas) and England (Ipswich, Rotherham and Plymouth). A trial period when Hibs were in the Caribbean in the winter shut-down convinced Alex McLeish that the man from the bizarrely named club Joe Public could prove useful. Sadly, he never really adapted to the rigours of the Scottish game and was released in the summer of 2000.

JOHANSSON, Jonatan

Striker

Born: Stockholm, 16 August 1975.
Career: TSP 1995, FC Flora Tallin 1997, Rangers 1997, Charlton Athletic 2000, Norwich City (loan) 2005, Malmo 2006, HIBERNIAN 2009.

■ Capped 91 times by Finland, Johansson was a former teammate of Mixu Paatelainen in the Finnish national side. A £500,000 transfer to Rangers in 1997 had brought him to the attention of Scottish football fans and in the 1998–99 season he scored against Hibs in November 1999 at Ibrox. Rangers made a near £3 million profit when they sold Jonathan to English Premiership club Charlton, he in turn responded by scoring over a dozen goals for the south London club. He made his debut for Hibs against Hearts at Tynecastle on 3 January 2009 and manager Paatelainen said of his former teammate 'As well as vast international experience he has experience of the Scottish Premier League, so I'm sure he will settle very quickly into our squad.'

JOHNSTON, Leslie

Centre-forward

Born: Glasgow, 16 August 1920.
Career: Clydebank Juniors, Clyde 1941, HIBERNIAN 1947, Clyde 1947, Celtic 1948, Stoke City 1949, Shrewsbury Town 1953, Hinckley Athletic.

■ The career of Leslie Hamilton Johnston merits recalling as he was a huge 'name' in his heyday and Hibernian capturing his signature was a clear mark of the club's intent. When Leslie Johnstone joined Hibernian for £10,000 on Valentine's Day 1947 his transfer was a Scottish record fee, and it matters little that by October 1948 he was returning to Clyde. Born in Glasgow on 16 August 1920, he had begun his career at Clydebank Juniors and then moved to Clyde in December 1941. Capped by Scotland during the war, he was viewed as a crafty, intelligent leader who was assured in front of goal. Hibs bought him in March 1947 but his debut away to Falkirk on 5 April turned into high farce with the game being abandoned due to a waterlogged pitch with only 15 minutes remaining. One week later he made a scoring bow against Celtic in a 2–0 Easter Road win. At the start of the 1947–48 season he lit up the Easter Road scene in dramatic fashion. His four-goal haul in the second match of the campaign (a 7–1 demolition of Airdrie) had the *Edinburgh Evening News* positively purring as they described him as 'the complete footballer, displaying expert dribbling and opening the game to all around him.' Few could have predicted that when he scored at Hampden in early October against Queen's Park he was netting his last goal for the club. Stories soon emerged that he had not settled with Hibs and wished to return to Glasgow and Clyde. For £8,000 Paddy Travers, the Clyde supremo, was able to take him back to Shawfield in October 1947. He had played only four League games of the new season but clearly he had been struck by wanderlust. His spell at Clyde was equally brief and soon Leslie was off to Celtic for £12,000, thus ensuring that a scarcely heard-of £30,000 had been spent on him in three quick transfers. His debut for Celtic in October 1948

BOBBY JOHNSTONE

Inside-right

Born: Selkirk, 7 September 1929.
Career: Selkirk, HIBERNIAN 1946, Manchester City 1955, HIBERNIAN 1959, Oldham Athletic 1960.

■ Nicknamed 'Nicker' by dint of his scurrying, probing style (which resembled the border collie of that name in a *Sunday Post* cartoon) he was in some ways the classic small Scottish inside-forward. His forte was not speed nor was it strength, rather it was an ability to dart between opponents, pass with unerring accuracy and entertain with his natural ball skills. That he was also a considerable goalscorer made him the complete footballer in his era.

Born and bred in the lovely border town of Selkirk, he joined Willie McCartney's Hibernian in 1946. He was only 17 at the time. The diminutive apprentice painter made traditional progress through the Hibernian reserve team before breaking into the first team in the late-1940s. His name was to be the final piece in the 'Famous Five' jigsaw and for almost a decade Easter Road became synonymous with great entertaining football. He made his debut at St Mirren in early April 1948 and it was in the 1948–49 season that he made the first-team spot his own. When Hibernian landed the title in 1951 and 1952 Johnstone was a key player. A simple glance at the record books will reveal just how good a player Bobby was. He won 17 caps for Scotland (scoring half a dozen goals), won two League Championship badges with Hibs (1951 and 1952) and scored in two consecutive FA Cup Finals (lifting the Cup in the second of those Finals). He was certainly a man for the big occasion. When Scotland beat England 3–2 at Wembley in April 1951 he scored on his debut, and Bobby Johnstone represented Great Britain in 1955 when the combined home nations tackled the Rest of Europe. When he moved to Manchester City in March 1955 it cost the Maine Road club £22,000. Within weeks he scored City's goal in the FA Cup Final against Newcastle. City lost that game but they won the following year and again Johnstone scored – this time with a header. He returned to Hibernian in September 1959, making his second debut in a 4–2 home win over Kilmarnock. Although he was thicker set by this time he had enough left to score his 100th goal for the club. October 1960 saw him return to Lancashire, this time with Oldham Athletic. Later he would play semi-professionally with non-League Whitton Albion before briefly managing Workington Town. Bobby died in August 2001.

was rather cheeky…scoring twice against Hibs as the Glasgow club won 2–1 at Easter Road! His career wound down with spells south of the border turning out for Stoke City and Shrewsbury Town.

JONELEIT, Torben

Central-defender

Born: Monte Carlo, 17 May 1987.
Career: AS Monaco 2006, HIBERNIAN (loan) 2007, AS Monaco 2008.

■ A German Under-21 international, Torben was signed by John Collins but was released in January 2008 by new Hibs boss Mixu Paatelainen. The 20-year-old central-defender had been signed on a one-year loan deal from French club Monaco. Collins had been keen on the youngster as he was clearly a 'thinking, football playing' central-defender. He played three League matches for the club, two of them as a substitute.

JONES, Mervyn

Full-back

Born: 6 October 1949.
Career: Edina Hearts, HIBERNIAN 1967, Falkirk 1971, Stirling Albion 1972, Cowdenbeath 1975, Newtongrange Star 1977.

■ Mervyn had a couple of seasons in the Hibernian fist team in the late-1960s. However, with the likes of John Brownlie and Erich Schaedler competing for full-back berths his options became quite limited. In July 1971 he joined Falkirk but he only spent one season at Brockville before moving to Stirling Albion. The remainder of his career was spent in the Second Division.

JONES, Rob

Centre-half

Born: Stockton-on-Tees, 3 November 1979.
Career: Gateshead, Stockport County 2003, Grimsby Town 2004, HIBERNIAN 2007.

■ Team captain as Hibernian lifted the Scottish League Cup in 2007, Jones was an inspirational signing. A commanding central-defender, he not only lifted the trophy but also scored the opening goal with a towering header. The 6ft 7in defender was signed by Tony Mowbray and the Hibs boss said at the time: 'Rob is a player we have been watching over the course of last season and we are convinced of his quality and good techniques'. Those qualities were needed as Gary Smith and Gary Caldwell had both left the club and Hibs were desperately short of height in central defence. Certainly it seemed like an inspired signing, indeed by August 2007 the Leeds United manager Dennis Wise was attempting to lure Jones back south. Dominant in defence, he was also a decided asset at Hibernian's attacking set-pieces and his dependable temperament made him 'a rock' in the club's defence.

K

KANE, John

Midfield

Born: Glasgow, 8 June 1987.
Career: HIBERNIAN, Motherwell, Partick Thistle 2006, Glenafton, Stranraer 2008.

■ A former Scotland Under-18 international, John played only one match for Hibs despite being part of the youth set up at Easter Road for five seasons. His big day came in April 2004 when he was a playing substitute against Livingston. A fairly combative defender, he perhaps lacked the pace necessary at the top level. He moved to Motherwell but was not quite able to break through there either, but he eventually put his 6ft 1in frame to good use with Stranraer.

KANE, Paul

Midfield

Born: Edinburgh, 20 June 1965.
Career: Salveson BC, HIBERNIAN 1982, Oldham Athletic 1991, Aberdeen 1991, Viking Stavanger, St Johnstone 1997, Clyde 2002.

■ Paul's father, Jimmy Kane, was on Hibs' books briefly before moving to Cowdenbeath in November 1959 without ever having played a League match (this largely due to a broken leg early in his career). Paul on the other hand made over 200 outings as a Hibee and became one of the most popular Hibs players of the modern era. Kane joined Hibs in 1982 from Salveson BC and as a life-long fan brought up in Leith was delighted to do so. His League debut came in a rather embarrassing away game to Dundee United during September 1983 which saw Hibs thrashed 5–0. But Kane was not to be deterred by such an inauspicious start. His game contained plenty of energy and sufficient strength to make him as combative a midfielder as any in the Scottish game at one stage. By 1986 he was part of the Hibs side that lost the League Cup Final to Aberdeen 0–3, indeed Aberdeen knocked Hibs out of the Scottish Cup at the semi-final stage, and Kane in later years would say that facing the experienced Alex McLeish, Willie Miller and Jim Leighton came just too soon for a young Hibs team. October 1987 gave Paul one of his finest memories. He scored the winning goal at Easter Road as Hibernian defeated Hearts 2–1 and in an era in which Hearts largely held the upper hand it was clearly a special moment. Kane spent nine seasons at Easter Road before moving on to Oldham in February 1991 and indeed was barely out of the door when the Wallace Mercer take-over bid surfaced. It says much for Paul's Hibernian leanings that he travelled up from Oldham to help in the 'Hands Off Hibs' movement. From Oldham he journeyed to Alex Smith's Aberdeen in November 1991 but he left Pittodrie a few years later to join Viking Stavanger of Norway in Scotland's first-ever Bosman transfer. He came back to Scotland when he was 31 and played with St Johnstone then Clyde before retiring in the summer of 2003, having accomplished a long-held ambition of completing 20 years in the senior game. Three times a League Cup Finalist (with Hibs, Aberdeen and St Johnstone) he was unlucky to never win a medal in his lengthy career.

KEAN, Sammy

Wing-half

Career: Kirkintilloch Rob Roy, HIBERNIAN 1938.

■ Wing-half Sammy Kean played an influential role in the Hibernian team which won the Scottish League Championship in 1948. A native of Dumbarton, he made a major contribution whenever he played, although his work was often overshadowed by more glamorous forwards in the same team. Signed from Kirkintilloch Rob Roy in 1938 by Willie McCartney he went on to win international honours with the Scottish League, but the war badly disrupted his career. In 1941, he teamed up with wartime guest player Matt Busby to form one of the strongest half-back lines in Scotland, and Kean always believed the pair's best performance together was the game when Hibs fought back from 0–2 down to take the Summer Cup from Rangers in 1941. Among the interesting items the winning Hibs players received was a specially commissioned recording of the BBC Radio commentary. Such was Kean's prowess that he and Tommy McIntyre were the subject of a £10,000 bid from Manchester United before the war…which Hibs turned down. Never the most prolific of marksmen he did however grab a goal in the Scottish Cup thriller against Raith Rovers which Hibs won 4–3 at Kirkcaldy in 1949, and he had been a scorer from all of 60 yards when Lawrie Reilly made his Hibs debut. A far less happy Cup memory was being part of the Hibernian side sensationally ditched from the competition by little Edinburgh City (despite the match having been moved to Easter Road!). When Willie McCartney died and Hugh Shaw took over as manager at Easter Road, Kean gave up playing and became assistant trainer to Jimmy McColl, and he instilled a great sense of spirit among the squad according to no less a judge than Lawrie Reilly. By July 1954 he was recognized as the first-team coach at Easter Road. 'He was one of the great characters of the game and I personally never saw him in a bad mood,' recalled Reilly. 'He was a super person to have around on the training ground and every morning I couldn't get into training quick enough. He was a real bundle of fun.' In 1957 Kean moved to Dundee and went on to help coach Bob Shankly's Championship-winning team of 1962. By 1965 Sammy was persuaded to take over the reins at Falkirk but his stint there was not a success and he moved on to resume coaching duties at Partick Thistle.

KEENAN, Joe

Midfield

Born: Southampton, 14 October 1982.
Career: Westerlo (Belgium), Willem II (Holland), Melbourne Victory, HIBERNIAN 2008.

■ Joe was signed by Mixu Paatelainen in the summer of 2008. Despite being born in Southampton he was aware of Hibs, having played in Australia alongside former Hibee Grant Brebner. The 25-year-old made his debut in a League defeat at Kilmarnock and then scored his opening goal for the club in the disastrous League Cup defeat at home to Morton.

KELLY, Colin

Goalkeeper

Born: London, 19 October 1961.
Career: Balloch Juveniles, HIBERNIAN 1980, Dundee 1981, Montrose (loan) 1981, Morton 1984.

■ Colin joined Hibs in April 1980 and the following season he made his only two League outings for the club in what was a promotion-winning First Division campaign. However, in February 1981 he was allowed to join Dundee and spent three seasons on Tayside before moving to Greenock Morton.

KERR, Brian

Midfield

Born: Bellshill, 12 October 1981.
Career: Newcastle United 2001, Motherwell 2004, HIBERNIAN 2007.

■ Brian had the unenviable task of filling the midfield void left by Scott Brown's transfer to Celtic. Signed on a Bosman from Motherwell in the summer of 2007, he made what can only be deemed the perfect start by scoring the only goal of the opening game of the season – away to Hearts! Brian had won three Scotland caps under Berti Vogts and ironically had been a 12-year-old schoolboy on Hibs' book of youngsters (this during the reign of Alex Miller). He was released by Hibs in the autumn of 2008.

KERR, Jimmy

Goalkeeper

Career: Ormiston Primrose, HIBERNIAN, Queen of the South 1952.

■ One of the bravest goalkeepers ever to serve Hibernian, Jimmy was signed by Willie McCartney in very unusual circumstances. Playing as a 15-year-old in a schools match at Easter Road he was spotted by the club's hierarchy from the stands. By the time he was 17 he was a Hibernian player. He played at juvenile level with Ormiston Former Pupils and was capped three times by Scotland at Schoolboy level. When Hibs secured his signature they almost immediately farmed him out to the tough learning grounds of Scottish junior football with Ormiston Primrose. Tall at 5ft 11in, and strong with his 12st 2lb frame, Kerr was highly mobile with a reassuring presence. During the war years he served in the RAF but he managed to play first-team football when on leave and he was in the Hibees side that won the Summer Cup Final against Rangers in 1941. A plumber by trade, he played in what was quite clearly a different era. Quality Hibs players of his age like Bobby Nutley, Sammy Kean and Arthur Milne worked in the Leith Shipyards during the war, while Davie Shaw was a miner and Tommy McIntyre worked away from football as a press photographer! Jimmy Kerr's place in Hibernian folklore was assured when he saved a penalty from George Hamilton in the 1947 Scottish Cup Final but to no avail as Aberdeen won a Hampden Park thriller 2–1. Earlier in the season he had been charged into the net by Brown of Motherwell and despite furious protests the goal was allowed to stand. Kerr was the reliable custodian when Hibs won the first of their post-war Championships in 1948 but missed two chunks of that season due to having been badly injured against Clyde in September at Easter Road. Prior to leaving to join Queen of the South he was presented with an inscribed lighter and cigarette case…a sign of a different era if ever there was one. Extremely highly thought of by his fellow players, he clearly impressed those who ran Hibernian too for he was invited onto the board long after his playing days were behind him. There was an element of irony in Kerr finally losing his place to understudy Tommy Younger, given that both goalkeepers would sit on the same board of directors at Easter Road when Tom Hart was in charge of affairs!

KILGOUR, Rab

Full-back

Born: Edinburgh, 20 October 1956.
Career: Tynecastle BC, Meadowbank 1975, Whitehill Welfare 1978, HIBERNIAN 1978, St Johnstone 1980.

■ Initially on Meadowbank Thistle's staff, Rab reverted to non-League football with Whitehill Welfare before Hibernian signed him in 1978. He made his debut against Rangers at right-back just weeks later and impressed all with his composure. However, he rarely scaled those heights again and was destined to be a fringe player at Easter Road. His short career at Hibs ended when he was granted a free-transfer and moved on to St Johnstone. Five seasons at Muirton Park followed and he had two goals in his first season with them, a feat he never achieved while a Hibee. That was a good haul for a man who started his career in Perth by managing to get sent off during his pre-season debut!

KILLEN, Chris

Centre-forward

Born: New Zealand, 8 October 1981.
Career: Manchester City 1999, Wrexham (loan) 2000, Port Vale (loan) 2001, Oldham Athletic 2002, HIBERNIAN 2006, Celtic 2007.

■ Recruited in January 2006 by Tony Mowbray, Killen was a powerful target man who had an all too brief Hibernian career. He had 21 caps and 13 international goals for New Zealand and arrived from Oldham having been on target 15 times in the season before he ventured north. In September 2006 he cemented his growing reputation in Edinburgh when he contrived to score both goals in a 2–1 home win over Rangers; and earned a red card to boot! Increasingly he became the fulcrum of Hibs' attacking options. By early-2007 Hibs were going well and Killen had the 'wind in his sails', but then he injured his Achilles tendon and without his presence to lead the attack Hibs were bereft of their spearhead. By the time he had regained his fitness it was time to renegotiate his one-year Hibernian contract. When he predictably moved to Celtic on a Bosman in the summer of 2007 he lifted the lid on events at Easter Road where it transpired he had only been offered a further one-year deal when clubs such as Cardiff City were offering a three-year deal. However, it was to Glasgow he journeyed and his loss was an undoubted blow to Hibernian, for he was a target man who had scored 16 League goals in only 25 matches.

KINLOCH, Bobby

Inside-forward

Career: Edinburgh Waverley, HIBERNIAN 1959, Greenock Morton 1962, Berwick Rangers 1964, Toronto City, Hamilton Steelers (Canada), Raith Rovers 1967, Dunfermline Athletic 1968.

■ Bobby broke into the Hibs side in the 1960–61 season and returned the most impressive figures of 10 goals in only 11 League matches. Considering that he also scored against Barcelona and Roma in Hibs' Fairs Cup adventures it was quite a season for Bobby. He will of course be forever remembered as the man who famously swapped jerseys with Joe Baker to confuse Barcelona. The following season he made only six League starts and it was clear that he was not going to be the answer to the post-Joe Baker era. He went to Greenock Morton in September 1962. From Scotland he emigrated to Canada where he played with Toronto City and Hamilton Steelers before the lure of Scotland called and he joined Raith Rovers. He was a reliable centre-back for Rovers in the same side as Ian Porterfield who would later make a name for himself with Sunderland at Wembley in 1973.

KIRKWOOD, Billy

Midfield/defender

Born: Edinburgh, 1 September 1958.
Career: Cornbank BC, Dundee United 1975, HIBERNIAN 1986, Dundee United 1987, Dunfermline 1987, Dundee 1988.

■ But for a brief stint at Easter Road, William John Kirkwood would surely have been a one-club man and that club would have been Dundee United. He joined the Tannadice outfit in 1976 and proved himself a versatile performer rattling in 67 goals in almost 400 outings despite many of them being as a defender. He won a Premier Division Championship badge in 1983 with United as well as two League Cup-winners' medals. He moved to Hibernian in 1986 and made his debut in the 'Souness match'. Impressively strong and economical, he was soon appointed club captain but his stay was short and he returned to Dundee United having played in only 26 League games for Hibs. Kirkwood was appointed manager of Dundee United but enjoyed greater success coaching at Hull, St Johnstone, Livingston and Dunfermline.

KONDE, Oumar

Defender

Born: Switzerland, 19 August 1979.
Career: FC Basle 1997, Blackburn Rovers 1998, Freiburg 1999, Hansa Rostock 2004, HIBERNIAN 2006, Panionios (Greece).

■ For a player that commanded £900,000 in transfer fees there is little doubt that Hibernian supporters remain mystified as to why. Konde rarely shone in his 14 outings as a Hibee and seemed ill-suited to the game in Scotland. He was aged 26 when Tony Mowbray convinced him to try Scotland. He had made 80 outings for Basle, where arguably he played his best football.

KONTE, Amadou

Forward

Born: Mali, 23 January 1981.
Career: Cambridge United 2004, HIBERNIAN 2003, Kalamata (Greece).

■ A brace of goals against Dinaburg in a second round Intertoto Cup tie in 2006 was perhaps the highlight of Amadou's two-year Hibernian career. He singularly failed to impress as a Hibs player and became a near cult figure following a series of hapless displays. Aged 25 he bought out the remainder of his contract in order to return to France to ponder a new career. At 6ft 3in he was an imposing figure when in full flight.

L

LAING, Dave
Wing-half
Born: Strathmiglo, 20 February 1942.
Career: Bayview YC, Hearts 1942, Clyde 1954, HIBERNIAN 1956, Gillingham 1957, Canterbury.

■ While with Hearts, Dave had been capped by the Scottish League before moving to Clyde for £5,000. He won a Scottish Cup-winners' badge as captain of Clyde but after two seasons at Shawfield moved to Hibernian. By this time his pace was going and he converted from wing-half to full-back. Alas, the move to Hibs had come too late and he only managed six games in the 1956–57 season before moving on. In August 1957 he joined Gillingham. It is interesting to note that Dave was the editor of the Hearts match programme at one stage and eventually ended up working as a sports reporter in England.

LAMBIE, Duncan
Winger
Born: Whitburn, 20 April 1952.

Career: Edina Hibs, Millwall 1968, Dundee 1971, St Johnstone 1974, Furth (West Germany) 1976, HIBERNIAN 1979.

■ Duncan was a flying winger who had enjoyed six years with Dundee and then three with St Johnstone before he arrived at Hibs via West Germany. He played only a handful of games for Hibernian but his haul of three goals in 13 League matches suggests he might have been a good addition had he arrived a few years earlier. Duncan made a most unusual Hibs debut, playing in the friendly at Tel Aviv in Israel. His brother was John Lambie who as a player was a solid full-back then began his coaching career at Hibs before managing Partick Thistle and Hamilton.

LARUSSON, Bjarnolfur
Midfield
Born: Iceland, 11 March 1976.

Career: IBV Iceland, HIBERNIAN 1997, Walsall 1998, Scunthorpe United 2000, IBV Iceland.

■ An Icelandic midfielder, Bjarni made his debut away to Kilmarnock in October 1997 and promptly scored. But he was unable to impose himself in Jim Duffy's team and as Hibs slipped to relegation under Alex McLeish he could not force his way back into the team. He failed to feature in Hibernian's First Division promotion campaign; in September 1988 he moved to the English midlands to join Walsall. He fitted in well there, helping the club achieve promotion to the First Division. He eventually returned to Iceland where he resumed his business and marketing studies, and he also did a little male modeling!

LATAPY, Russell

Midfield

Born: Trinidad, 2 August 1968.
Career: Trintoc, Port Morant, Newton, Porto 1995, Academica Coimbra 1996, Boavista 1997, HIBERNIAN 1998, Rangers 2001, Dundee United 2003, Falkirk 2003.

■ Russell Nigel Latapy was one of the most remarkably gifted players to serve Hibernian in the post-war era. The diminutive Russell had all of the skills to justify his nickname 'Little Magician'. He had over 50 caps for Trinidad and Tobago before he moved to Portugal and by the time he retired from international football had taken that total to over 100. His stint in the Iberian peninsular reached its zenith with Porto, and in Bobby Robson's side he was a UEFA Cup quarter-finalists and the first Trinidadian to play in the Champions League. Alas, in the aforementioned UEFA Cup he missed a vital spot-kick in a shoot-out against Sampdoria that cost the Portuguese club the tie. Signed during Hibernian's successful First Division campaign of 1998–99 he quickly won a host of admirers. His trickery, hard shooting and sheer entertainment value marked him out as the outstanding player not only at Hibs but in the First Division, and he was duly voted First Division Player of the Year in 1999. In the Scottish Premier League he found a fitting stage and his incisive play was a delight to watch. He scored in the famous 6–2 rout of Hearts and was generally Hibs' most direct weapon. Sadly, Russell's career at Hibernian ended in tawdry fashion. As the year 2001 got underway he was negotiating a new contract and was seemingly too far from the club's figures. A late-night drinking session in the spring saw him miss training. This was one indiscretion too many for the club and he did not play again for Hibs. Given that these events happened in the very season in which the club was chasing a Champions League spot and Scottish Cup glory this was sad indeed. In the summer of 2001 Russell moved to Rangers. Better perhaps to dwell on Russell's huge contribution to the revival of Hibernian which went before his fall from grace. He won both League Cup and Scottish Cup medals with Rangers, was promoted with Hibs and Falkirk and added a Challenge Cup medal while at the Bairns. He returned to the West Indies in late 2008.

LAURSEN, Ulrik

Full-back

Born: Denmark, 28 February 1976.
Career: OB Odense 1993, HIBERNIAN 2000, Celtic 2002, OB Odense 2006, FC Copenhagen 2008.

■ Ulrik was a Danish wing-back who always impressed with both his physique and his application. One of Alex McLeish's finest captures, the athletic Dane slotted into the Hibernian side with ease. Ulrik made his debut in the 0–0 draw with Hearts in July 2000 at Tynecastle, missed only a handful of games in his first season and even chipped in with a couple of League goals. Capped 26 times by Denmark at Under-21 level he was signed from OB Odense. Sadly, his second season at the club was compromised by injury, and when he returned to full fitness he left to join Celtic in a deal which the club could hardly refuse as a harsher economic climate swept through the game. He did not feature in Martin O'Neill's Celtic side with anything like the frequency he had Hibs'.

LAVETY, Barry

Centre-forward

Born: Johnstone, 21 August 1974.
Career: Gleniffer Thistle, St Mirren 1991, HIBERNIAN 1996, St Mirren (loan), Clydebank 2001, Team Bath 2002, St Mirren 2003.

■ 'Basher' was a £200,000 capture from St Mirren in August 1996. He scored on his debut against Brechin City and looked likely to become a successful Hibernian striker but unfortunately he was hit with a mystery virus soon afterwards and never seemed quite the same force again. He did score the opening goal of Hibs' season in the First Division (a winner at Greenock) but flitted in and out of the team; even re-joining St Mirren on loan at one stage. The general impression was that he was too out of condition to figure in Alex McLeish's First Division promotion-winning team. Eventually released, he returned to St Mirren but injury problems beset him and he was forced out of the game at a relatively early age. His first spell with St Mirren had been somewhat blighted by

a drug-related problem although he did find the net with impressive regularity. Between 1993 and 1995 he was capped nine times by Scotland at Under-21 level. He re-emerged in the game via a study course spent at Bath University where he represented Team Bath in the 2002–03 FA Cup trail.

LEHMANN, Dirk

Forward

Born: Aachen, Germany, 16 August 1971.
Career: FC Energie Cottbus, RWD Molenbeek, IFC Koln, Fulham, HIBERNIAN 1999, Brighton, Motherwell 2002.

■ A German striker with prodigious skills in the air, Dirk joined Hibernian in July 1999 and scored twice on his debut against Motherwell. He joined that select band of Hibees to have been sent-off in a friendly when he was sent packing against Caribbean opposition as Hibs spent the 1999–2000 winter shut-down in Tobago. That said, Lehmann had been subjected to almost continuous provocation and had previously never been sent off in his career. Dirk grabbed headlines in his early days at Hibs by virtue of wearing earings, which he would cover up with huge elastoplasts on match day. The sight of him running around with large white squares hanging from his ears

inevitably drew comments. However, he also earned column inches in the press for a few important goals in his time as a Hibs player. He netted in the 3–0 romp at Hearts in December 1999 and had two in a pulsating 5–2 win over Dundee at home in August 2000. Dirk played 59 games for Hibs in the League (most of them as substitute) and scored 16 goals. He gradually slipped down the pecking order as the likes of Zitelli and Libbra came on board, and he eventually moved to Brighton when he was unable to negotiate an extension to his contract. Prior to playing for Hibs he had been with FC Energie Cottbus, RWD Molenbeek, Cologne and Fulham. He returned to Scotland from Brighton to join Motherwell and was at Fir Park during the turbulence of 2002.

LEIGHTON, Jim

Goalkeeper

Born: Johnstone, 24 July 1958.
Career: Dalry Thistle, Aberdeen 1976, Manchester United 1988, Dundee 1992, HIBERNIAN 1993, Aberdeen 1997.

■ Arguably the greatest Scottish goalkeeper of his generation, Jim won League, Scottish Cup, League Cup and European Cup-winners' Cup medals – without ever representing the Old Firm! Indeed, Jim played 552 League games in Scotland alone. Leighton was hugely dependable, and crucially a wonderful performer for Scotland (his international career brought 81 caps and ran from 1982–1998!). His heroics at Pittodrie earned him a lucrative move to Manchester United and initially he flourished under Alex Ferguson at Old Trafford. It seemed that his 1988 switch for £750,000 was a master stroke by Fergie. Leighton cemented his place as Scotland's number-one goalkeeper while at Manchester until the fateful 1990 FA Cup Final against Crystal Palace when his manager blamed him for several mistakes. Crestfallen, Jim returned to Scotland and played with Dundee before Hibernian stepped in. He was a great performer for Hibs. Snapped up in July 1993 he was an ever present in the 1993–94 season and indeed over the four seasons he was a Hibee he missed only one League match in 154 games. The 6ft tall, slimly built custodian steered Hibs to a League Cup Final and was methodical in his match preparation. It is interesting to note that Jim played in goal against Hibernian for Deveronvale in a pre-season friendly in 1977 while on loan from Aberdeen (Hibs showed no mercy in a 6–0 win).

LEISHMAN, Tommy

Wing-half

Born: Stenhousemuir, 3 September 1937.
Career: Cowie Juveniles, St Mirren 1955, Liverpool 1959, HIBERNIAN 1963, Linfield 1965, Stranraer 1968.

■ Unthinkable perhaps today, but Leishman was signed by Hibernian from Liverpool. Recruited in January 1963 during the great freeze, he scored his first goal for Hibs against Falkirk but thereafter flitted in and out of the team for two and a half seasons. By 1964 it was clear he was not going to be a regular and he moved on to Linfield in Belfast, where he became player-manager. He did return to

Scotland in April 1968 when he joined Stranraer, and this was his second west of Scotland club for he had started his senior career in Paisley with St Mirren. Indeed, in 1959 he was part of their Scottish Cup-winning team that beat Aberdeen in a thrilling Hampden Final. This earned him a move to Liverpool and the English Second Division in 1962.

LENNON, Danny

Midfield

Born: Whitburn, 6 April 1970.
Career: Hutcheson Vale BC, HIBERNIAN 1985, Raith Rovers 1994, Ayr United 1999, Ross County 1999, Partick Thistle 1999, Gretna 2003.

■ Danny enjoyed a remarkably lengthy football career in Scotland and it is not unfair to say that Hibernian never really got the best from him. He was one of a talented group of youngsters at the club in the late-1980s. Signed on an 'S' form by John Blackley, Danny established himself in the Hibernian reserve side before breaking into the first team. In seven seasons with Hibs he played 37 times. He left Hibs for Raith Rovers, was a member of their famous League Cup-winning team and scored in their remarkable UEFA Cup clash with Bayern Munich. Capped by Northern Ireland at B international level, Danny undoubtedly got better as his career developed and probably reached his peak with Partick Thistle. In 2001 he was club captain as the Jags won the Second Division Championship in a canter, and by 2008 he was manager of Cowdenbeath.

LESLIE, Lawrie

Goalkeeper

Born: Edinburgh, 17 March 1935.
Career: Newtongrange Star, HIBERNIAN 1956, Airdrie 1959, West Ham United 1961, Stoke City 1963, Millwall 1966, Southend United 1968.

■ A reliable 5ft 11in goalkeeper, Lawrie caught the eye of Hibernian when playing with Newtongrange Star and the army. Manager Hugh Shaw signed him in 1956 and two years later the wisdom of that signing was apparent as Leslie gave an inspired display against

Rangers in the Scottish Cup semi-final. Unfortunately for the lad who was raised in Niddrie, Hibs slipped to defeat in the Final against Clyde. Surprisingly, Hibs allowed Leslie to move to Airdrie in November 1959 and such was his popularity that Lawrie was captain for a spell at Broomfield. He then enjoyed a career in England that saw useful stints in London and Stoke-on-Trent. His first port of call in London was with West Ham United where his time was blighted by injury – but he did play outfield against Arsenal! Capped five times by Scotland and four times by the Scottish League, Lawrie certainly enjoyed his career. Not bad for a lad who was almost killed in a road accident at the age of 10 and had a metal pin in his leg from that age onwards.

LIBBRA, Marc

Centre-forward

Born: France, 5 August 1982.
Career: Cannes, Marseilles, Toulouse 1999, HIBERNIAN 2001, Norwich City 2001, Creteil 2002, Ajaccio 2003, Livingston 2004.

■ An exceptional centre-forward, Alex Mcleish brought this French striker to Hibs during the 2000–01 season. Tall and powerful, he was, at

Marc Libbra

6ft 2in, also very good on the ground and scored some exceptional goals for Hibs. Indeed, he scored at Parkhead on his debut against Celtic and then gave the Glaswegians a torrid time in the 2001 Scottish Cup Final. Sadly, in the summer of 2001 he was unable to secure a suitable deal at Hibernian and he joined English First Division side Norwich. He scored a stunning hat-trick in a pre-season friendly match for Norwich against Fakenham Town, then netted within 11 seconds of his full League debut against Manchester City. He was released from his contract by Norwich in September 2002. Interestingly, he came back to Scotland in 2004 when he joined Livingston from French football.

LINWOOD, Alex

Midfield

Born: Glasgow, 13 March 1920.
Career: Muirkirk Juniors, St Mirren 1939, Middlesbrough 1946, HIBERNIAN 1947, Clyde 1948, Morton 1951.

■ Before Lawrie Reilly claimed the Hibs number-nine jersey as his own a number of players tried manfully to fill the position. Alex Linwood was among the quality recruits that Willie McCartney lured to the club and in truth he was an accomplished finisher (22 League goals in only 36 starts). Linwood was with Hibernian in 1947 and won a Scottish League Championship medal in his very first season. However, for all Alex was a most talented forward he was unable to command a regular spot. It was thus almost inevitable that Alex would move on and he duly joined Clyde in 1948. Alexander Bryce Linwood had begun his senior career with St Mirren in 1939 and dominated their goalscoring tables throughout the war years. For seven consecutive seasons he topped their scoring charts. Indeed, he scored 148 goals for St Mirren, a tally which included their Summer Cup Final winner against Rangers in 1943. His goalscoring heroics earned him a move to Middlesbrough in June 1946 for £5,000, and it was from 'Boro that Hibs bought the lively striker. He was a prolific marksman but frequently upstaged. The 8–0 win over Third Lanark in November 1947 was a point in case. He scored a hat-trick that day, but it was largely uncommented on because Gordon Smith scored the other five goals! From Hibs he moved to Clyde in October 1948 and then on to Morton, and he served the Greenock club as a prolific marksman from 1951 to 1955. While with the Bully Wee he played in the 1949 Scottish Cup Final. That was also the year in which he gained his only Scotland cap, scoring against Wales in a 2–0 win.

LOVE, Graeme

Midfield

Born: Bathgate, 7 December 1973.
Career: Salveson BC, HIBERNIAN 1991, Ayr United 1997, Queen of the South 1998, Clydebank 1999, East Fife 1999, Stirling Albion 2000, Bathgate Thistle 2002.

■ Graeme James Love spent six years as a Hibee and between 1991 and 1997 made 39 League appearances. He never managed more

than a dozen or so games in any one season so it is probably fair to say he was something of a fringe player. Graeme earned a Scotland Under-21 cap against Russia in November 1994. He moved to Ayr United in the summer of 1997 and his full-back talents were put to use there until he moved on to Queen of the South then Clydebank. When junior football began its Premier League in 2002 Graham was in the Bathgate side that took part.

LOVELL, Stuart

Midfield

Born: Sydney, Australia, 9 January 1972.
Career: Reading 1990, HIBERNIAN 1998, Livingston 2001, Queen of the South 2005.

■ Signed by Alex McLeish when Hibernian dropped into the First Division, Lovell was an outstanding success and arguably underrated by many. He came to Hibs having scored 67 goals in 150 matches for Reading and matched his prowess with industry. An eloquent speaker on the game, he provided much of the graft in a midfield boasting players such as Latapy and Sauzee and helped the club not only achieve promotion but also contributed 11 goals from a midfield position. A member of the Hibernian Scottish Cup Final team, he was rather surprisingly allowed to leave in the summer of 2001 and joined a thriving Livingston where he proved his worth rather quickly. How ironic that in the League Cup Final of 2004 he was in the Livingston side that beat Hibs 2–0.

LOVERING, Paul

Full-back

Born: Glasgow, 25 November 1975.
Career: Neilston Juniors, Clydebank 1995, HIBERNIAN 1998, Ayr United 2000, St Johnstone 2003, Airdrie United 2004.

■ Paul was a left-back with a prodigious talent in the air. He was recruited to Hibs by Alex McLeish from Clydebank in October 1998. Clydebank had farmed him out to Neilston Juniors and then used him from March 1995 onwards. He was Second Division Player of the Year and a promotion winner with the Bankies. His career with Hibernian started well and his phenomenal heading ability caught the eye. However, he failed to build upon a solid start and let the team downly badly when he was sent off along with Franck Sauzee in a 2–0 Easter Road reversal to Celtic in September

1999. Eventually Paul was allowed to join Ayr United. He had the last laugh; playing for Ayr in the shock League Cup semi-final victory they achieved over Hibernian in 2001. His stint at Airdrie saw him as player-coach by 2008.

LUNA, Francisco 'Paco'

Forward

Born: Spain, 23 September 1971.
Career: Almeria, Albacete, Sporting Gijon, Dundee 2000, Monterrey (Mexico), HIBERNIAN 2001, Almeria 2003.

■ 'Paco' Luna joined Hibernian from Mexican side Monterray in 2001. A Spanish-born centre-forward, he had played at the highest level in Spain with Sporting Gijon and with lesser lights Almeria and Albacete. In season 1999–200 he had a short stint with Dundee and it was while at Dens Park that Hibs boss Alex McLeish saw him first hand. He was a clever forward and while not the tallest (5ft 10in) he was excellent in the air. When Hibernian met AEK Athens in the UEFA Cup he almost won the tie for Hibs, scoring twice in regulation time and then going ever so close in the final seconds to securing what would have been a stunning win. He returned to Spain in January 2003.

LYNCH, Sean

Midfield

Born: Edinburgh, 31 January 1987.
Career: HIBERNIAN 2006.

■ Sean made his Hibees debut at Aberdeen in a 2–2 draw, pushed into the first team by John Collins. It was to be the first of five outings before he was sent to St Johnstone for a loan spell. Sadly, he was injured in his first outing for the Perth club and returned to Easter Road to recover. Capped by Scotland at both Under-19 and Under-20 level he was unfortunate not to make more of a breakthrough at Hibs.

M

McALLISTER, Kevin

Left-wing

Born: Falkirk, 8 November 1962.
Career: Camelon Juniors, Falkirk 1982, Chelsea 1985, Falkirk 1988, HIBERNIAN 1993, Falkirk 1997, Albion Rovers 2002.

■ Frail, speedy and extremely direct, Kevin was an exciting winger who enjoyed a marvellously lengthy career (21 years). He went from Camelon Juniors to Falkirk and was a huge hit before moving south. He cost Chelsea £34,000 in June 1985 and won a Second Division Championship badge and two Full Members' Cups. His August 1991 transfer back to Brockville cost Falkirk £225,000. It was Alex Miller who signed Kevin for Hibs, seizing upon the fact that the Bairns had been relegated and would inevitably have to trim their staff. Signed around the same time as Jim Leighton and Michael O'Neill, he joined a Hibs team that reached a Cup Final and proved solid and dependable. Ten days after the arrival of Jim Duffy as Hibs' boss Kevin was on his way back to Falkirk. He reached a Scottish Cup Final with the Bairns and won a Challenge Cup medal in what proved a fairly prolonged 'Indian Summer'. Throughout his career the enduring quality that Kevin brought to football was entertainment value. One interesting story surrounds Kevin McAllister's later career. He came back with Falkirk to play at Easter Road during Hibernian's brief exile in that League and noted prior to the game that he would be up against Paul Lovering. Remarkably, 16 years prior McAllister had played for Camelon Juniors alongside Paul's father Frank Lovering!

McARTHUR, Jim

Goalkeeper

Born: Dunfermline, 27 February 1952.
Career: Jubilee Athletic, Halbeath BC, Cowdenbeath 1968, HIBERNIAN 1972, Meadowbank Thistle 1983, Cowdenbeath 1983, Raith Rovers 1984.

■ A goalkeeper of considerable talent, Jim joined Hibs in 1972 from Cowdenbeath for £8,000. Born in February 1952 he was only 16 when he moved from Jubilee Athletic to Cowdenbeath. He played a few games in the late-1960s and by season 1971–72 was the Fife club's regular number one. Hibernian noted his progress and for less than £10,000 acquired the services of a 'keeper who was both brave and smart. He made his debut against Dumbarton a few months after signing but had to be patient and spent some time on the sidelines watching Mike McDonald put together an impressive run of outings. Patience is, they say, a virtue and Jim proved the theory. When he finally won the first-team jersey he held it for the most part until 1983 (except in the 1976–77 and 1977–78 seasons in which he failed to make a single League outing). That allowed him to clock up over 200 appearances as a Hibee and such loyalty was rewarded by a

testimonial against Hearts. A modest player, he attributed much of his success to good defences in front of him – Brownlie, Blackley, Black and Schaedler, then Bremner, McNamara and Stewart – but the truth is he was a very capable performer. Away from football he was a physical education instructor but he later became a noted football agent in Scotland and was often seen at Easter Road in a professional capacity.

McBRIDE, Joe (Junior)

Left-winger

Born: Glasgow, 17 August 1960.
Career: Celtic BC, Everton 1976, Rotherham United, Oldham Athletic, HIBERNIAN 1985, Dundee 1988, Queen of the South, East Fife 1991, Albion Rovers 1994, Livingston 1996, Hamilton 1996.

■ A clever winger, Joe was quite unlike his father in terms of build and style. McBride Junior started his career in England with Everton and by the time he came to Hibs he was a confident and experienced performer. His time at Hibernian was eventful, not least a marvellous performance in a 2–2 draw at Tynecastle when Hibs battled back from 2–0 down thanks to two quite stunning free-kicks from Joe. After giving up the game he gradually moved into coaching, and in the early-2000s Joe was youth coach at Celtic, a post he held for six and a half years. Around the same time Joe was also a stalwart in the Everton 'masters' side that performed ably in indoor tournaments.

McCABE, Thomas

Wing-half

Career: Wishaw, HIBERNIAN 1944, Hamilton Accies 1948, Falkirk 1949, Stirling Albion 1953.

■ At the start of the 1946–47 season (the first official post-war season) Tom McCabe wore the number-six jersey until 7 September when he turned out against Hearts. Shortly afterwards he suffered an injury at work and he was out of the team until early 1947. He played his last game for Hibernian in the home defeat to Motherwell on 1 February 1947 and by September 1948 he had joined Hamilton Accies.

McCAFFREY, Dermot

Defender

Born: Omagh, 29 March 1986.
Career: HIBERNIAN 2004, Queen of the South (loan) 2006, Livingston (loan) 2007, Falkirk 2008.

■ Dermot had what can only be described as a busy debut. His big day came in April 2007 away to Aberdeen and sadly it was cut short when he was sent off. Alas this proved to be the only first-team appearance that Dermot, who was a Northern Ireland Under-21 international, made for Hibs and in 2008 he joined Falkirk.

McCAFFREY, Stuart

Defender

Born: Glasgow, 30 May 1979.
Career: HIBERNIAN 1996, Aberdeen 1998, Inverness CT 2000, St Johnstone 2008.

■ Stuart made only a handful of outings for Hibernian before moving to Aberdeen in the summer of 1999. His transfer was settled by a tribunal with Aberdeen being required to play £60,000 when Hibernian had asked for £100,000 compared to the Dons' £37,5000 valuation. He never made the expected progress at Pittodrie and drifted to Inverness Caledonian Thistle. Here he settled well and went on to make over 100 appearances for the Highlanders before moving to St Johnstone in July 2008.

McCANN, Kevin

Full-back

Born: Glasgow, 11 September 1987.
Career: HIBERNIAN 2006.

■ The departure of Steven Whittaker to Rangers opened the door for 19-year-old Kevin McCann to step into the Hibernian limelight. He made his debut against Aberdeen in 2007 and quickly won over Hibs boss John Collins. Indeed in January 2008 new Scotland Under-21 manager Billy Stark called Kevin up to his

JOE McBRIDE — HERO

Centre-forward
Born: Kilmarnock, 10 June 1938.
Career: Shettleston Juniors, Kirkintilloch Rob Roy Juniors, Kilmarnock 1956, Wolves 1959, Luton Town 1960, Partick Thistle 1960, Motherwell 1962, Celtic 1965, HIBERNIAN 1968, Dunfermline 1970, Clyde 1971.

■ Joe McBride was simply a wonderful goalscorer. He was a man of many clubs but it would hard to avoid the conclusion that he gave each of them wonderful service. Only Ally McCoist and Willie Wallace in the post-war era scored more goals than McBride who bagged 221 League goals in Scotland. He arrived at Hibernian in the wake of Colin Stein's departure to Rangers and very quickly allowed the Hibs fans to forget a player who had been a fans' favourite. As a youngster McBride was an outside-right and it was in that position that Kilmarnock spotted him playing Glasgow schools football with St Gerards. Concerned by his lack of bulk (which would not be a problem later in his career) Killie promptly farmed Joe out to Kirkintilloch Rob Roy Juniors. He was something of an instant hit in their senior side when 'called-up', and goals against both halves of the Old Firm paved the way to a move down south. But in a truly Scottish context McBride had burst to prominence when playing at Motherwell, after which he then became one of Jock Stein's finest ever Celtic signings. But for an appalling piece of bad luck he would have been one of the famous Lisbon Lions, but an injury picked up at Christmas in that epoch-making season saw him miss out…nevertheless he was still the top scorer in Scotland that term, despite not playing in a match after Christmas! Joe McBride made 94 appearances for Celtic scoring 86 goals and famously scored four times for the Celts at Easter Road in a 5–3 Celtic win. He was thus well known to Hibs fans when he was signed in early November 1968 to replace the recently departed Colin Stein. Quickly settling in he grabbed 19 goals in 23 League games and five European goals in only four matches. His debut saw him score at Ibrox and he then hit a hat-trick against Lokomotiv Leipzig and four against Morton in a truly sensational start in Edinburgh. Soon afterwards he scored for Hibs at Celtic, but when the delayed League Cup Final against the same opponents came round Joe was forced to watch from the stand as Hibs slumped to a 2–6 defeat (this because Joe was Cup-tied). In total, Joe scored 24 goals in his first season and as that haul was achieved in only 30 matches his wonderful strike rate was clear to see. His departure to Dunfermline was widely lamented in Edinburgh but on reflection he was perhaps on the wane. Slightly heavier, he was by now a goalmouth poacher, but one possessed of wonderful instincts.

squad, a sure sign that Hibs had a youngster with good potential on their books. Sadly, a bad knee injury hampered Kevin's early progress with Hibs. Desperate to play when Mixu Paatelainen replaced Collins as manager he unwisely battled through the pain barrier until club doctors pointed out the chance that he would do irreparable damage if he did not rest the injured knee.

McCLELLAND, Joe

Left-back

Born: Edinburgh, 12 October 1935.
Career: Edinburgh Thistle, Armadale Thistle, HIBERNIAN 1954, Wrexham 1964, Rhyl 1965.

■ Joe was Hibs' groundsman in the late 1950s. Harry Reading ran a club called Edinburgh Thistle and it was from this nursery club that Hibs recruited many of their players, Joe McClelland was one such signing. He had played for Scotland Youth against their Welsh counterparts and had also been a Scotland Secondary Schools pick so he came highly recommended. By season 1957–58 he was established as left-back and he played in the disappointing 1958 Scottish Cup Final defeat against Clyde. Away from Easter Road he was an industrious lad and coached the Americans who wanted to play soccer at the US Air Base in Kirknewton, Edinburgh. This was perhaps a throw back to his national service days when he served with The Royal Scots as a motor mechanic. In June 1964 Joe joined Wrexham and he played in 32 games for the Welsh club in the mid-1960s.

McCLUSKEY, George

Centre-forward

Born: Hamilton, 19 September 1957.
Career: Thorniewood United, Celtic 1974, Leeds United 1983, HIBERNIAN 1986, Hamilton 1989, Kilmarnock 1992, Clyde 1995.

■ It was John Blackley who signed George from Leeds United in 1986. The clever striker had spent three years at Elland Road but made his name at Celtic with whom he won all the major Scottish domestic honours. He spent eight seasons at Celtic and scored 52 League goals for them, before rattling in 16 goals in 73 League outings for Leeds. A former Under-21 international, he continued to score for Hibs in a five-year career at Easter Road. George is well remembered as the victim of 'that tackle' by Graeme Souness in a particularly tempestuous clash with Rangers at Easter Road in 1986. He left for Hamilton after a three-year spell with Hibs and cost the Lanarkshire club £35,000. George later played with Kilmarnock and Clyde.

McCLUSKEY, Jamie

Winger

Born: Bellshill, 6 November 1987.
Career: HIBERNIAN, St Johnstone 2007.

■ Jamie became the youngest player to play for Hibs in 40 years when he made his debut against Kilmarnock at Rugby Park during the tail end of the 2003–04 season; indeed he was the then youngest debutant in the Scottish Premier League. Diminutive, he was nevertheless extremely tricky and brave for his size. A shining example of this came in the League Cup tie

against Peterhead in 2006 when he audaciously chipped home a penalty-kick in a 4–0 win. Alas, he was not able to make the grade at Easter Road and he was transferred to St Johnstone after failing to become a regular in the Hibs team. In September 2008 the then 20-year-old, having been released by St Johnstone, went on trial with Serbian club Partizan Belgrade.

McCORMACK, Darren

Defender

Born: 29 September 1988.
Career: HIBERNIAN 2007.

■ Darren made his League bow for Hibs in the 4–1 win over Kilmarnock in September 2007. His popularity at this point was extremely high given that it was revealed he had turned down an attempt by Celtic to lure him to Glasgow before he had even made his Hibs debut. Quickly impressive, he was rewarded for his early Hibs showings by being included in the Scotland Under-21 squads in 2008 for matches against Lithuania and Norway.

McCREADIE, Harvey

Centre-forward

Born: Stranraer, 1 October 1942.
Career: Accrington Stanley 1958, Luton Town 1960, Wrexham 1960, Mossley 1961, HIBERNIAN 1962, Altrincham 1963.

■ Harvey began his interesting career south of the border. His first professional contract was earned at Accrington Stanley and after only three months he was sold to Luton Town for £5,500 (a transfer that owed as much to Stanley's impending financial doom as to Harvey's ability). It was to be with Mossley in non-League football that Harvey made his mark, grabbing 36 goals in 44 matches. In September 1962 Hibs forked out a £1,000 fee to lure Harvey to Edinburgh. He scored three goals in nine matches as a Hibee before returning to the north-west of England.

McCURDY, Pat

Midfield

Born: Greenock, 12 November 1964.
Career: Largs Thistle, Shamrock BC, HIBERNIAN 1982, Hamilton 1984, Morton 1985, Stranraer 1986, Dalry Thistle, Largs Thistle.

■ The offer of a contract at Hibs was enough for the Greenock youngster to abandon his painting and decorating apprenticeship in 1982. He did not regret his decision as he scored on his debut for Hibs in an 8–1 rout of Kilmarnock in April 1983. He played his last game in the 1983–84 season and failed to make a more lasting impression. In 1984 he became a member of John Lambie's Hamilton Accies squad but his left-wing talents did not really blossom there either. Subsequent moves carried him to Morton, Stranraer and Alloa. He enjoyed greater success in the junior ranks serving Dalry Thistle and then netting the winner in the 1994 Scottish Junior Cup Final for Largs Thistle (Alan Rough was in the opposition dug-out as Glenafton manager).

McDONALD, Kevin

Midfield

Born: Newcastle, 26 August 1985.
Career: HIBERNIAN 2001, Airdrie 2007.

■ Linked with Sunderland as a boy, Kevin was ultimately a product of Hibernian's prolific youth system. The 5ft 10in midfielder was not able to command a regular spot and following a stint on loan at Second Division Airdrie he made the move to Lanarkshire permanent in July 2007. He had made his Hibs debut on the final day of the 2003–04 season but was unable to build upon his early promise.

McDONALD, Mike

Goalkeeper

Born: Glasgow, 8 November 1950.
Career: St Rochs Juniors, Clydebank 1968, Stoke City 1972, HIBERNIAN 1976, Berwick Rangers 1980, Hawick Royal Albert 1981, St Johnstone 1982, Arbroath 1984.

■ A solid goalkeeper, Mike arrived at Easter Road intent on fulfilling his promise. He had started his career with Clydebank shortly after the club entered the Scottish League in 1965.

Mike McDonald

Mike was 'a Bankie' for five years before moving on to Stoke City where he was apprentice to not just Gordon Banks but also Peter Shilton. Not surprisingly, first team openings were limited! Eddie Turnbull signed Mike for Hibs for £25,000 in January 1976 and this was soon proved to be money well spent. Mike made his debut in a 5–0 win versus St Johnstone in late January 1976. He played in over 100 League games for Hibs and was an able shot stopper. There was, however, one bitter disappointment. In the League Cup semi-final of 1978 against Aberdeen he was beaten by a very long distance lob by Stewart Kennedy after 107 minutes of a tense game at Dens Park. After leaving Easter Road he played with Berwick before making the short journey to Tynecastle in order to coach Hearts' reserves. However, the game still pulled at him and he returned to playing with Hawick and then St Johnstone. A good after-dinner speaker, he would return to former clubs, most notably Stoke, in this capacity.

MacDONALD, Tommy

Outside-right

Born: Glasgow, 24 May 1930.
Career: Hill O'Beath, HIBERNIAN 1947, Wolverhampton Wanderers 1954, Leicester City 1956, Dunfermline 1960, Raith Rovers 1962, Queen of the South 1963, Stirling Albion 1963, Cowdenbeath 1964.

■ A talented winger, Tommy came to Hibs from Fife junior club Hill O'Beath. Of course he could hardly have set himself a harder task than trying to prise the number-seven jersey off the incomparable Gordon Smith. That said, Tommy made a real go of the assignment he faced. He made his Hibernian debut in a 2–0 win at home to Aberdeen in October 1949 and just one week later was part of the Hibernian team that tackled Dunfermline in the Scottish League Cup semi-final at Tynecastle Park. Alas, Hibs slumped to a 0–2 reversal and Tommy did not play again that season. Indeed, he had to wait until the 1953–54 season to feature again. He was a surprise inclusion in the side that traveled to Airdrie in December 1953 and scored with a header in a 2–0 win. He stayed in the team until late in the season and clearly got a taste for first XI activity. So much so that in April 1954 he signed for Wolves but played only five games before moving on to Leicester City. At Filbert Street he enjoyed three very successful seasons and scored 27 goals in only 113 matches. In 1960, aged 30, he signed for Dunfermline and he was able to help them reach the 1961 Scottish Cup Final, although sadly he missed the Final through appendicitis. A couple of years later he joined Raith Rovers.

McEWAN, Willie

Midfield

Born: Wishaw, 20 June 1951.
Career: Pumpherston, Uphall Saints, HIBERNIAN 1968, Blackpool 1973, Brighton 1974, Chesterfield 1974, Mansfield 1977, Peterborough 1979.

■ Signed in 1967 from Uphall Saints, Willie was essentially a fringe player at Hibs. A half-back, he found it hard to break into the first team but did celebrate scoring a European winner against Malmö. In January 1971 he earned a Scotland Under-23 cap and between 1969 and 1973 he played for Hibs on 61 occasions. He then embarked on what was a most impressively varied English career (where he was better known as Billy), representing a number of clubs as a player before moving into management with equal fluidity. Among the clubs he managed were Sheffield United, Rotherham, Darlington, Derby County, York City and Mansfield Town. McEwan had a dry sense of humour and once famously told York City supporters to remember that he was Billy McEwan and not Billy Graham, the evangelist preacher!

MacFARLANE, Willie

Left-back

Career: Tranent, HIBERNIAN 1949, Raith Rovers 1958, Morton 1960.

■ Willie was one of that select band of Hibernian players who returned to manage the

club. His father had played for Leith and St Bernards so Willie was of good footballing stock. An impressive schoolboy player, he starred with Tynecastle School, Hutchison Vale and then Tranent before rolling up at Easter Road. A full-back himself, he was signed in 1949 by Hugh Shaw and made his debut in a friendly against Tottenham Hotspur. He went on to play in the great European nights that saw Hibs reach the European Cup semi-final. Willie moved to Raith Rovers in October 1958 and in October 1960 he joined his final senior playing club – Morton. This was a sound move for it brought him into close contact with Hal Stewart the ebullient, innovative and charismatic manager of Morton. From there it was into management; a career that began in the humble surrounds of Galashiels then carried him to Hawick and Stirling Albion. He was a part-time manager at Stirling, working during the days as a plant-transport manager and concentrating on Albion in the evenings. However, when Bob Shankly left Hibs Willie was invited to concentrate solely on football as the Easter Road boss. One of his first acts was to bring young Stirling defender Erich Schaedler to Hibernian. Willie made a good start at Hibs, including a win at Tynecastle, but he was to last just over a year and was sacked in quite remarkable circumstances. In December 1970 Hibs were just 24 hours away from a Fairs Cup tie with the mighty Liverpool when the Hibernian board intervened in team matters in the most stunning way. Chairman Tom Hart told MacFarlane that both Joe McBride and Johnny Graham should be withdrawn from his squad to face the Merseyside giants. Initially MacFarlane consented but then on reflection decided that he would decide who was, and who was not, in his squad. In an emotional statement to the press he stated: 'Thinking things over I have decided to restore the two players and also Hamilton to my party. It is the only logical thing I can do to keep my self-respect. At the moment I will be picking the team for tomorrow night. I am not in the slightest bit interested in the political situation at Hibs.' The key wording within that phrase was 'at the moment'. Within hours Tom Hart had sacked MacFarlane and even the Hibs public relations officer – former player Tommy Younger – steered clear of the controversy by telling waiting pressmen that he would not comment because he '…didn't want to become involved'. Thus Hibernian were seeking their fifth manager in nine years on the eve of one of their most prestigious matches. Of course, Hart had in the eyes of many been waiting to rid the club of MacFarlane for some weeks, indeed he had recruited a ready-made replacement in Dave Ewing just a month earlier. The press were generally supportive of MacFarlane's plight and few disagreed that he was placed in an intolerable position by having his team selections dictated to him from the boardroom. In all, his dismissal must rank as one of the more shoddy episodes in Hibs' rich history.

McGACHIE, John

Centre-forward

Born: Edinburgh, 13 November 1965.
Career: Savleson BC, Aberdeen 1981, HIBERNIAN 1984, Hamilton 1984, Meadowbank Thistle 1985, Hamilton Accies 1989, Stirling Albion 1990, Montrose 1991, Peterhead, Keith.

■ Signed by Hibs from Aberdeen in 1984, John was a Scotland Schoolboy international. He did not make the expected impact at Easter Road and moved on to Hamilton Accies having made 11 outings for Hibs. He did score a notable counter against Aberdeen at the business end of the 1983–84 season, a goal against his former employers that must have given some satisfaction. He netted on his debut for Accies but proved a much more useful marksman for his next club, Meadowbank.

McGHEE, Alex

Forward

Born: 2 June 1955.
Career: Edinburgh Thistle, HIBERNIAN 1972, Morton 1974, Dundee 1978, Cowdenbeath 1980.

■ A versatile forward, Alex could play in a number of forward positions, which was perhaps a hindrance to his career. He made his debut for Hibernian in the 1971–72 season, turning out in the final League game of the season as Hibs went to Ibrox and beat Rangers 2–1 on the eve of their European Cup-winners' Cup triumph. Ordinarily that would herald the start of a satisfying career, but in Alex's case it was a false dawn. He did not play first-team football again for Hibs and was off to Greenock in March 1974.

McGINLAY, Pat

Midfield

Born: Glasgow, 30 May 1967.
Career: Anniesland Waverley, Blackpool 1986, HIBERNIAN 1987, Celtic 1993, HIBERNIAN 1994, Ayr United 2000.

■ Pat was a veritable midfield powerhouse, with the added bonus of having a flair for scoring goals. His senior career began with Blackpool and he had made a dozen outings for the seaside club when Hibs first signed him in July 1987. He proved himself such a quality player that Celtic persuaded him to move to Glasgow in July 1993 for a substantial sum. That £525,000 fee came just as he seemed destined to become the next Hibernian player to play for Scotland. In a near 18-month stint in the east end of Glasgow he was an adept goalscorer and a very popular player with the fans. Not surprisingly, he was badly missed at Hibernian and when he was brought back to the club it was amid much rejoicing among the support. His return was a little strange in that he had been a consistent marksman for the Celts, but nevertheless he did not quite seem to 'fit' and Hibs were able to lure him back. Although it was a close run thing as he very nearly joined Motherwell in the deal that took Phil O'Donnell to Celtic. Hibs broke their transfer record to buy him back for £425,000 and did not regret the big outlay. He was a key player in Hibernian's 1998 promotion success, scoring – from midfield – a highly impressive 12 goals in just 30 matches. Given that he had won the League Cup with Hibs in 1991 he was rare in the modern era in having more than one Hibs winners-medals to his name.

McGLINCHEY, Paul

Midfield

Career: Tynecastle BC, HIBERNIAN 1979, Berwick Rangers 1981, Postal United 1982.

■ An Edinburgh-born midfielder, Paul joined Hibs from Tynecastle Boys Club and by 1980 had made seven League appearances. A silk-screen printer by trade, his stay at Easter Road was short but he did manage an outing for Scotland's Professional Youth side while a Hibee.

McGLYNN, Tony

Inside-forward

Career: Edinburgh Thistle, HIBERNIAN 1961, Airdrie, Third Lanark 1964.

■ Tony 'JP' McGlynn may not have a spectacular entry in the Hibernian hall of fame but he can at least point to two goals from only three starts. Early in the 1961–62 season he made a successful outing as a Hibee and promptly scored the winner against Raith Rovers in a 3–2 victory at Easter Road. Unfortunately it did not herald the start of a wonderful career and he had to wait an entire season before popping up on the team sheet again, this time in a 3–1 win over Motherwell. However, there was no breakthrough and he was soon on his way to Airdrie. He later turned up at Third Lanark in September 1964, but unfortunately the club folded in 1967 after a slow decline.

McGOVERN, Paul

Centre-forward

Born: Edinburgh, 31 October 1968.
Career: Royston Rosebery, HIBERNIAN 1985, Partick Thistle 1990.

■ Paul made his debut in August 1987 in a 3–2 League Cup victory over Montrose. He then managed a run in the League side and scored his only goal for the club in January 1988 during a 1–1 draw at Greenock Morton. But that season was to mark the high point in his Hibernian career and in July 1990 he moved to Partick Thistle. Despite a handful of goals for Thistle he never really settled in Maryhill and thereafter his career took in varied locations like Cyprus, Ayr United (as an unused trialist) and Gala Fairydean.

McGRAW, Allan

Centre-forward

Born: Glasgow, 1939.
Career: Renfrew Juniors, Morton 1961, HIBERNIAN 1966, Linfield 1969.

■ A superb striker with Morton, it was rather unfortunate that Hibs did not sign Allan until July 1966, by which time he was already being plagued by the knee injuries that would ultimately end his career. His spell with Morton was so good that it merits retelling even in a publication about Hibs. Such was the prolific nature of McGraw's scoring he earned the sobriquet 'Quick Draw' McGraw. He once scored over 50 goals in a season for Morton and twice helped the club gain promotion, as well as reach the 1963 League Cup Final. He had five seasons with Morton and recorded figures of 116 goals in 137 League games. In the League Cup semi-final of 1963 he scored the goal that denied Hibs a Final place at the expense of the Greenock club. As a Hibs player McGraw, while hampered by injury, looked every bit the complete professional. His commitment was beyond reproach and while not as prolific as he had been at Cappielow he was a useful goalscorer. In 1968 he scored a League Cup semi-final winner against Dundee that entered Easter Road folklore (despite being scored at Tynecastle). The circumstances were unusual in that he was effectively 'a lame duck' at the time, having been badly injured but remaining on the field as Hibs had already used their only substitute (Jim O'Rourke). He moved to Linfield in May 1969, by which time he was playing a deeper role, with the intention of helping them in their European campaign. In 1999 Allan stood as an independent candidate in the West Renfrewshire constituency in the Scottish Parliamentary elections. He had just over 14 years as Morton manager and as a shrewd operator brought in over £4 million in transfer fees; a sum that included selling his son Mark to Hibs!

McGRAW, Mark

Centre-forward

Born: Rutherglen, 5 January 1971.
Career: Port Glasgow Rangers, Morton 1989, HIBERNIAN 1990, Falkirk 1995, Morton 1997, Clyde 1998, Stirling 2000, Forfar Athletic 2000.

■ Son of Alan McGraw, the ex-Hibs and Morton striker, Mark began his senior career at Morton while his father was the boss. He had played only a handful of matches for Morton when Alex Miller signed him for Hibs in February 1990. He tore ankle ligaments not long into his Hibs career and was arguably

never the same player again. He scored a couple of goals for Hibs in the 1994–95 season but rarely reached the heights expected of him. After his five-year stint with Hibs he turned out for several smaller clubs including Falkirk and Clyde.

McGURK, Dennis

Inside-forward

Career: Dunkeld Amateurs, HIBERNIAN 1948.

■ Football was in Dennis's family; his father had played with Portadown in Northern Ireland. At 5ft 8in and weighing just over the 10st mark he was light for a professional footballer, but in the 1949–50 season he showed real promise in Hibernian's second team scoring 12 League goals in 12 matches. Like many promising young players at Easter Road his misfortune was to be at the club at the same time as the Famous Five were dominating not just Edinburgh but Scottish football in general. Thus Dennis managed but a single senior League outing. That came in the 1949–50 season on 4 March at home to Third Lanark and proved a notable match. Hibs lost 0–1, their only defeat in the final 14 League matches of the season, and given that they lost the League title to Rangers by a single point it was a very significant defeat. A Dundonian, he used to travel every day from the Tay to the Forth to join Hibs for training and was training to be a radiographer while he dabbled with first-team football at Easter Road.

McINTOSH, Martin

Centre-half

Born: East Kilbride, 19 March 1971.
Career: Tottenham Hotspur, St Mirren 1988, Clydebank 1991, Hamilton Accies 1994, Stockport County 1997, HIBERNIAN 2000, Rotherham 2001.

■ When Martin moved to Stockport County in England he earned Hamilton Accies £80,000. A tall, powerful and aggressive centre-half, he had caught the eye with Accies and clearly Alex McLeish had been impressed for he wasted no time in luring Martin back to Scotland when the opportunity arose. Alas the move did not work out. Having made nine outings in the tail end of the season he was rather surprisingly used only four times the very next season. Completely out of favour he was moved on to Rotherham in 2001.

McINTYRE, Tommy

Centre-half

Born: Bellshill, 26 December 1963.
Career: Fir Park BC, Aberdeen 1981, HIBERNIAN 1986, Airdrie 1994.

■ A scorer in the 1991 League Cup Final triumph, Tommy joined Hibs in December 1986 from Aberdeen. Signed within hours of Graham Mitchell, both players made their debut in January 1987 against Falkirk. Tommy proved to be good value at £30,000 and delivered an unexpected bonus as something of a goalscorer, lending height and physical strength to set pieces. He was also a noted penalty-kick converter, as he proved in that League Cup Final. In July 1994 he joined Airdrie in the Scottish First Division.

McKAY, Jim

Goalkeeper

Born: 14 February 1953.
Career: Wick Academy 1973, Brora Rangers 1975, HIBERNIAN 1977, Brora Rangers 1977, Ross County 1978, Elgin City 1980, Brora Rangers 1983.

■ Jim was signed on a one-month loan deal from Highland League club Brora Rangers in 1977 and was fielded as a trialist against Partick

Thistle in September 1977. He scored a goal against Blackburn Rovers in the Anglo-Scottish Cup and also played against Newcastle United in a 3–0 friendly win but his stint in the Premier League was to be short lived. His crack at professional football over, Jim returned to his work in a mill back in the Highlands.

McKEE, Kevin

Full-back

Born: Edinburgh, 10 June 1966.
Career: Whitburn BC, HIBERNIAN 1982, Hamilton Accies 1986, Partick 1993, Stenhousemuir 1996.

■ A clever young full-back, Kevin joined Hibs in 1982 having played with Whitburn and Polbeth. He made his bow in May 1983 while still only 16 and began to impress all and sundry with his speed of thought and neat distribution. His time at Easter Road will be forever associated with a match at Rangers in 1984 when he was assaulted by a home supporter and required four stitches in a mouth wound. Openings were limited at Easter Road and after four seasons on the books at Hibs he moved on to Hamilton where he won League and Cup medals. Later in his career he moved to Glasgow with Partick Thistle and then on to Stenhousemuir.

McKENZIE, Roddy

Goalkeeper

Born: 31 July 1945.
Career: Drumchapel Amateurs, Airdrie 1963, HIBERNIAN 1973, Clydebank 1975.

■ A vastly experienced 'keeper, Roddy had been with Airdrie for over a decade when he joined Hibernian in August 1973. Hibs were, of course, well served for goalkeepers at this time and thus Roddy made only seven appearances, all them in his first season at Easter Road. Disillusioned by the lack of openings he took the opportunity to join Clydebank in August 1975.

McLAREN, Billy

Midfield

Born: Glasgow, 7 June 1948.

Career: Kirkintilloch Rob Roy, Dunfermline 1969, East Fife 1971, Raith Rovers 1972, Queen of the South 1973, Morton 1978, HIBERNIAN 1980, Clyde 1982, Queen of the South 1983, Partick Thistle 1984.

■ With well over 400 senior games in Scotland, Willie enjoyed a lengthy career. He joined a struggling Hibs in December 1980 from Morton and helped the club regain Premier League status. Back in the top flight he played in half of Hibs' games before being moved on to Clyde. A rugged defender, he took 'few prisoners' but there was more to his game than brawn and he displayed this by enjoying a lengthy coaching career after he quit playing. Never a full-time player, he was also a civil servant and as such was determined to avoid the potential pit-falls of fully professional football. He was known as one of the game's great practical jokers. During his time at Morton there was quite a Hibs connection with Roy Baines, Neil Orr, Joe McLaughlin, Ally Scott and Bobby Thomson all part of the same Morton side as McLaren.

McLAUGHLIN, Joe

Centre-half

Born: Greenock, 2 June 1960.
Career: Morton 1977, Chelsea 1983, Charlton 1989, Watford 1990, Falkirk 1992, HIBERNIAN 1996, Clydebank 1997, St Mirren 2000.

■ Joe McLaughlin was a tall, whole-hearted central-defender who relied on his skilled reading of the game to a great extent. Never the quickest of defenders, he was strong in the air and decisive on the ground. Another major plus point was his steady temperament when under pressure. He made his breakthrough in the 1970s with Greenock Morton, winning 10 Under-21 caps, and was a big buy for Chelsea. After six seasons at Stamford Bridge he moved in 1989 to Charlton before coming back to Scotland with Falkirk. Joe joined Hibernian in February 1996 and helped shore up a leaky defence. He played nine matches that season and nine in the following campaign before moving on to Clydebank in the summer of 1997. After hanging up his boots Joe had a go at coaching with Millwall (working with Mark McGhee) and briefly managed Morton in a caretaker capacity during 2004, but by 2008 he was running a business providing young players for American Universities.

MacLEOD, Ally (1)

Outside-left

Born: Glasgow, 26 February 1931.
Career: Third Lanark 1949, St Mirren 1955, Blackburn Rovers 1956, HIBERNIAN 1961, Third Lanark 1963, Ayr United 1964.

■ Few men have impacted on the Scottish game with quite the same mixture of fun and ebullience as Ally MacLeod. Raised on the south side of Glasgow, he rose to be the most charismatic manager the Scottish national side has had, and his association with Ayr United reaped rewards out of all proportion to the size of the club. Alistair Reid MacLeod's senior playing career began at Third Lanark. His odd running style saw him nicknamed 'Noddy' but he was a solid performer and half a dozen seasons later was on his way to St Mirren. By now a flying winger, he was soon snapped up by Blackburn Rovers. In 1960 he played in an FA Cup Final but a contractual dispute saw him made available for transfer in the summer of 1961. In July 1961 he joined Hibernian and in two seasons played in 52 League games and chipped in with six goals. He returned briefly to Third Lanark and then his association with Ayr United began. Lifting the club from the doldrums, he was Ayr's 'Citizen of the Year' by 1973 as he led them to Hampden semi-finals. In 1976 MacLeod was lured to Aberdeen and he quickly steered them to a League Cup Final win over Celtic. In 1977 he was Scotland manager and 12 months later (after stirring wins over Czechoslovakia and Wales) he led the club into the World Cup Finals in Argentina. A defeat, a draw and a win against Peru, Iran and Holland respectively saw Scotland crash out in what was a disappointing campaign. He soon returned to domestic management and Motherwell, Airdrie, Ayr and Queen of the South enjoyed his bizarre mix of humour and talent. Ally suffered from Alzheimer's disease in his later years and died aged 72.

MacLEOD, Ally (2)

Centre-forward

Born: Glasgow, 1 January 1951.
Career: St Mirren 1970, Southampton 1973, HIBERNIAN 1974, Dundee United 1982, Stenhousemuir 1983.

■ Although known throughout his career as Ally MacLeod, he should not to be confused with **the** Ally MacLeod of Scotland, Argentina and Ayr United fame. For although they shared a name and a connection with Hibs they were indeed very different footballers, representing very different eras. The MacLeod in question here was Alexander Hector McMillan MacLeod. A fairly sensational young striker with St Mirren, he served notice of his ability by scoring all four Saints goals in a 4–1 win at Rangers in 1971. That earned him a move to Southampton but he failed to settle on the south coast. In December 1974 Hibs signed him and in so doing completed one of their sharpest pieces of business. He may have appeared a little heavy and non too quick but he went on to play over 300 games as a Hibee

and was a prolific marksman in the modern 'defensively coached' era. His debut came in a goalless draw at Airdrie in December 1974. In the season that Hearts were relegated for the first time in their history, MacLeod scored a vital derby winner and his glut of goals late in the season ensured Hibs did not go down. He was also on target in the 1979 Scottish Cup Final when Hibs lost to Rangers after two replays. He played 208 League games and netted 72 goals. In a strange ending to his career he signed for Jim McLean's Dundee United, only to pick up an injury in training that all but ended his career. He never actually played a game for United.

MacLEOD, Johnny

Outside-left

Born: 23 November 1938.
Career: Armadale Thistle, HIBERNIAN 1957, Arsenal 1961, Aston Villa 1964, Mechelen KV (Belgium), Raith Rovers 1971, Newtongrange Star 1972.

■ Although Johnny was only with Hibernian from 1957 until the summer of 1961 he made a considerable impact. A tall, rangy winger he was a notable goalscorer and that, allied to his speed and trickery, made him a firm favourite with the fans. He played in 85 League games for Hibs and his return of 27 goals gives a good idea of just what a dangerous forward he was. In season 1959–60 Hibs won away matches at Airdrie and Partick Thistle 11–1 and 10–2 respectively; Johnny had five goals in those two games. He also scored in the famous 4–4 draw at Barcelona in the Fairs Cities Cup. Strangely, when he left Hibernian he was replaced by another MacLeod – Ally – and thus the surname remained on the Hibernian team sheet. MacLeod joined George Swindin's Arsenal in 1961 when he was aged just 22 and was clearly a super prospect. In September 1963 he wrote his name into the Arsenal record books by scoring the Londoners' first-ever goal in European competition. He managed over 100 matches for the Gunners but never made quite the impression in London as he had in Edinburgh. Nevertheless, he was good enough to join Aston Villa in 1964 and rack up another century-plus of appearances. His career wound down firstly in Belgium with KV Mechelen and then nearer to home in Kirkcaldy with Raith Rovers.

MacLEOD, Murdo

Midfield

Born: Glasgow, 24 September 1958.
Career: Dumbarton 1974, Celtic 1978, Borussia Dortmund 1987, HIBERNIAN 1990, Dumbarton (player-coach) 1993.

Murdo Mcleod

■ A product of Glasgow amateur football, Murdo joined Dumbarton in 1974 and had four years with the Boghead side before moving to Celtic in November 1978 for a fee of £100,000. His stay at Parkhead was highly successful, picking up four League Championship medals, two Scottish Cup-winners' medals and one League Cup-winners' badge. He gained Under-21 and full caps for Scotland while in Glasgow. A battling midfielder, he was known for the power and accuracy of his long-range shooting and he used this to good effect for Celtic and Scotland. He coveted possession of the ball and in short was a player who mixed dynamism with genuine skill. The Scotland caps continued when he had a spell in Germany with Borussia Dortmund. Joining in the summer of 1987, he won a German Cup medal – and duly became the first Scot to do so. He returned to Scotland with Hibs in October 1990, after a fierce tug of war between Hibernian and Dunfermline, and promptly won a League Cup-winners' badge in 1991 in a Final that saw Hibs beat the Pars! He later entered coaching and made his mark with Dumbarton, Partick Thistle and Celtic, serving under Wim Jansen at Parkhead. He then went into the media working as a pundit for BBC Scotland

McMANUS, Michael

Midfield

Born: Bathgate, 24 October 1967.
Career: Edina Hibs, HIBERNIAN 1984.

■ Michael joined Hibs in March 1984 and made his single outing as a Hibee in the following season. That single appearance came as a substitute in a home fixture against St Mirren in December 1984. It was not a good time to break into the Hibs team and only the presence of very poor Morton and Dumbarton sides saved Hibernian from relegation.

McMANUS, Tom

Forward

Born: Glasgow, 28 February 1981.
Career: HIBERNIAN 1997, East Fife (loan) 1999, Airdrie (loan) 2001, Boston United 2004, *Dundee 2005, Falkirk 2006, Dunfermline 2007, Colorado Rapids 2008.*

■ Tom joined Hibs straight from school and his pacy, snappy style of forward play made him a favourite with the Easter Road support. A bubbly personality and very approachable manner helped too. He had loan spells with Airdrie and East Fife, scoring three times in 11 games for the latter before really making his mark at Hibs. His Scottish Cup quarter-final winner at Kilmarnock helped the club reach the 2001 Scottish Cup Final and he won several Under-21 caps before settling into first-team duties. However, he was rather unfortunate with injury and sustained a broken ankle against Dundee in January 2002 that hampered his career. From making his debut in May 1999 at Stranraer to playing a key role in the 2002–03 campaign he matured as a player and became a regular marksman for the side. By 2008 Tom was playing his football in North America with Colorado Rapids.

McNAMEE, John

Centre-half

Born: Coatbridge, 11 June 1941.
Career: Bellshill Athletic, Celtic 1959, HIBERNIAN 1964, Newcastle United 1966, Blackburn Rovers 1971, Morton 1973, Lancaster City 1973.

■ A huge centre-half, John was Jock Stein's first Hibernian signing, coming to the club from Celtic in April 1964. In short he was an uncompromising player who could frighten his own players as much as opposition players. Pat Stanton tells a lovely story of how John would turn to the Hibs players before a match and remark: 'Any of yous goes hidin' today an' you'll have me to answer to'. He arrived at Easter Road with quite a reputation. His vendetta with the Celts' John Hughes was a quirky but hugely entertaining side-show during his spell with Celtic. Hughes, a considerable success, was one of the first players at Celtic to own a car. He would drive past McNamee, who would be standing at a bus stop on his way to work. This fuelled the animosity that existed and this

JACKIE McNAMARA   HERO

Sweeper

Born: Glasgow, 19 September 1952.
Career: Cumbernauld United, Celtic 1970, HIBERNIAN 1976, Morton 1985.

■ Jackie was suffering dreadfully with his knees at Celtic when Eddie Turnbull offered him the chance to come to Hibs in 1976. Two years earlier he had scored for Celtic against Hibs and in doing so created an impression on Turnbull. Hibs physio John McNiven suggested that 24-year-old Jackie could recover, and McNiven's expertise was vital because within months of arriving McNamara had to undergo a cartilage operation and extensive recuperation. In signing for Hibs what Jackie never knew throughout the negotiations was that the legendary Pat Stanton would be going in the other direction. So he arrived at Easter Road to be greeted with simmering resentment as one of Hibernian's true legends departed. However, McNamara had almost 10 years at Hibs and received a testimonial against Newcastle United after over 200 matches. His testimonial entered Easter Road folklore when George Best returned to take part and was close to being sent off when he told the referee: 'Do you realize that all these people here have come to see me…oh, and Jackie too!' There were many highs in his career at Easter Road including the 1979 Scottish Cup Final run that saw Hibs beat Aberdeen and Hearts en route to a twice replayed Final with Rangers. The low point was being relegated in 1980. Not noted for his goalscoring, he got his first against Leicester City in a friendly in the Midlands and then went 64 games before popping up with a cracker in a Cup-tie at Rangers. McNamara enjoyed both goals but always put his Hibernian career in a wider perspective saying: 'Hibs stood by me when I had the knee injury. They saved my career and gave me 10 wonderful years. I owe them everything.' John Blackley freed McNamara when his knees were deemed to be pretty well 'gone' and John McNiven had done all he could. Allan McGraw had just been made Morton manager and convinced McNamara that he could continue at a less demanding level. Little did Jackie know that a wonderful 'swan-song' was about to unfold. McNamara, who had always hated playing at Greenock, joined when the 'Ton were bottom of the First Division but helped them embark on a 17-match unbeaten run. His son played with Dunfermline before moving successfully to Celtic, Wolves and Aberdeen as well as earning many Scotland caps. Jackie Senior for his part had a brief spell as Hibernian assistant manager under Jim Duffy in December 1996. But even upon leaving that post he attended Hibs games home and away as a genuine Hibernian

would spill out at training where Hughes and McNamee would go at each other with gusto. McNamee was legendary for his rough-house tactics and was once booked for fighting his own goalkeeper, the notorious Frank Haffey, in a reserve match. With such a reputation it was therefore with considerable glee and trepidation that Hibs fans welcomed their new centre-half. He did not let them down. A veritable man-mountain, he was as uncompromising as he was fearsome. He served Hibs from 1964 to December 1966 when he moved on to Newcastle United.

McNEIL, Andy

Goalkeeper

Born: Edinburgh, 19 January 1987.
Career: Southampton, HIBERNIAN 2006.

■ Recruited from English Premiership football, Andy made his Hibernian debut one year after joining the club, in January 2007 against Dunfermline. He was quickly viewed as a solid shot-stopper and a fairly talented youngster. Recognition of his talent came with the award of a Scotland Under-21 cap but like his predecessor Zibi Malkowski he was prone to costly errors, and although he was the Hibs goalkeeper going into the 2008–09 season the jury to some extent was still out.

McNEIL, George

Outside-right

Career: Tranent, HIBERNIAN 1964, Morton 1968, Stirling Albion 1969.

■ Arguably better known as a sprinter, McNeil joined Hibs in the mid-1960s. An apprentice quantity surveyor, he had shown athletic prowess at Ross High School in Tranent and by the time he was with Hibs he was competing in the prestigious Powderhall New Year's Day Sprint. Sadly he played only one game for Hibs, during the 1965–66 season. A move to Morton in 1968 brought a slightly more productive season but he never played more than 12 games in one season; a figure he achieved at Stirling Albion in the 1968–69 campaign.

McNEIL, Matt

Centre-half

Born: Glasgow, 28 July 1927.
Career: HIBERNIAN, Newcastle United 1949, Barnsley 1951, Brighton 1953, Norwich City 1956.

■ Sold to Newcastle United in December 1949 having made a single outing in the 1949–50 season. The big centre-half made just nine outings for United but increased that total by 60 when moving to Barnsley, and he was just as consistent for Brighton and Norwich whom he joined subsequently. Born in Glasgow in July 1927 his only problem at Easter Road was clearly the level of competition in what was a Championship-winning side.

McQUEEN, Tommy

Goalkeeper

Born: West Calder, 21 February 1929.
Career: Burnbank Athletic, Motherwell 1946, Leith Athletic 1947, Alloa Athletic 1947, Kilbirnie Ladeside 1948, HIBERNIAN 1952, Queen of the South 1953, Accrington Stanley 1954, East Fife 1957, Berwick 1957, Stranraer 1960.

■ With only three appearances for Hibs, Tommy is unlikely to ever feature in an all-time great Hibs XI. Yet here was a goalkeeper who knew his stuff. After leaving Hibs for Queen of the South in 1953, he moved on to Accrington Stanley before returning to Scottish football with East Fife.

McQUILKEN, Jamie

Full-back

Born: Glasgow, 3 October 1974.
Career: Gorbals United, Celtic BC, Giffnock North BC, Celtic 1993, Dundee United 1995, HIBERNIAN 1996, Falkirk 1998, Aberdeen 2003, St Johnstone 2004, Gretna 2004, Queen of the South 2007.

■ Jamie served an apprenticeship at Celtic that included stints under Liam Brady and Lou Macari before moving to Dundee United. Unable to command a place when Tommy McLean arrived he signed for Hibernian in 1996. Jim Duffy used Jamie in the 1996 season but he slipped badly from the team and over the course of the next season he played just a single game. Thereafter he moved around considerably. In January 2007 he moved from Gretna to Queen of the South, a fortuitous move given that Gretna went into administration in March 2008.

McWILLIAMS, Derek

Midfield

Born: Broxburn, 16 January 1966.
Career: Whitburn BC, HIBERNIAN 1982, Broxburn Athletic 1983, Dundee 1984, Stirling Albion 1986, Falkirk 1987, Dunfermline Athletic 1991, Partick Thistle 1994, Clydebank 1997, Partick Thistle 2000, East Stirlingshire 2000, East Fife 2000, Airdrie 2001.

■ Pitched into the Hibernian side as a raw 16-year-old in 1982, Derek showed enough in his early games (both against Clydebank) to suggest a decent career could lie ahead. However, that career was to be spent largely away from Easter Road. More readily associated with Falkirk, Partick Thistle and Dunfermline, Derek was a strong running midfielder with a degree of 'bite' to his game.

McWILLIAMS, Walter

Forward

Born: Pumpherston, 1935.
Career: Broughton Star, Livingston United, Ards, Distillery, HIBERNIAN 1956, Cowdenbeath 1957, Peebles Rovers.

■ Walter was one of four smiling faces that graced the cover of the *Hibernian Handbook* in the summer of 1956. The 5ft 11in striker was newly recruited from Livingston United and the handbook giving a glowing introduction: 'Walter played for Irish League clubs Ards and Distillery while in the RAF and played for the Irish League against the Scottish League. Scored 111 goals for unbeaten Livingston last season.' Clearly his exploits at Livingston could not be repeated at senior level and as things transpired he played just two League games for Hibs but scored once; so he could be reasonably happy with his contribution. Both of his matches for Hibs came in the 1956–57 season. He moved to Cowdenbeath in May 1957 and after a couple of seasons in the B Division moved from senior football into the non-League ranks.

MADSEN, John

Defender

Born: Esbjerg, Denmark, 14 May 1937.
Career: Esbjerg, Morton 1965, HIBERNIAN 1967.

■ An experienced Danish international centre-half (he made his debut against Norway in Oslo in 1961), John was signed from Morton in July 1966. His early performances were said by some to be compromised by his insistence on staying in Greenock and travelling by train to Edinburgh. However, a move to Barnton soon

settled him. By 1968 Hibs were finishing third in the League and the rock-solid defensive talents of Madsen were a big part of that. He returned to Denmark in the summer of 1968 to resume his career as an architect. However, he was still under contract to Hibs and returned to Easter Road in the autumn (had he not he would be been banned *sine die* by the SFA). He played 21 games in the 1967–68 season and then returned permanently to Denmark.

MA-KALAMBAY, Yves

Goalkeeper

Born: Brussels, Belgium, 31 January 1986.
Career: PSV Eindhoven, Chelsea 2003, HIBERNIAN 2007.

■ A towering goalkeeper, standing at 6ft 6in, Yves joined Hibernian when John Collins was in charge. He had been a reserve 'keeper at Chelsea and as such had trained with some of the finest players in Britain including both Petr Cech and Carlo Cudicini. Born to Congolese parents in Belgium, he was associated with Eindhoven before moving to Chelsea. First-team openings were limited at Stamford Bridge and he had a period on loan with Watford before moving to Hibs in June 2007. Debut day was a challenging derby against Hearts but he came through that well and soon had deposed Malkowski as the Hibernian number one. On the eve of the 2008 season he was selected for the Belgian 2008 Olympic squad thus throwing Mixu Paatelainen's early season plans into confusion.

MALKOWSKI, Zbigniew

Goalkeeper

Born: Olsztyn, Poland, 19 January 1978.
Career: Stomil Olsztyn 1997, Excelsior 2002, HIBERNIAN 2005, Gretna (loan) 2006, Inverness CT (loan) 2007.

■ Signed by Tony Mowbray and initially very secure, 'Zibi' gradually became error-prone and as a goalkeeper his errors were horribly magnified. He reached a nadir in the Scottish Cup semi-final against Hearts at Hampden Park in 2006 when he conceded two goals that contributed hugely to a resounding 0–4 defeat. One of them was the cardinal sin of leaving too much room on his front post – so much room in fact that he virtually invited Hearts' Paul Hartley to place the ball in the unguarded net. Loaned out to Gretna (where he helped them win promotion to the Premier League) and Inverness he eventually left the Easter Road payroll when released from his contract in late-August 2008.

MARINELLO, Peter

Winger

Born: Edinburgh, 20 February 1950.
Career: Salveson BC, HIBERNIAN 1966, Arsenal 1970, Portsmouth 1973, Motherwell 1975, Fulham 1978, Phoenix Inferno, Hearts 1981, Partick Thistle 1983, Whitburn 1984.

■ Marinello was perhaps the Hibernian player who promised most and delivered least, such were the expectations placed on his young shoulders. Born in Edinburgh in February 1950, he joined Hibs in 1966 from Salveson BC and by the time he had reached 18 he was a first-team regular. In little over two seasons he made 45 League outings for Hibs and chipped in with five goals; it helped that he reserved some of his best showings for matches against the Old Firm. The 1969–70 season saw him

reach his peak at Easter Road and when he scored twice in an impressive 3–1 win over Rangers it was not just Hibs that thought he looked good, Arsenal did too. In January 1970 the big London club broke their own transfer record and signed Marinello for £100,000. With his long dark hair, good looks and youthful wing skills he was rather unfortunately compared to George Best. One Highbury director even went as far as to say: 'We've just signed the nearest thing football has to The Beatles.' Arriving in London he was saddled with this impossible comparison but scored on his debut with a dazzling goal at Old Trafford. But five goals in 51 matches was not good enough for the Gunners and his career went into decline. He followed his Highbury days with spells at Portsmouth, Motherwell, Fulham, Canberra City, Phoenix Inferno and, in a return to Edinburgh, Hearts. He wrote an autobiography titled *Fallen Idle* and this became something of a best-seller as it was a frank and fulsome account of his career.

MARINKOV, Alex

Centre-half

Born: Grenoble, France, 1967.
Career: Annency, Martigue, Limoges, Raon L'Etape. Scarborough 1998, HIBERNIAN 1999.

■ Tall and dark-haired, the easy going Marinkov was signed by Alex McLeish as Hibs stormed towards promotion from the First Division. He played his part (nine games and one goal) but left early the following season to revert to playing amateur football in France. For Alex it seemed that professional football was not quite the dream he harboured. In France Marinkov had played with a range of smaller French sides such as Annency, Martigue, Limoges and Raon L'Etape. He then tried his luck in England with Scarborough before joining Hibernian, but the feeling was that Alex did not relish being a full-time footballer and preferred the part-time option. His career record shows that he retired in May 2000.

MARJORIBANKS, Brian

Centre-forward

Career: Airth Castle Rovers, HIBERNIAN 1961.

■ Brian made his Hibernian debut in the 1961–62 campaign and slotted into the team with ease. Three goals in just four matches suggested a player who would enjoy his time at

Easter Road. But the following season was a disaster both for Brian and Hibernian. The club tried a few players at centre-forward and ultimately relied on the arrival of Gerry Baker to avoid relegation; as it was they finished 16th in an 18-club top flight. Brian had lost his first-team place and he was soon on his way out of Easter Road.

MARSHALL, Gordon

Goalkeeper

Born: Farnham, 2 July 1939.
Career: Balgreen Rovers, Hearts 1956, Newcastle United 1963, Nottingham Forest 1968, HIBERNIAN 1969, Celtic 1971, Aberdeen 1972, Arbroath 1972.

■ Few Hibs players have had such an inauspicious start to their careers as Gordon Marshall. A highly rated goalkeeper, he conceded two goals within six minutes of his debut. He was signed in 1969 by Bob Shankly, having earned an England Under-23 cap and played with Hearts, Newcastle and Nottingham Forest. Indeed, he had won League and League Cup-winners' medals while at Tynecastle so it was clear that he knew his stuff. After leaving Hibs he joined Celtic, Aberdeen and then Arbroath. While with Arbroath he played against Hibs and helped the minnows achieve a memorable Cup shock in March 1977 when they won a fourth round Scottish Cup replay 2–1 at Easter Road. Gordon's son (also called Gordon) became a noted goalkeeper too, playing with the like of Kilmarnock and Celtic. Gordon Senior played 389 League games in Scotland alone so the longevity of his career is beyond doubt.

MARTIN, Lilian

Full-back

Born: Valreas, France, 28 May 1971.
Career: ASOA Valence 1988, AS Nancy 1990, Dijon 1992, Dunkerque 1993, Monaco 1996, Marseille 1999, Derby County (loan) 2000, HIBERNIAN 2002.

■ The last signing made by Franck Sauzee, Lilian arrived as the Sauzee slump hit crisis point. He managed only one outing before Franck parted company with Hibs and it was perhaps inevitable that the veteran would leave at the same time.

MARTIN, Neil

Centre-forward

Born: Tranent, 20 October 1940.
Career: Tranent Juniors, Alloa Athletic 1959, Queen of the South 1961, HIBERNIAN 1963, Sunderland 1965, Coventry City 1968, Nottingham Forest 1971, Brighton 1975, Crystal Palace 1976, St Patrick's Athletic 1976.

■ A most accomplished finisher, Neil had the full striking package – presence, height and power. His haul of 53 goals for Hibs in 65 matches easily explains why he was heavily sought after and unfortunately why he only remained at Easter Road for a couple of seasons. Bought from Queen of the South in late-1963, Martin had been raised in Tranent and relished joining Hibs. Prior to playing with Queen of the South he had been at Alloa and gained renown for his heading ability and eye for goal. He proved a great signing for Hibs, netting goals with gusto. He was with Hibs when Jock Stein was in charge and remained

Neil Martin

during the immediate aftermath of Stein's bitterly disappointing departure to Celtic. Neil was sold to Sunderland in October 1965 and was an instant hit on Wearside, and he scored 38 goals in 86 matches for the Rokerites then moved to Coventry and Nottingham Forest where he was equally prolific. He later played with Brighton and Crystal Palace and upon his retirement could reflect on a career that brought three Scotland caps, including a key role against the mighty Italians at Hampden Park when Scotland famously won 1–0 in November 1965.

MARTIS, Shelton

Centre-half

Born: Dutch Antilles, 29 November 1982.
Career: Excelsior 2002, FC Eindhoven 2004, Darlington 2005, HIBERNIAN 2006, West Bromwich Albion 2007.

■ A powerful centre-half, Shelton arrived at Easter Road in August 2006 having played in

Holland and England. Manager Tony Mowbray was glowing in his reference saying that Martis was 'someone we have watched for a long time, he is composed, athletic and competitive'. However, he had a fairly torrid time at Hibs and along with Zieb Malkowski his name became something of a by-word for calamity. It was perhaps best all round that Shelton moved on to Tony Mowbray's West Bromwich Albion for £50,000 in July 2007.

MATHISEN, Svein

Midfield

Born: Sauda, Norway, 30 September 1952.
Career: IFK Start 1973, HIBERNIAN 1978, IFK Start 1979.

■ Svein was one of two Norwegian players Hibernian tried to sign in trying circumstances in 1978. He was a full international with seven caps and therefore more likely to acquire the, then, essential Department of Employment clearance. He had actually played for Norway against Scotland in a European Nations Cup match and made his Hibs debut along with Isak Refvik against Morton in a dramatic League Cup quarter-final tie, when Hibs turned a 1–0 first-leg deficit into a 2–1 aggregate win. But despite Hibernian chairman Tom Hart's finest efforts neither Matheson or Refvik could be signed permanently. Mathisen, who was nicknamed 'Matta', was a teacher and made the most of his return to Norway. He ended with career with two Norwegian Championship medals, played in 327 games (scoring 106 goals) and ended up winning 25 caps. When his playing days were over he carved out a career in the media, covering matches for both television and radio.

MATYUS, Janos

Full-back

Born: Budapest, Hungary, 20 December 1974.
Career: Budapest Honved 1993, Ferencváros 1998, Energie Cottbus (Germany) 2000, HIBERNIAN 2002, Admira Wacker (Austria) 2003, Gyori ETO 2005, Ferencváros 2007.

■ International Hungarian full-back Janos was signed by Bobby Williamson early in the 2002–03 season when Hibs endured a wretched start to the season and badly needed to shore up a leaky defence. It seemed a sound signing as Janos had won 30 under-23 and 34 senior caps and was clearly a quality performer. He fitted in well and was composed and constructive when on the ball. But the suspicion was that he was in the veteran phase of his career and when he injured his Achilles tendon against Dundee United in October 2002 he relinquished his first-team place. Matyus had actually played at Easter Road in 1996 for Hungary under-23s. He fitted in well at Hibs and was a steady performer but, alas, his stay lasted only a year before he returned to Hungary via Austria.

MAY, Eddie

Utility

Born: Edinburgh, 30 August 1967.
Career: Hutcheson Vale BC, Dundee United, HIBERNIAN 1985, Brentford 1989, Falkirk 1990, Motherwell 1993, Dunfermline 1999, Airdrie 2001, Berwick Rangers, Western Knights (Australia).

■ A sprightly and direct player, capable of playing as a scoring midfielder or a defensive full-back, May was one of a clutch of promising youngsters at Easter Road in the mid-1980s. He made his debut at Dundee on 14 September 1985 and scored his first goal at home to Clydebank the following January. It was a good season to break into the first team as the club reached the League Cup Final and the semi-finals of the Scottish Cup. The following season Eddie established himself as a regular and his versatility was evident as he wore no fewer than five different jerseys (in the days when one to 11 were all that was on offer!) and contributed five goals to the 'goals for' column. In January 1989 he had the only goal in a derby triumph over Hearts. Steady progress alerted others to Eddie's talents and the offer of a cheque for £165,000 from Brentford in 1989 was too good for a cash-strapped Hibs to turn down. He performed well in England but in 1990 Jim Jefferies took May to Falkirk where he was an integral part of their revival in the early-1990s. Thereafter he played with several clubs, always impressing with his versatility and commitment. His extraordinary fitness served him well when he retired from playing, and in 2007 he was part of the Motherwell 'masters' side that won the Scottish Football Masters indoor tournament.

MILLEN, Andy

Defender

Born: Glasgow, 10 June 1965.
Career: Pollok Juniors, St Johnstone 1983, Alloa 1987, Hamilton Accies 1990, Kilmarnock 1994, HIBERNIAN 1995, Raith Rovers 1997, Ayr United 1997, Morton 1999, Clyde 2001, St Mirren 2004.

■ Born in Kilmarnock in 1965, Andy played with St Johnstone, Alloa, Hamilton Accies and Killie before joining Hibs in March 1995. He came to Easter Road in a deal that took Billy Findlay to Kilmarnock in exchange. He was a fringe player with Hibs but had won a B International cap for Scotland against Wales and picked up two B&Q Cup-winners' badges

from his time at Hamilton. Upon leaving Hibs he played with Raith Rovers, Ayr United and Morton during the infamous years of Hugh Scott's chairmanship, before he moved to Clyde where he provided much needed experience in a team recruited largely from the ranks of junior clubs. However, there was a remarkable finale to his senior career. He joined the St Mirren coaching staff as a player-assistant and on 5 May 2007 he played against Dundee United when aged 41 years and 329 days; thus becoming the oldest player ever to feature in an SPL game.

MILLER, Graeme

Midfield

Born: Glasgow, 21 February 1973.
Career: Tynecastle BC, HIBERNIAN 1990, Berwick Rangers 1996.

■ Born in 1973, Graeme joined Hibs straight from school. He played outside-left and was part of the 'Miller' dynasty at Easter Road as his father Alex managed the club at one point and younger brother Greg was also on the playing staff. Whereas Greg was able to eke out a career away from Edinburgh, Graeme struggled to fulfill his undoubted potential and drifted from the Scottish game without making any great impact. He had a single start as a Hibee, in the 1992–93 campaign.

MILLER, Greg

Midfield

Born: Glasgow, 1 April 1976.
Career: Hutchison Vale BC, HIBERNIAN 1994, Livingston 1998, Motherwell 1998, Clydebank 1999, Vasteras (Sweden) 2000, Brechin City 2001, Arbroath 2004.

■ Brother of Graeme, and son of manager Alex, accusations of family favouritism cannot have made life easy for Greg at Hibernian. He made his debut in an away defeat at Falkirk in November 1995 as a substitute and started for the first team a few months later against Raith Rovers. However, first-team outings were rare (but there was a home goal against Kilmarnock to savour). Unable to make the expected impact at Easter Road, Greg moved to Motherwell and then on to Clydebank. With the Bankies in deep financial trouble he was forced to move on again and joined Swedish Second Division side Vasteras. He returned to Scotland to join Brechin City in January 2000.

MILLER, Kenny

Centre-forward

Born: Edinburgh, 23 December 1979.
Career: Hutchison Vale BC, HIBERNIAN 1996, Rangers 2000, Wolverhampton 2001, Celtic 2006, Derby County 2007, Rangers 2008.

■ A live-wire striker, Miller burst into the Hibs first team during Alex McLeish's reign and was hot-property from the off. Goals against the Old Firm and Hearts (following a confidence boosting loan spell with Stenhousemuir) had the cheque books at the ready and he was off to Rangers. But before he departed for £2 million he was capped by Scotland at Under-21 level and was on the verge of a full call-up. He was unlucky not to make more of his spell at Ibrox for despite scoring five in one game against St Mirren the Glasgow club were unconvinced and they sold Kenny to Wolves (ironically just as Alex McLeish arrived as Rangers manager). That was not to be the last twist in his career. In 2006 he joined Celtic and thus achieved that rare feat of representing both halves of the Old Firm. As if that were not enough, in 2008 he rejoined Rangers, this time in a £1.9 million deal after a spell with Derby County.

MILLER, Willie (1)

Goalkeeper

Born: Glasgow, 20 October 1924.
Career: Maryhill Harp, Celtic 1942, Clyde 1950, HIBERNIAN 1954.

■ A vastly experienced 'custodian', Willie joined Hibernian after serving Celtic and Clyde with some panache. A Scottish League international, he was signed in an injury crisis at the tail end of the 1953–54 season and made his debut in an impressive 3–0 home win over Aberdeen. In his next game he played against Rangers in front of an unusually small 17,000 crowd. By the start of the 1954–55 season Tommy Younger was back and Miller was ultimately given a free transfer in April 1955 and retired shortly afterwards. Away from football he has worked as a locomotive engineer in the huge Glasgow St Rollox works but success as a goalkeeper allowed him to establish Miller's Bar in the Townhead district of the city.

MILLER, Willie (2)

Full-back

Born: Edinburgh, 1 November 1969.
Career: Edina Hibs, HIBERNIAN 1987, Dundee 1998, Raith Rovers (loan), Cowdenbeath 2002.

■ During Alex Miller's time in charge there was a solid backbone to the Hibernian side. Willie Miller (no relation to the Aberdeen player or Alex Miller himself) was a key part of that strength and would play 239 League games for Hibs. A fiercely competitive full-back, Willie was signed from Edina Hibs in 1987 and made his debut in February 1990 against Celtic. He made swift progress thereafter and was capped seven times by Scotland at Under-21 level. Miller was popular with the Hibernian support, largely by dint of his physical approach to the game and whole-hearted commitment. Between 1989 and 1998 he made an excellent 246 appearances of which seven were as a substitute. Highlight of his time at Easter Road was surely being part of the side that won the League Cup against Dunfermline in 1991. He could never be called a cultured player or a particularly creative individual but few got past him without considerable effort or guile. From Easter Road Willie moved to Dundee where he was a regular for a few seasons until joining Keith Wright at Cowdenbeath. There were some Hibernian fans who suggested that Miller took the role of 'man marking' quite literally!

MILNE, Arthur

Centre-forward

Born: Brechin, 1915.
Career: Brechin Victoria, Dundee United 1934, Liverpool 1937, HIBERNIAN 1937, St Mirren 1946, Coleraine 1950.

■ Arthur moved from Brechin Victoria to Dundee United and thus began a most interesting career. A prolific marksman, he travelled to Liverpool in March 1937 ostensibly on loan but was not returned to Dundee United. An unseemly squabble broke out and Hibernian exploited this indecision to sign Milne. Dundee United had claimed he was a Liverpool player and they were due a transfer fee. *The Dundee Courier* neatly, and rather bluntly, summed up the Merseyside club's views: 'Liverpool did not accept the offer of his transfer, they decided they were rather afflicted with too many stocky little forwards'. Thus he joined Willie McCartney's Hibernian as a free agent and in June 1941 scored within 20 seconds of the start of a famous 5–2 Hibs win at Celtic (indeed he bagged a hat-trick that day). Alas, his Easter Road career was nearing an end when official League football resumed after World War Two. He did play in three matches in the 1946–47 season but in September that season he moved to St Mirren for £1,650. Interestingly, the vacancy at the Paisley club had arisen due their star striker Alex Linwood moving to Middlesbrough. Linwood would in due course come to Easter Road. Milne left Saints in the summer of 1950 and played briefly in Northern Ireland with Coleraine. He died in Edinburgh in May 1997.

MILNE, Callum

Full-back

Born: Edinburgh, 27 August 1965.
Career: Salveson BC, HIBERNIAN 1983, Partick Thistle 1993, Whitburn 1998.

■ Callum was only 17 when Hibs signed him from Salveson Boys Club in April 1983. He flitted in and out of the team and after almost a decade at the club had only just made the 50 appearances mark. His career was clearly hampered by injury and perhaps less so by indiscipline. He was sent off against Rangers in 1991; a dismissal that infuriated Hibs boss Alex Miller and stalled the progress that Milne was making. He was sent off a few times at his next club too, Partick Thistle, where he clocked up a century of appearances.

MITCHELL, Graham

Defender

Born: Hamilton, 2 November 1962.
Career: Auchengill BC, Hamilton Accies 1979, HIBERNIAN 1986, Falkirk 1996.

■ Graham joined Hamilton Accies from local nursery club Auchengill Star BC in 1979. He became one of Accies' finest defenders and stayed with them until late December 1986 when he joined Hibs. Few could have imagined that having carved out a notable career with Accies he would do likewise at Easter Road. He soon forged a strong defensive partnership with Gordon Rae and this would continue when Gordon Hunter moved into central defence. Strong in the tackle and reliable when games became frantic, he was coolness personified. This excellent temperament made him a leading member in the Hibernian team and one of the first names on the team sheet for several years. Against Dunfermline Athletic in 1991 he won a League Cup-winners' badge and he was still an automatic selection for the side that was beaten by Rangers in the Final of the same tournament two years later. After a long and distinguished career with Hibs, which brought almost 300 senior outings, he was freed in May 1996 and made the short journey to Falkirk. A quiet, unassuming, very dependable player indeed. For a player who rarely ventured into opposition territory it is ironic that he is well remembered for one of his goals. The strike in question came against Videoton of Hungary in a first round UEFA Cup tie in September 1989 and sent Hibs on the way to a memorable European triumph.

MORAIS, Filipe

Winger

Born: Lisbon, 21 November 1985.
Career: Chelsea 2005, MK Dons (loan), Millwall, St Johnstone (loan), HIBERNIAN 2007, Inverness (loan) 2008.

■ A Portuguese Under-21 international but raised in London, Filipe was on loan to St Johnstone from Millwall when he appeared against Hibs in the CIS Cup semi-final at Tynecastle early in 2007. In July of the same year John Collins signed Morais for Hibs noting at the time: 'Filipe came very highly recommended by contacts at Chelsea, I saw him for myself last season when he was on loan to St Johnstone both before the CIS Cup match and in that game itself.' He made his Hibs debut in a pre-season win over Middlesbrough in the month that he joined the club.

MORAN, Dougie

Centre-forward

Born: Musselburgh, 29 July 1934.
Career: Musselburgh Union, HIBERNIAN 1951, Falkirk 1957, Ipswich Town 1961, Dundee United 1964, Falkirk 1964, Cowdenbeath 1968.

■ Little Dougie Moran had the kind of debut schoolboys dream of. Pitched in to the Hibs team in place of the great Scotland striker Lawrie Reilly he responded by scoring a debut winner. That was in March 1954 against St Mirren, but soon he would be off doing his national service and almost inevitably his Hibernian career suffered. He went to Falkirk in January 1957 and scored a Scottish Cup Final winner for them in 1958. A prolific marksman as a Bairn, he even stayed with them when they were relegated but in July 1961 he moved on to Ipswich Town for £12,000. Life in East Anglia suited him well and he was an integral part of their finest years, helping himself to an English Championship medal in the process. He returned to Scotland with Dundee United but could not settle and joined Falkirk once more.

MORROW, Sam

Midfield

Born: Londonderry, 3 March 1985
Career: Ipswich Town, HIBERNIAN 2004, Livingston (loan) 2006, Partick Thistle (loan) 2007, Derry City 2007.

■ Signed in the summer of 2004 by Tony Mowbray, Morrow had been through Ipswich Town's impressive youth system and was a Northern Ireland Under-21 international. He made his Hibs debut against Killie in August 2004 and impressed immediately with his intelligent distribution. Sadly he failed to build on a good start and was soon off to the likes of Livingston and Partick Thistle on loan. He was eventually released by John Collins and trained with both St Mirren and Derry City before joining the latter in July 2007. It would be fair to say that injuries plagued Morrow's progress at both Hibs and Derry.

MUIR, George

Left-back

Career: Cowdenbeath Royals, Edinburgh Thistle, HIBERNIAN 1953.

■ George was a left-back who made his debut in the opening game of the 1955–56 season, as Hibs slumped horribly to lose 6–2 at Aberdeen. Indeed, George did well to bounce back from that horror show and in the next season he made two dozen League appearances. Versatile enough to play both right and left-back he was at his peak in the mid-1950s. By 1960 he was fading rapidly from the Easter Road first-team scene and he played his final game in a 3–3 draw against Airdrie in March. George was born in Lochgelly, Fife.

MUIR, Lindsay

Midfield

Born: Linlithgow, 10 May 1956.
Career: HIBERNIAN 1974, St Johnstone 1978, Berwick Rangers 1980, Cowdenbeath 1987, Berwick 1988.

■ Small, wiry and with a head of thick black curly hair, Lindsay was among the most prominent Scotland Schoolboy internationals of his era. He clearly made an impression on Eddie Turnbull for he was in the Hibs first team within months of coming to Easter Road, having impressed on a pre-season tour of Ireland. But although he made a mark in the 1975–76 campaign he faded just as quickly from the picture. In 1978 he joined St Johnstone and he stayed there for two seasons before moving south to Berwick Rangers.

MUIRHEAD, Billy

Goalkeeper

Career: Arniston Rangers, HIBERNIAN 1959, Raith Rovers 1962, Toronto City, Stenhousemuir 1968, Berwick Rangers 1969.

■ Billy made his Hibernian debut in January 1960 against Rangers at Ibrox shortly after being signed as a raw 19-year-old from Arniston Rangers. He had only eight reserve matches under his belt when he was called upon to counter the Rangers attack. Standing in for Jackie Wren (who had flu) and Billy Wilson (who was injured) he played out the remainder of the 1959–60 season. It was a season that slumped horribly after Christmas and Muirhead shipped five goals against Clyde and six against Dundee. At 5ft 11in this young apprentice joiner had all the hallmarks of a good goalkeeper but seemed to lack the presence to make a lasting impression. As a schoolboy he played for Edinburgh Schools and it was said that Dunfermline were keen on him before he joined Hibs.

MULKERRIN, Jim

Centre-forward

Born: Dumbarton, 25 December 1931.
Career: Dumbarton Stroller Juveniles, HIBERNIAN 1950, Accrington Stanley 1957, Tranmere Rovers 1959.

■ A centre-forward, Jim was only 5ft 6in and had to have that little extra to succeed. He made his debut in the 1951 Championship-winning team, playing in a 2–2 draw at Dundee in April and leading the line a few days later at Clyde when Hibs officially won the League. Hibs retained the Championship title the following season but Jimmy was only called upon once, and that was when Hibs were missing Johnstone and Reilly on international duty. He stood in for Reilly once in the 1952–53 season but clearly was going to struggle to oust the master from the first team. He hung on for a while and was rewarded with five goals in eight matches in the 1955–56 season (as well as a Scotland B cap against England) but elected to move on in March 1957 when Accrington Stanley called. It was a move that worked well and he scored a very impressive 36 goals in 70 matches for them. In his early days at Easter Road he worked as a painter in Dumbarton and trained at Boghead Park to cut down on his travel.

MUNRO, Iain

Midfield/full-back

Born: Uddingston, 24 August 1951.
Career: Drumchapel Amateurs, St Mirren 1968, HIBERNIAN 1973, Rangers 1976, St Mirren 1977, Stoke City 1980, Sunderland 1981, Dundee United 1984, HIBERNIAN 1985.

■ A refined and cultured player, Iain Munro was a delight to watch. His cerebral approach and almost artistic use of the ball allied to a wonderfully balanced athleticism made him a tremendous team player. There was a considerable gnashing of teeth when he left Hibs for Rangers in 1976, a feeling which lingered when the players received in exchange – Ally Scott and Graham Fyfe – failed to live up to expectations. Ian joined St Mirren in 1968 from Glasgow amateur football but was farmed out to Cambuslang Rangers and Blantyre Vics before joining officially in 1969. A physical education teacher by trade he was part-time at St Mirren until Hibs signed him in May 1973, and he played in the 1973 Dryburgh Cup Final win over Celtic and the 1974 League Cup Final which the club lost 3–6 to Celtic. Ironically, his home debut had come against former club St Mirren in a Dryburgh Cup tie at Easter Road. Alas, he was sold to Rangers but that did not work out and he returned to St Mirren when their young boss Alex Ferguson convinced him to join the likes of Fitzpatrick, Richardson and Stark in a flourishing Paisley side. Iain won seven Scotland caps before joining Stoke City and then Sunderland before returning to Scotland with Dundee United. John Blackley persuaded Iain to return to Hibs and he enjoyed a fine twilight to his career playing in another League Cup Final (1985–86) and a Scottish Cup semi-final. Retiring at 35 he then entered coaching and managed Dunfermline, Dundee, Hamilton Accies and Raith Rovers. He then moved to Ayr United to be assistant to Gordon Dalziel.

MUNRO, John

Outside-right

Born: Linlithgow, 1930.
Career: Bathgate Thistle, HIBERNIAN 1948.

■ John was another of the youngsters given the unenviable task of being understudy to Gordon Smith. He played a single League game for Hibs, against Raith Rovers at the tail end of the 1950–51 League season. His career was perhaps badly affected by the then requirement to complete national service and while in the RAF he clearly lost out on footballing opportunities. He spent much of the 1952–53 season playing in Hibs' third team (eight goals in 11 matches) and in the summer of 1953 he was given a free transfer.

MURDOCK, Colin

Centre-half

Born: Ballymena, 2 July 1976.
Career: Manchester United, Preston North End 1997, HIBERNIAN 2003, Crewe Alexandra 2004, Rotherham United 2005, Shrewsbury Town 2007, Accrington Stanley 2008.

■ Hibernian supporters were initially sceptical about the qualities Colin possessed. Standing at 6ft 3in and occasionally gangling and lumbering in his approach, Colin could appear like the accident prone centre-half football fans dread. Much of that changed one night at Hampden Park in 2003. In a thrilling CIS League Cup semi-final penalty-shoot out against Rangers Colin converted the decisive penalty and thus earned his niche at the club. But there were unfortunately too many detractors on the terraces who, despite Colin's international status with Northern Ireland, would not be won over. His huge physical presence was a wonderful asset at set-pieces but there were no hiding places for such a huge player when mistakes were made. Having joined Hibs in the summer of 2003 he barely reached the 50-game mark before moving to Crewe Alexandra in 2004. A very articulate man off the field he had at one time harboured ambitions to be a lawyer.

MURPHY, David

Left-back

Born: Hartlepool, 1 March 1984.
Career: Middlesbrough 2001, Barnsley (loan) 2003, HIBERNIAN 2004, Birmingham City 2008.

■ In October 2007 Hibs went to the top of the SPL when David Murphy headed the only goal in a surprise 1–0 win at Rangers. It was perhaps the clearest sign that the club would struggle to hang on to a player who had grasped the chance Hibs had offered and simply got better and better with three years of regular first-team football. Signed by Tony Mowbray in July 2004, Murphy impressed with his forays down the left wing and developed a knack for tucking away opportunities. Creative, energetic and technically very sound he quickly won over the Hibs support with his consistency. By the time of the Rangers match he was the finished article and one of the first names on the team sheet. When John Collins took over from Mowbray he had no hesitation in endorsing Murphy as his regular left-back. Clearly Alex McLeish had continued to watch events unfold at Hibernian for it was the former boss who came back to Easter Road in January 2008 to prise Murphy away. The 23-year-old Murphy thus slipped back down south for a fee of £1.5 million; good business for Hibs who had acquired the player on a Bosman from Middlesbrough.

MURPHY, John

Wing-half

Born: 26 November 1949.
Career: Tynecastle BC, HIBERNIAN 1966, Morton 1971, Stirling Albion 1973, Cowdenbeath 1975, Newtongrange Star 1977.

■ A talented Hibs youngster under Bob Shankly, John made fleeting first-team appearances and played on the tour of Nigeria. In June 1971 he left Hibs to join Morton but after 70 games for the Greenock club he was on his travels once more, this time Stirling Albion being the destination. He brought the curtain down on his senior career with a spell at Cowdenbeath.

MURRAY, Antonio

Midfield

Born: Cambridge, 15 September 1984.
Career: Ipswich Town 2003, HIBERNIAN 2005, Histon Town 2007.

■ Antonio was a product of Ipswich Town's youth system and it was there that he had impressed the then youth coach Tony Mowbray. When Mowbray was at Hibs he signed Murray in the hope that the youngster, who had made a handful of first-team outings for Ipswich, would provide some much-needed spark. Signed in the January 2005 transfer window he was viewed on a short-term contract initially but soon earned a longer deal. Unfortunately he was badly hit by injuries and had made just over a dozen outings when he was released in 2006.

MURRAY, Gary

Centre-forward

Born: Dundee, 19 August 1959.

Career: Blairgowrie, Montrose 1977, HIBERNIAN 1980, Forfar Athletic 1984, Montrose 1986.

■ Born in Dundee in 1959, Gary was signed in December 1980 for £50,000 from Montrose where he was a prolific marksman (he had 39 goals in 85 matches). The fee was a record for the little Angus club. One of Gary's great strengths was that he could play wide on the left as well as straight down the centre. Strong in the air, he was also adept at cutting in from wide positions and using his shooting power to good effect. He made his debut for Hibs in the First Division against Stirling Albion and had his first goal a few weeks later in a 1–0 win over Dumbarton. His stay in Edinburgh would bring 16 goals in 79 matches and while this is not the most prolific return by a Hibs centre-forward it was nevertheless a credit-worthy contribution. Slipping out of favour in 1984 he elected to join Forfar. Although he did well there it was clear that he was at heart a Montrose lad and in 1986 he returned there as a veteran. It was a highly successful return and he scored 53 times in 157 matches in his second spell at Links Park. In 1991 Gary retired through injury. Perhaps never the most artistic of players he was nonetheless a very robust marksman and clearly a solid performer at a certain level.

MURRAY, Ian

Left-midfield

Born: Edinburgh, 20 March 1981.
Career: HIBERNIAN, Rangers 2005, Norwich City 2007, HIBERNIAN 2008.

■ A product of the Hibernian youth system, Ian Murray epitomised all that was good in a young player. Full of enthusiasm, dedicated to learning and with the additional bonus of being a big Hibernian supporter. He quickly progressed from being a fringe player at Easter Road and benefited enormously from a loan spell at Alloa Athletic in January 2001. Thereafter he would quickly progress to being a member of Scotland's Under-21 side and rather fittingly won his first full Scotland cap at Easter Road in 2002 (against Canada and in opposition to teammate Paul Fenwick). By that time he had played in a Scottish Cup Final and had briefly captained Hibs. His enormous work-rate allied to good all-round skills had made him a key performer at the club. As a boy he had been associated with Dundee United but things really took off for him when he switched to Easter Road. He made his Hibs debut against that club in January 1999. His first goal came in a Scottish Cup tie against Dunfermline and by 2002–03 he was leading the Hibernian goalscoring charts...from midfield! One of Ian's key qualities was being able to raise his game in crunch matches, and he scored valuable goals against St Johnstone in a relegation battle and scored with composure in the derby against Hearts. Against the city rivals he earned one note of notoriety by dying the date 1973 into his hair, a clear reference to the famous 7–0 Hibs win of that year and one guaranteed to rile the Hearts supporters. A move to Rangers in the summer of 2005 did not work out quite as expected and illness (reactive arthritis) hampered his progress. Salvation appeared to come in the form of a free-transfer to Norwich City in August 2007 but Ian, then aged 26, failed to settle in Norfolk and returned to Hibernian in the January transfer window of 2008 for a second spell. He

re-adjusted quickly but was sent off against Motherwell in February 2008 as he came to terms again with the frenetic pace of the SPL.

MURRAY, Willie

Winger

Born: Edinburgh, 28 August 1954.
Career: Salveson BC, HIBERNIAN 1971, Sydney 1980, Cowdenbeath 1981.

■ A speedy, long-haired forward, Willie was a fringe player in the Eddie Turnbull years. He could take a chance when presented and was the kind of busy winger that supporters could relate to. Although a member of the Scotland Youth team, and linked to the club from 1970, patience was required on Willie's part before making his Hibernian breakthrough because he did not make his first-team debut until July 1972 against Waterford in a pre-season tour of Ireland. At the time the outside-right position was a bit of an issue, the usual number seven Alex Edwards being more of a midfielder than a conventional winger. Willie made his League bow in the 1973–74 season when Hibs pushed Jock Stein's strong Celtic side all the way in the title race. He was a playing substitute in a 3–1

win at Dundee in April 1974 but a few days later started in a damaging 3–2 defeat to lowly Arbroath. His best season was in 1977–78 when he was a regular, but by 1980 he was slipping from the reckoning and he went to Australia briefly before moving on to Cowdenbeath.

N

NELSON, Dennis
Midfield

Born: Edinburgh, 25 February 1950.
Career: Broxburn Athletic, HIBERNIAN 1970, Dunfermline Athletic 1972, Crewe Alexandra 1974, Reading 1976, Crewe Alexandra 1978.

■ Dennis made just one appearance for Hibs, in the 1971–72 season, a 1–3 reversal at home to Airdrie. This solitary outing proved scant reward for this powerful little centre-forward. There is no doubt that a broken leg which he endured early in his Hibs career (during a practice match) did his Easter Road prospects great harm. Better times lay in store when he went to Dunfermline in the 1973–74 season and he barely missed a game as the Pars headed to promotion in the Second Division. He hit 13 goals for Dunfermline that season including four in an 8–0 rout over Brechin. Dennis later tried his luck south of the border with Crewe, Reading and back to Crewe – where he was always a regular.

NICHOLLS, Dave
Midfield

Born: Bellshill, 5 April 1972.
Career: Chelsea BC, Ferguslie United, HIBERNIAN 1989, Coleraine, Hamilton Accies 1994, Cork City, Clydebank 1995, Falkirk 1999, Dunfermline 2001, Falkirk 2003, Gretna 2005.

■ From Chelsea BC to Ferguslie United and then on to Hibernian was the early career route of this solid midfielder. Dave joined Hibs in 1989 but never quite held down a permanent first-team position and eventually moved to Coleraine in Northern Ireland. From Ireland he returned to Scotland in 1994 to join Hamilton Academicals. Failure to establish himself there saw a move to Southern Ireland and Cork before Clydebank snapped him up. At this stage his promise began to mature and by the time he joined Falkirk he was a very competent midfielder indeed. He had two spells with the Bairns and was part of the Gretna story as the little Borders club raced through the Scottish Leagues in the early-21st century and he played in the 2006 Scottish Cup Final. With over 300 matches at senior level his had been quite a productive career.

NICOL, Kevin
Midfield

Born: Kirkcaldy, 19 January 1982.
Career: Hill o'Beath, Raith Rovers 1998, HIBERNIAN 2002, Brechin City (loan) 2006, Peterhead 2006.

■ One of the few signings made by Franck Sauzee, Kevin could not quite make a mark at Easter Road. His signing was something of a surprise as he had hardly been a regular for Rovers. When Grant Brebner was seriously injured at home to Rangers in a 2004 Scottish Cup tie he stepped into the breach, but such outings were the exception rather than the norm. He found first-team openings very limited in Edinburgh, his best season being 2003–04 when he made over a dozen starts. The very next season he broke bones in his foot and his progress was halted. He moved briefly to Brechin on loan early in 2006 and then signed permanently for Peterhead in February 2006. He was capped three times by Scotland at Under-19 level.

NICOL, Robert
Wing-half

Born: Edinburgh, 11 May 1936.
Career: Ashton, Edinburgh City, HIBERNIAN 1952, Barnsley 1962, Berwick Rangers 1963.

■ In 1952 Hibs went to Edinburgh City to secure the services of Schoolboy international, and apprentice fitter, Bobby Nicol. This right-sided wing-half and occasional inside-forward broke into the Hibernian first team in the mid-1950s but in 1962 he was freed, this despite having earned Scotland Under-23 caps against England (1956) and Holland (1958). His problem was that he was never quite able to

make himself an automatic selection. Robert Benjamin Mathieson Nicol then moved to Barnsley before returning to Scotland with Berwick Rangers. In all he played 37 League games for Hibs and scored two goals.

NISH, Colin

Forward

Born: Edinburgh, 7 March 1981.
Career: Rosyth Recreation, Dunfermline Athletic 1997, Alloa (loan) 2000, Clyde 2002, Kilmarnock 2003, HIBERNIAN 2008.

■ Colin was signed by Mixu Paatelainen in the January 2008 transfer window. A powerful 6ft 3in striker he had been with Kilmarnock since July 2003, indeed one of his first goals for Killie came against Hibernian, and he had played against Hibernian in the 2007 League Cup Final (which Hibs won 5–1). He must have had mixed feelings that day for Nish was brought up in Edinburgh and was a Hibbee as a youngster! While not a prolific marksman at Kilmarnock he was nevertheless a regular goalscorer, and he would have been a Bosman signing for Hibs had Killie not accepted a nominal fee in the transfer window. Something of a bad boy on the field he was sent off at Motherwell in April 2008, his second sending off in a short period of time.

NOUBISSIE, Patrick

Defender

Born: Bourg-la-Riene, 25 June 1983.
Career: CS Brétigny-sur-Orge, Le Mée-sur-Seine SF, CS Sedan, Crewe Alexandra 2006, Stockport County, Grimsby Town, Swindon Town, HIBERNIAN 2007, Livingston (loan) 2007, Dundee (loan) 2007, released from contract 2008.

■ Signed by John Collins, Patrick must have been surprised to be sent out on loan immediately. The feeling was that he needed match fitness after his release by Swindon Town. He did gain some valuable experience but was off on loan again when Mixu Paatelainen allowed him to join Dundee. Patrick's Hibernian career amounted to four games before he was released from his contract.

NUTLEY, Robert

Winger

Born: Paisley, 10 September 1916.
Died: Paisley, 1996.
Career: Blantyre Victoria, HIBERNIAN 1946, Portsmouth 1946, Queen of the South 1947.

■ Bobby was another player whose best years were lost to the Second World War. He was born in Paisley in September 1916 and broke into the Hibernian side in the 1937–38 season, scoring eight goals in 26 League fixtures. Alas, what would have been his prime years coincided with the Second World War and he only played in a single match for Hibs in the 1946–47 season – a 1–0 win at Queen's Park on 17 August – before moving to Portsmouth in August 1946. He was 30 by the time he joined Pompey and he only managed nine matches for them before bringing the curtain down on his career by returning briefly to Scotland with Queen of the South.

O'BRIEN, Alan

Winger

Born: Republic of Ireland, 20 February 1985.
Career: Newcastle United 2004, Carlisle United (loan) 2005, HIBERNIAN 2007.

■ Signed from Newcastle United in 2007, Alan saw his career at Easter Road badly hampered by injury. John Collins was hardly able to field him and Collins's successor Mixu Paatelainen was equally unlucky. A Republic of Ireland international, his career at Newcastle had been dogged by injury and at one point he had been loaned to Carlisle United to keep his fitness on track. This was all a great loss to the Easter Road club who had hoped O'Brien would fill the void left by the departure of Ivan Sproule.

O'BRIEN, Gerry

Outside-left

Born: Glasgow, 10 November 1949.
Career: Drumchapel Amateurs, Clydebank 1968, Southampton 1970, Bristol Rovers (loan) 1974, Swindon Town 1976, Clydebank 1977, HIBERNIAN 1978, Rutherglen Glencairn.

■ Eddie Turnbull went to Clydebank in May 1978 to secure the services of Gerry and he quickly scored the winner in an East of Scotland Shield Final to win over the supporters. But alas this was a false dawn, and when Gerry left Hibernian in July 1979 he had made only seven League outings, five of those as a substitute. His career had started with Clydebank and by the late-1960s he was looking like a very competent player indeed. In March 1970 he was lured to Lawrie McMenemy's Southampton and he had five excellent years there.

O'CONNOR, Garry

Centre-forward

Born: Edinburgh, 7 May 1983.
Career: HIBERNIAN 2000, Lokomotiv Moscow 2006, Birmingham City 2007.

■ A glut of goals in the Hibernian Under-18 and Under-21 sides catapulted young Garry straight into the Hibernian first team in the summer of 2000. He responded with all four goals in a 4–0 pre-season win at Gala Fairydean. A powerful young striker he netted his first competitive strike in a 1–1 draw against Celtic in February 2002. Thereafter he was a frequent scorer, so much so that he was capped by Scotland at full international level before making any appearances at Under-21 or lesser ranks. There was a precedent here as he had been voted Scotland's Player of the Month in April 2002 without ever having won the young version of the award. Some of his goals were the stuff of local legend. He hit a real 'belter' in a 3–0 win at Partick and scored the famous 90th-minute winner against Hearts at Easter Road when Hibs won with only 10 men in 2003. He continued to make sound progression and although not great in the air he was both powerful and clever with the ball at his feet. By the time other clubs were circling around Easter Road looking for his signature he had contributed 58 goals in 166 appearances. O'Connor was sold to Russian side Lokomotiv Moscow in February 2006 for £1.6 million. The terms were magnificent with the young striker reputed to have signed a five-year deal earning him roughly £16,000 per week. But for all that wealth he did not really settle in Russia despite being able to produce the goals when needed, including the only one in Lokomotiv's victory in the May 2007 Russian Cup Final over FC Moscow in the Luzhniki Stadium. His stay in Eastern Europe lasted 15 months before he was signed by Birmingham City of the English Premiership in a £2.65 million deal in late June 2007. Birmingham boss Steve Bruce had no doubt been influenced by O'Connor's successful return to the international fold. He had walked out on Scotland prior to a match in Ukraine in 2007, but after a cooling off period, Alex McLeish reintroduced him and he rewarded his former boss with goals against Austria and the Faroe Islands as Scotland pushed towards the 2008 European Championships. How ironic that McLeish should succeed Bruce in the Birmingham hot seat.

Garry O'Connor

WILLIE ORMOND　HERO

Winger

Born: Falkirk, 23 February 1927.
Career: Gairdoch Juveniles, Stenhousemuir 1946, HIBERNIAN 1946, Falkirk 1961.

■ Willie Ormond enjoyed what can truly be described as one of the most distinguished careers in Scottish football. As a player he was the outside-left in the renowned Hibernian forward line 'The Famous Five'. As a manager he took St Johnstone to new heights before winning a nation's heart as the quietly effective manager of Scotland. But Ormond was much more than a soaring success. He was a universally popular figure in the Scottish game. His cherubic looks, beguiling smile and approachable manner made him a favourite wherever he went. Here was a 'man of the people' the fans could relate to. When he died in 1984 he was mourned the length and breadth of Scotland.

Ormond was the only member of the Hibernian 'Famous Five' to cost a transfer fee. He actually started his career with Stenhousemuir (where he played only a handful of games in his six months) and joined Willie McCartney's Hibs in November 1946 for the princely sum of £1,200. That proved a sound piece of business for the Hibees and Ormond stayed at Easter Road for 15 years. Willie would score 133 goals for Hibs in 348 matches, including a last-minute winner against Rangers in front of 40,000 in his home Hibs debut. He overcame a catalogue of injuries to achieve those figures. Three leg-breaks, a broken arm and ruptured ligaments were at the top of an appalling list. But in an age before the concept of 'bouncebackability' was in vogue, Ormond was the archetypal survivor. Three Championship medals came Willie's way in his Easter Road career. When Hibs retained their title in 1952 they did so with a 3–1 win over Dundee in which the mercurial Ormond scored twice. He could not add a domestic Cup medal, however, and that was not for lack of trying. Willie played in the 1947 Scottish Cup Final and was on the losing side again in 1958. He reached the League Cup Final with Hibs in 1950 but once more Lady Luck deserted the Edinburgh men. But the national stadium was not always unkind and he won six caps for Scotland (to go with seven Scottish League caps). Willie stayed at Hibs until the summer of 1961 when he moved to Falkirk, but he rather ungraciously

returned to Easter Road in October of that year to score both Bairns goals in a 2–2 draw. How Falkirk were glad of that point. Season 1961–62 proved a close call for the Brockville men and they stayed in the top flight by the narrowest of margins, finishing ahead of relegated St Johnstone by a single point. Ormond had little more than a year as a Falkirk player (he was the third member of the Ormond family to play for the Bairns; his brothers Bert and Gibby also playing professional football) before becoming joint trainer-coach. But it was further north in Perth that Willie really made his mark. St Johnstone had lost their boss of eight years Bobby Brown to Scotland and when Harold Davis (the former Rangers and East Fife wing-half and Queen's Park coach) turned the post down they looked to the former Hibee to revive their flagging fortunes. Ormond was appointed St Johnstone boss in March 1967. When he walked through the door of the long-gone Muirton Park he arrived full of enthusiasm. Aged just 41 he was helped by the great success his good friend and

former Hibernian teammate Eddie Turnbull had made of the Aberdeen job. Perhaps fortunate to go from trainer to manager of a First Division club in one simple leap, he was clearly grateful for the opportunity as he made crystal clear at the time, saying: 'It has long been my ambition to manage a club, and to go to such a well established outfit as St Johnstone is a great honour. I think there are great prospects here. I have just got to put the confidence into the boys and get them working together. I don't see why we shouldn't do well.' Ormond was to stay until 1973 and as he fell in love with Perth so Saints fell in love with him. Clever in the transfer market, he was equally shrewd when it came to spotting and promoting talented youngsters. During his reign he took St Johnstone to new heights. They reached the League Cup Final in 1969 and a third place finish in the League the following season gave them entry to the Fairs Cup. Remarkably, Saints took to Europe with ease and they despatched the likes of Hamburg and Vasas Budapest in a thrilling run that captivated Perthshire. St Johnstone supporters still recall the Ormond years with great fondness. His was the side of Connolly, Hall and Pearson and excitement was always high on the Perth agenda. Just how popular Ormond was is clear when you drive up to McDiarmid Park and see his name emblazoned on the respectfully named Ormond Stand, a sure sign of his celebrity status. If his spell at St Johnstone marked the high spot of his domestic career then 1974 marked his international high point. In December 1972 Scotland boss Tommy Docherty left to take the vacant Manchester United job. On 4 January 1973 Willie Ormond, then aged 46, was announced as Docherty's successor. It was a blow to St Johnstone but great news for Scotland. Although not instantly! On 14 February the Scottish FA celebrated its centenary with a match against England at Hampden Park, and a stunned crowd saw England romp home by an embarrassing 5–0 scoreline. It was hardly the bow that Ormond had dreamt of making. Yet Ormond turned things around. So much so that they were able to qualify for the 1974 World Cup Finals in Germany, returning home unbeaten. Ormond was rewarded with an OBE 12 months later. Ormond's love of Edinburgh was never far from the surface and in May 1977 he became Hearts boss. Sadly that did not work out the way he had hoped and in January 1980 he moved out of Tynecastle. Naturally enough his next port of call was Easter Road, where he worked with Eddie Turnbull briefly before taking over from Eddie in March 1980. Alas, poor health had begun to take its toll and his stay in the Hibs hot seat was short-lived. He slipped out of football to concentrate on running his public house in Musselburgh. Willie Ormond died in Edinburgh's Eastern General Hospital on 4 May 1984, aged just 59. He was mourned throughout the Scottish game, such was the high esteem with which this highly likeable man was held. To this day his record in the World Cup as Scotland manager remains unsurpassed and mention of his name in both Edinburgh and Perth brings nothing but praise.

HIBERNIAN: The Players and Managers 1946–2009

John O'Neil

OGILVIE, John

Left-back

Born: Motherwell, 28 October 1928.
Career: Thorniewood United, HIBERNIAN 1946, Leicester City 1955, Mansfield Town 1960.

■ In the 1951 Scottish Cup semi-final at Tynecastle against Motherwell John suffered a transverse fraction of his leg. There was some irony that he himself was a native of Motherwell and indeed spent much of his recuperation using Motherwell's swimming baths. He had broken into the side in the late-1940s and with his swift tackling and no-nonsense approach was a popular figure. Having said that the facts remain that he only played 35 League games for Hibs over a period of eight seasons. Hibernian granted him a free transfer in April 1955. This was his cue to try his luck elsewhere and in September 1955 he joined Leicester City and made almost 100 appearances for the Foxes.

O'NEIL, John

Midfield

Born: Bellshill, 6 July 1971.
Career: Fir Park BC, Dundee United 1988, St Johnstone 1994, HIBERNIAN 2000, Falkirk 2003, Gretna 2006, Cowdenbeath 2007.

■ John was a Scotland Under-18 Schoolboy international and a product of Fir Park Boys' Club before joining Dundee United. He flourished under Jim McLean's shrewd management, bagged five goals in a single Premier League Reserve game and progressed to the stage where he scored in the thrilling 1991 Scottish Cup Final. From United it was up the Tay to St Johnstone before Alex Mcleish took him to Hibernian. John was an industrious midfielder and he was able to ensure that the craft of the likes of Latapy and Sauzee had an engine to match. His first goal for Hibs came in the famous 6–2 thrashing of Hearts at Easter Road, and although never a regular marksman he was able to add the odd goal throughout his Hibs career. In April 2001 he earned a Scotland cap when he played against Poland and there was little doubt that he was one of the most talented and reliable midfielders of the day. It is fair to say there was some regret on the terraces at Easter Road when he headed to Falkirk. With League new boys Gretna he had a remarkable spell that saw him win two Championship badges and play in the 2006 Scottish Cup Final against Hearts. He joined Brian Welsh's Cowdenbeath in July 2007 which reunited him with a former Dundee United teammate.

O'NEILL, Michael

Centre-forward

Born: Portadown, 5 July 1969.
Career: Coleraine 1984, Newcastle United 1987, Dundee United 1989, HIBERNIAN 1993, Coventry City 1996, Aberdeen (loan) 1997, Reading (loan) 1998, St Johnstone 2000, Clydebank 2001, Wigan 2001, Portland Timbers 2001, Glentoran 2002, Ayr United 2004.

■ Michael Andrew Martin O'Neill spent three seasons with Hibernian and impressed as a speedy and thoughtful player, in the mould of an old-fashioned inside-forward. One of his key strengths was his eye for goal and his tally while at Easter Road was impressive. At his peak he commanded considerable transfer fees and when Dundee United bought him for £300,000 from Newcastle they broke their transfer fee record. Capped 34 times by Northern Ireland, Michael had a nomadic career which was sadly blighted by injury, particularly a major groin problem that necessitated five operations. If ever a spell at a single club proved a player's injury problems then it was Michael's at Coventry where he suffered a dislocated shoulder and no fewer than three hernias! However, to his Hibernian career. Recruited by Alex Miller in the summer of 1993 he joined the club at the same time as Kevin McAllister and Jim Leighton and they were all celebrating a League Cup Final outing within months of arriving. He made his debut in a 1–0 defeat at Tynecastle Park in August 1993 and scored his first goal in a 3–1 win over St Johnstone. His international career also had the full quota of highs and lows, including a brace in a sensational 5–3 win over Austria. He was short tempered at times and had the notoriety of being sent off in an Edinburgh derby. Michael made the step up into management with Brechin City in the summer of 2007 and given the number of distinguished managers he had played under there were high hopes that he would rejuvenate the little Angus club. He did well enough to be appointed Shamrock Rovers boss in late 2008.

ORMAN, Alen

Midfield/full-back

Born: Bosnia, 31 May 1978.
Career: Admira Wacker (Austria), Royal Antwerp (Belgium), HIBERNIAN 2001, FC Thun (Switzerland) 2005.

■ A Bosnian by birth, Alen and his family moved to Austria when civil war erupted in what was then Yugoslavia. He made football his career and earned a contract with Admira Wacker in Vienna. His displays there were sufficiently good to interest Belgian side Royal Antwerp. He joined Hibernian for £100,000 in the summer of 2001 and looked a pacy overlapping full-back. His stock on the terraces at Easter Road rose considerably when he scored a real 'screamer' at Ibrox Park in a 2–2 draw. He was extremely industrious and showed pace when going forward, so much so that he became the first Hibs player to be capped by Austria when he played against Norway in late-2002. A dramatic end to the year followed with Alen suffering an epileptic fit before a match against Rangers, but he quickly recovered and was none the worse for his experience. Never that frequent a 'pick' under Bobby Williamson he did better under Tony Mowbray and rediscovered his scoring touch in late-2004. By the time he left Hibs he had played 73 matches.

ORR, Neil

Defender/midfield

Born: Greenock, 13 May 1959.
Career: Gourock School, Morton 1975, West Ham United 1982, HIBERNIAN 1987, St Mirren 1993, Queen of the South 1995.

■ Neil's father Tommy had been a respected international with Scotland and a local hero with Morton, and Neil proved equally popular in Greenock. He played over 200 games for Morton (League Cup and Scottish Cup semi-finals included) before earning a big money move to West Ham in December 1981 (the fee was said to total £300,000). He spent just over five seasons in London before Hibs came calling with a £100,000 cheque. His debut came against Queen of the South at Easter Road and Neil scored in a 3–1 win. However, it was primarily as a strong defensive midfielder that he had been signed and his goals were an added bonus. The goals trickled in and he was one of Hibernian's 'forgotten' scorers against Morton on the day that goalkeeper Andy Goram scored with a downfield punt. Capped seven times by Scotland at Under-21 level, he was part of Hibs' League Cup-winning side in 1991.

Alen Orman

JIMMY O'ROURKE — HERO

Inside-forward

Born: Edinburgh, 18 September 1946.
Career: HIBERNIAN 1962, St Johnstone 1974, Motherwell 1976.

■ One of the most popular Hibernian players of the Eddie Turnbull management era, it is often overlooked that Jim O'Rourke was with Hibernian long before Eddie was appointed boss. Jim joined Hibernian in 1962 from schools football and stayed until 1974. His subsequent career took him to St Johnstone and then Motherwell before he returned to Easter Road as reserve team coach to Eddie Turnbull. Brought up as a Hibernian supporter he had watched the team from 1951 onwards. As he once confessed to me: 'Every game as a Hibernian player was a great occasion for me because for so long I had followed the club from the terraces'. His debut came on 9 December 1962 against Utrecht of Holland in the Fairs Cup. Only 16 at the time, manager Walter Galbraith shrewdly delayed telling Jim of his bow until the very afternoon of the match. O'Rourke played well and his career was underway, and it flourished when he found the route to goal. Quite simply, O'Rourke loved scoring goals and he had the good fortune to play in sides that provided him with plenty of opportunities. Playing up front with Alan Gordon was perhaps his zenith, but the partner he most enjoyed was Joe Baker who had been a particular boyhood hero. The absolute pinnacle of O'Rourke's spell at Easter Road was never in any doubt. In an emotional interview Jim once told me: 'For me the highlight of my time at Easter Road was the 1972 League Cup Final when we finally got our hands on the silverware we thoroughly deserved. It was such an important win for the players and for their families. Personally, coming from a Hibs family it provided a wonderful sense of achievement.' December 1972 and January 1973 were the halcyon days for Hibernian fans, when the team truly delivered the supporters to the football equivalent of 'the Promised Land'. On 9 December Hibs defeated Celtic 2–1 in the League Cup Final and then on the following Saturday not only was the Cup paraded around Easter Road but Hibs crushed Ayr United 8–1. With a goal in the Final, a hat-trick against Ayr and then a brace in the January 1973 massacre of Hearts at Tynecastle (when 7–0 was scant reward for the most one-sided derby in history) the part played by O'Rourke could never be overstated. Jim left for St Johnstone in 1974, where ex-Hibs coach John Lambie was on the staff, and with a wonderful sense of irony his first goal for the Saints came in a 1–0 win over Hibernian at Easter Road on 28 September 1974. He would later play with Motherwell but it is as a Hibernian player he is best remembered and his 210 League outings (with 81 goals) were marked by competitiveness and bravery.

P

PAATELAINEN, Mika-Matti

Centre-forward

Born: Helsinki, Finland, 3 February 1967.
Career: FC Haka, Dundee United 1987, Aberdeen 1992, Bolton Wanderers 1994, Wolverhampton Wanderers 1997, HIBERNIAN 1998, Strasbourg 2001, HIBERNIAN 2002, St Johnstone 2003, St Mirren 2004, Cowdenbeath 2005.

■ A Finnish international, 'Mixu' joined Hibernian in 1998 from Wolverhampton Wanderers and proved a most astute purchase. His goals not only helped Hibs escape from the First Division, but once back in the Premier League he showed enough experience and goal awareness to be a major player. Famously he scored three times against Hearts in a 6–2 win at Easter Road. Mixu came to Scotland with Dundee United and scored 33 goals for Jim McLean's side before moving to Aberdeen in a £400,000 deal. He rewarded the Dons by scoring 23 goals prior to taking his undoubted talents, not to mention imposing frame, to England where he starred with Bolton (15 goals) before joining Wolves. At just £75,000 he proved one of Alex Mcleish's finest acquisitions. Barrel-chested, and clever as well as powerful, he led the line with a mixture of never-say-die commitment and real craft. Aged 31 he had detractors initially who thought him a bit heavy, but Paatelainen was, to use a cricket analogy, almost like the fast bowler brought on to soften up the batsmen. A handful for any defender, he relished the physical side of the game and was astute enough to use his body well and to link with those around him. In the summer of 2001 he moved to Strasbourg in France but spent an unhappy season there in which he played only eight matches. He rejoined Hibernian shortly into the start of the 2002–03 campaign and scored his first goal in the awful 4–1 home defeat by Dunfermline. However, things picked up

following that defeat and he led the line with his usual mix of enthusiasm and know-how as the season wore on. When his playing days ended he was a player-coach at both St Mirren and St Johnstone before becoming player-manager of Cowdenbeath. He steered Cowdenbeath to the Third Division title in 2005–06 (winning the divisional Manager of the Year award) and this earned him the job of manager of TPS Turku back in his native Finland. It was therefore no surprise when he was selected to take over as Hibs boss when John Collins walked out on the club in late-2007. His experience as a Hibernian player was by this stage only a small part of a most impressive career and background. Mixu scored 18 goals in gaining 70 full Finland international caps and his father had captained Finland and won 50 caps. His two younger brothers Markus and Mikko also played professional football.

PARKE, John

Left-back

Born: Belfast, 6 August 1937.
Career: Cliftonville, Linfield 1955, HIBERNIAN 1963, Sunderland 1964, Mechelen (Belgium) 1968.

■ A talented full-back, John signed from Linfield in October 1963. Although he played in only 21 League games for Hibs it was clear that he was a very talented individual indeed, and with every performance he seemed to improve. It was always going to be a battle hanging on to such a solid talent and he was sold to Sunderland in November 1964. He settled well on Wearside and played in a century of games for Sunderland. John won 14 caps for Northern Ireland and ended his senior career playing in Belgium.

PATERSON, Craig

Centre-half

Born: South Queensferry, 2 October 1959.
Career: Bonnyrigg Rose, HIBERNIAN 1977, Rangers 1982, Motherwell 1987, Kilmarnock 1991, Hamilton Accies 1995, Glenafton Athletic, Forth Wanderers.

■ The son of John 'Jock' Paterson, Craig quickly proved himself to be an outstanding prospect at centre-half and while commanding in the air and solid on the ground he also displayed a neat use of the ball. Craig was signed in December 1977 and made his debut against Dundee in a friendly fixture at Dens Park in February 1978; although his League bow did not come until August 1979. Thereafter he edged his way increasingly into the first-team picture. Capped by Scotland at Under-21 level he was a rock at the heart of the Hibs defence by the early-1980s and was voted Hibernian Player of the Year in 1981. Sadly, he left for Rangers in July 1982 for a fee in the region of £225,000, he had played over 100 games for Hibs and would easily have tripled that total had he stayed at Easter Road. It was nevertheless money that cash-strapped Hibs could hardly refuse; and at the time it represented a record fee for the Glasgow club. He won a League Cup-winners' badge at Rangers, a Scottish Cup medal at Motherwell and then finished his top flight career at Kilmarnock. An astute observer of the game, he flirted with the notion of coaching. He squeezed in spells with Hamilton, Glenafton and Forth Wanderers before settling on a career in the media as a radio pundit. In his role as Radio Forth match summariser I would bump into Craig in many of the press rooms up and down Scotland and he always had a cheery word. His tales of his career were enormously entertaining. It was little surprise that he was lured to the bigger stage offered by the BBC such was his eloquence and clarity of thought.

PATERSON, John 'Jock'

Centre-half

Born: Colchester.
Career: Penicuik Athletic, HIBERNIAN 1944, Ayr United 1959.

■ Born in Colchester, England, 'Jock' worked as a representative for a brewery firm and was a versatile defender, capable of playing either centre-back or left-back. Signed from Penicuik Thistle in 1944 he was capped by the Scottish League against Wales in 1953 and it was probably only the strict rules concerning eligibility based on place of birth that denied him a full Scotland cap. Playing first-team football from 1948 through to 1960 there is little doubt that Jock was one of the great Hibernian servants. He was an ever present in both the 1951 and 1952 Championship-winning sides and in all played in a staggering 283 League games for Hibs. There was a degree of stability in the Hibs defence at this time and Paterson's fitness served him well. He did not venture into the opposition half too often hence the distinction he has that no outfield player played as many games in Hibs colours without scoring a single goal. Jock's debut came on 11 December 1948 in an away League match at Falkirk. Peter Aird, Hugh Howie and Simon Waldie had all tried the number-five jersey earlier in the season but the introduction of Paterson alongside Sammy Kean and Archie Buchanan suited Hibs well, and the introduction a couple of weeks later of Jock Ogilvie further strengthened what was already a strong rearguard. He spent a couple of seasons with Ayr in the early-1960s but it is a Hibee that he will always be remembered. The great newspaper man of the 1950s – Jack Harkness – once famously described Paterson as: 'The Rock of Gibraltar in a green-and-white jersey'. Jock's son Craig (*see above*) continued the family tradition by becoming Hibernian centre-half and captain in the 1970s.

PATERSON, Willie

Outside-right

Born: 30 April 1957.
Career: Burnley, HIBERNIAN 1975, Falkirk 1979, Kirkintilloch Roy Roy 1981.

■ Signed in 1975 as a teenager, Willie had been with Burnley for two seasons before becoming homesick. He made his debut at Motherwell late in the 1975–76 season, earning a penalty within minutes of coming on as a substitute. But over the following three seasons he was barely able to muster a place in the starting XI and in March 1979 he made a switch to Falkirk.

PATON, Eric

Midfield

Born: Glasgow, 1 August 1978.
Career: Hutcheson Vale BC, HIBERNIAN 1994, Stenhousemuir (loan) 1998, Partick Thistle 1999, Clydebank 2000, Queen of the South 2002.

■ Eric was a short and stocky youngster who could not quite impose himself on the Hibernian scene during Alex McLeish's years. There were four League outings in the successful First Division promotion campaign but it was clear he would not be able to force his way into a side containing the likes of Sauzee, Latapy and Zitelli. He later played for Partick Thistle and Morton having gone on loan to Stenhousemuir while at Hibs. He was unfortunate to find himself at Clydebank as that club headed for collapse but when he joined Queen of the South he had much more success. He played in over 200 games for the Doonhamers and was up against Hibernian in the Scottish Cup in 2007.

PEAT, Willie

Inside-forward

Career: HIBERNIAN 1944, St Johnstone 1947, Brechin City 1953.

■ A very versatile left-sided player, Willie scored three goals from 11 outings in the 1946–47 season. This was a good season in which to break into Hibs' team as the club finished a very close second in the League race. His debut had come on the final day of August 1946 away to Motherwell and although he scored Hibs lost 1–2. He was back in the team by November and scored in a victory at Queen of the South. When Jock Weir moved to Blackburn, Peat was tried as a centre-forward but without success, although he did score in the final game of the season (a 3–2 win over Falkirk). However, he hankered for more regular first-team football and elected to try his luck elsewhere. He moved to St Johnstone in 1947 and played over 100 games for the Perth outfit between 1947 and 1952.

PETERS, Allan

Right-back

Born: Edinburgh, 4 April 1969.
Career: Tynecastle BC, HIBERNIAN 1984, East Stirlingshire 1989.

■ A solitary game as a substitute during the 1986–87 season was all that Hibs were able to muster for this young defender. He took his leave of Hibs in March 1989 and enjoyed more regular football in a couple of seasons with Falkirk-based East Stirlingshire.

PINAU, Steven

Forward

Born: Le Mans, France 11 March 1988.
Career: Monaco, Genoa, HIBERNIAN (loan) 2008.

■ Signed on a one-year loan deal by Mixu Paatelainen, Steven made his debut in a 1–1 draw at Inverness in August 2008. A few days later he scored in the disastrous 3–4 home League Cup defeat to Morton at Easter Road. It was hardly the start the 20-year-old had dreamed of but Paatelainen was convinced of Pinau's pedigree: 'It's a good sign when a club like Genoa signs you on a five-year contract from another big club like Monaco'. Pinau had been capped by France at Under-19 level.

PLENDERLEITH, John

Centre-half

Born: Bellshill, 6 October 1937.
Career: Armadale Thistle, HIBERNIAN 1953, Manchester City 1960, Queen of the South 1963, Cape Town (South Africa).

■ A joiner by trade, Jackie (as he was known) was a Scottish Youth international. He made his Hibernian debut on 30 October 1954 at home to Kilmarnock and Hibs edged home by the odd goal in five. By the late-1950s he was a regular but not entirely settled at the club. In the winter of 1958 the *Daily Express* noted that:

'Arsenal, who are seeking the services of 19-year-old centre-half Jackie Plenderleith of Hibs, are advised to make a quick open-cheque bid or they will miss one of the greatest centre-halves since John Charles.' Arsenal did dither and in July 1960 Plenderleith moved to Manchester City and spent two seasons at Maine Road. John won one full Scotland cap as a City player (in a 5–2 win over Northern Ireland) and five Under-23 caps while a Hibee.

PLUMB, Angus

Centre-forward

Career: Armadale Thistle, HIBERNIAN 1948, Falkirk 1949, East Fife 1955.

■ This delightfully named forward joined Hibernian in 1948 from Armadale Thistle. Manager Hugh Shaw could be well pleased with his signing (who made his debut at Hearts on 1 January 1949), from his second match in 1949 Plumb scored in five consecutive League games; add three Scottish Cup ties and the record was eight straight games with Plumb on the score sheet. Sadly, competition was fierce at Easter Road and Angus was perhaps prematurely sold to Falkirk in December 1949. He had played seven League games and scored seven goals, and rarely can a player with such an exemplary record have been sold. His debut for Falkirk entered the stuff of folklore as Falkirk traveled to Raith Rovers and lost a 10-goal thriller 4–6! He did not forgive Hibs easily, as he scored against his former club at Brockville in March, and netted for the Bairns within 30 seconds in a thrilling 5–4 Hibs League Cup win (Hibs going on to reach the Final against Motherwell in that season). Nevertheless, Angus still delighted Hibs fans from time to time even while at Falkirk…most notably by scoring three for the Bairns in a 5–4 win over Hearts in March 1951. After Falkirk he played with East Fife where he returned a healthy goal haul that included 11 strikes in his first nine games. He wound his career down with a season at East Stirlingshire in the 1957–58 campaign. His statistics make for most impressive reading. He played 184 Scottish League games and scored 103 goals. In 41 League Cup ties he bagged 33 goals and 15 Scottish Cup ties brought seven goals. All in all he was a most accomplished finisher and from a Hibs perspective quite clearly 'one who got away'.

POWER, Lee

Forward

Born: Lewisham, 30 June 1972.
Career: Norwich City 1990, Charlton (loan) 1992, Sunderland (loan) 1993, Portsmouth (loan) 1993, Bradford City 1994, Millwall (loan) 1995, Peterborough United 1995, Dundee 1997, HIBERNIAN 1997, Ayr United 1998, Plymouth Argyle 1998, Halifax Town (loan) 1998, 1999.

■ It was in the later stages of his career that Lee joined Jim Duffy's struggling Hibernian, along with Paul Tosh, in a £200,000 deal. Power had been a journeyman player in England and had served a host of clubs without ever really scaling the heights. At 6ft tall he should have been able to lift Jim Duffy's side but failed to have the expected impact. In all Lee played only 11 League games in the colours of Hibernian but he did chip in with a couple of goals. Alas, when Hibs slipped into the First Division Lee was not part of Alex McLeish's long-term plans for the club. Power had to retire from the game at the age of 28 having suffered two broken legs but he made a surprise return at the age of 34…this time as chairman of English non-League side Cambridge United.

PRENDERVILLE, Barry

Full-back

Born: Dublin, 16 October 1976.
Career: Coventry City 1994, HIBERNIAN (loan) 1998, Ayr United 1999, St Patrick's Athletic 1999, Oldham Athletic 2000, Shelbourne 2001, Shamrock Rovers 2006.

■ Barry joined Hibs in September 1998 on loan from Coventry City and proved a most able full-back. With his strong heading ability and dynamic style he would have been an ideal asset for Hibs long-term but after his loan spell expired he was unable to come to a more permanent arrangement. Barry played 13 League games in Hibernian's promotion-winning season of 1998–99 and scored goals against both Morton and St Mirren. He came back to Scotland to play with Ayr United at one stage, then served St Patrick's Athletic and Oldham Athletic.

PRESTON, Tommy

Centre-forward

Career: Juniper Thistle, Edinburgh Thistle, Newtongrange Star, HIBERNIAN 1953, St Mirren 1964.

■ A very versatile player, Tommy could play any of the inside positions, and at one point he was a centre-forward replacement for Lawrie Reilly. Signed by Hugh Shaw, Tommy, who was 5ft 11½in, was given his first-team debut in 1954 against Celtic. He played three matches at the tail end of the 1953–54 season and by his own admission was greatly reliant upon the advice of Sammy Kean during his early days at Easter Road. At the end of that first season he toured Germany and Czechoslovakia with the club and stood in at centre-forward for the ill Lawrie Reilly. The goals came easily and at the start of the 1954–55 season he was a prolific marksman before Lawrie returned to first-team duties. Just how prolific he was is best gauged by the following statistics. He played in six League Cup sectional ties and scored eight goals (amazingly that was not good enough to ensure that Hibs qualified for the quarter-final stages!). He also scored Hibs' opening goal of the League campaign that term when they drew

1-1 at Rangers. Tommy figured in some magnificent Hibernian matches. High in that list would be the epic Fairs Cup clashes with Barcelona, Tommy himself reckoning that the 4-4 draw Hibs achieved in the Nou Camp was even better than the 3-2 victory at Easter Road in the return leg. No recollection of Tommy could possibly be complete without reference to his four goals in an amazing 11-1 away win at Airdrie which he followed up with goals in the 10-2 victory at Partick Thistle just weeks later. The latter two games came in the 1959-60 season which was a 'purple' period for Tommy as he bagged 12 goals in only 17 matches. A charming man to talk to, Tommy once told me that he was more famous in Edinburgh for his non-footballing activities. Sniffing a scent of scandal I asked him more, but the explanation was quite innocent. 'An interesting thing that happened to me in my career was doing a bit of modelling. It was for the Ideal Homes Exhibition at Waverley Station and was during the close season. I used to joke that I earned more doing this than I did playing football! It meant my face became well known in Edinburgh because the show was featured regularly in *The Scotsman*.' From Easter Road he moved to St Mirren but that did not last long (he played but a solitary game) and with 228 League appearances for Hibs (with 35 goals) it is understandable that he is forever associated with Hibernian.

PRINGLE, Alex

Wing-half
Born: 8 November 1948.
Career: Glasgow United, HIBERNIAN 1966, Dundee 1972, Clyde 1974.

■ Essentially a left-half, Alex made his first-team debut against St Johnstone in April 1969, and within a few years he was helping the club in Scottish Cup semi-final ties and jousting with the best in Scotland. After his spell with Hibs he was granted a free transfer in 1970 and was set to emigrate to South Africa when Hibs changed their mind. He did, however, manage to sample football abroad in two spells with North American clubs.

QUINN, Pat

Inside-left

Born: Glasgow, 26 April 1936.
Career: Bridgeton Waverley, Motherwell 1955, Blackpool 1962, HIBERNIAN 1963, East Fife 1969.

■ Prior to Mixu Paatelainen, Pat had the honour of being the last Hibernian player to score a hat-trick against Hearts. Signed in October 1963 from Blackpool, Pat was a clever, creative midfielder possessed of a very cultured left-foot. He had made his name in Motherwell's talented 'Ancell Babes' midfield, whom he joined in 1955 from Bridgeton Waverley. A contemporary of the likes of Ian St John and Andy Weir, he was skilled and exciting to watch. While at Fir Park he was capped four times by Scotland and six times by the Scottish League, making a rather unfortunate international debut in the infamous 9–3 debacle against England at Wembley in 1961. Pat joined Blackpool in 1962 but did not fit and a year later he joined Walter Galbraith's Hibernian side for £30,000. He settled quickly and had a goal at St Mirren just weeks later in a 1-1 draw. With his subtle promptings several players thrived around him and Neil Martin went on to finish with 20 goals in his 28 League games that season. The following season (1964–65) Pat grabbed eight goals for himself and was a part of the side that reached the Scottish Cup semi-final only to lose to Dunfermline at Tynecastle Park. After his Edinburgh playing days, with 131 League

outings, ended he moved to East Fife as player-assistant manager before taking up coaching roles with Partick Thistle, Hibs, Motherwell and Hamilton Academicals.

R

RAE, Robin

Goalkeeper

Born: Musselburgh, 18 January 1964.
Career: Musselburgh Windsor, HIBERNIAN 1981, Morton 1985, Hamilton Accies 1986, Ormiston Primrose, Bonnyrigg Rose.

■ Robin was an early prospect in the Scottish goalkeeping world, playing with the triumphant Scotland Under-18 side that won the European Youth Cup in the early-1980s. In his first season at Easter Road he made three outings but was very much second fiddle to firstly Jim McArthur, then Alan Rough, so he moved on fairly swiftly. In September 1985 he joined Morton and he made a handful of outings before winding down his career firstly with Hamilton Accies and then in the East of Scotland Leagues. Remarkably, when he dropped into junior football he played as a striker for both Ormiston Primrose and Bonnyrigg Rose.

RANKIN, John

Midfield

Born: Bellshill, 27 June 1973.
Career: Manchester United, Ross County 2003, Inverness CT, HIBERNIAN 2008.

■ John was a forceful midfielder who joined Mixu Paatelainen's side in the January transfer window of 2008. John had been a talented youngster and was on the books of Manchester United for a while before joining Ross County in Dingwall. He was a regular in the County side for several seasons until moving to Inverness CT. Hibs were among those monitoring his progress and when he fell from favour in Inverness Mixu Paatelainen wasted no time in making John a Hibee. He scored a famous winner against Celtic from near the halfway line in November 2008.

RAYNES, Steven

Midfield

Born: Edinburgh, 4 September 1971.
Career: Hutcheson Vale BC, HIBERNIAN 1989, Dundalk (Republic of Ireland), Livingston 1997, Forfar 1998, Brechin 1999, Cowdenbeath 2001.

■ Steven was on the fringes of first-team football at Hibs and played two matches in the 1992–93 season but was unable to eke out a regular starting place. He tried his luck in the Republic of Ireland and then enjoyed some stability with Livingston where he was almost ever present in the 1997–98 season. From West Lothian it was on to the likes of Forfar, Brechin and Cowdenbeath. Steven played over 100 games in the top three Scottish Leagues and scored three goals.

REFVIK, Isak

Inside-forward

Born: Bergen, Norway, 25 December 1956.
Career: Viking Stavanger, Tornado, HIBERNIAN 1978, Viking Stavanger 1979.

■ When Tom Hart brought Norwegians Isak Arne Refvik and Svein Mathisen to Easter Road in 1978 he could hardly have imagined the political issue that would erupt. Refvik had seven Norway Under-21 caps to his name and Mathisen the same number of full caps. It hardly seemed possible that their signing would provoke any problems, but gaining work permits proved to be a real issue. Both players made their Hibernian debut against Morton on 15 November. The match was a League Cup quarter-final and Hibs were trailing 1–0 from the first leg in Greenock. Ninety minutes later Hibs had won 2–0 and Refvik in scoring both goals had won over a quizzical Hibernian support. In his first eight matches with Hibs the little man from Bergen scored three times. But issues were surfacing and it soon became clear that Hibs would have a real fight on their hands to secure a work permit. Mathisen, as a full international, was not an issue. Both players eventually went back to Norway; Refvik to Viking Stavanger and Mathisen to IFK Start.

GORDON RAE — HERO

Central-defender

Born: Edinburgh, 3 May 1958.
Career: Whitehill Welfare, HIBERNIAN 1975, Partick Thistle 1990, Hamilton Accies 1992, Meadowbank Thistle 1992.

■ The considerable frame and enormous heart of Gordon Rae served Hibs for 13 seasons and whether he played as a centre-forward or a centre-half he proved extremely effective. He joined the club in 1975 from Whitehill Welfare and made his debut against Queen of the South in 1977, three days later he scored in a 2–0 win at Rangers and his Hibs career was up and running. Tall and strong, it was his determination that won Gordon a special place in the thoughts of Hibernian supporters. Over 13 seasons he grew to personify Hibs and the supporters loved his never-say-die commitment.

Those were the qualities that impressed Eddie Turnbull enough to sign Gordon and persuade the 17-year-old to give up an apprenticeship to concentrate on football. During his stint at Easter Road Rae won a First Division Championship medal, played in the Scottish Cup Final and sampled European nights. He was perhaps unlucky not to land silverware during his Hibs career. Beaten by a freakish goal against Aberdeen in a 1978 League Cup semi-final, Hibs then gamely battled through to the Scottish Cup Final only to lose the marathon match against Rangers in a second replay. Getting to Hampden gave Rae some of his finest moments in green. Among his many goals (there were 47 from 348 League games alone) was a very important strike in a tense quarter-final tie against Hearts at Easter Road in 1979. As if that were not contribution enough he bettered that feat by scoring against Aberdeen in the semi-final. He could not score in the Final, however, and the Cup was lost to Rangers; ironically a few days later Hibs beat Rangers in the League and Rae did score on that occasion. Several managers occupied the hot seat while Gordon was at Hibs, Eddie Turnbull giving way to Willie Ormond, Bertie Auld, Pat Stanton and Alex Miller. When Gordon left it was with a heavy heart to join Partick Thistle for £65,000 in March 1990. At Maryhill he won a promotion and made a favourable impression, and when he returned to Easter Road in 1992 on Scottish Cup business he was afforded a most generous welcome. Later he served in either playing or coaching capacities at Hamilton, Meadowbank, Gala Fairydean, East Fife, Edinburgh City, Coldstream, Newtongrange Star, Tranent and Linlithgow Rose. He returned to Hibernian behind the scenes to help in John Park's youth academy but by 2007 was assistant manager at Linlithgow Rose as the junior side entered the Scottish Cup with some style. Away from football he owned Clean Easy Laundry Services which specialized in cleaning football kits.

Alan Reid

REID, Alan

Midfield

Born: Paisley, 21 October 1980.
Career: Renfrew Victoria, HIBERNIAN 1998, East Fife (loan) 2001, Morton (loan) 2001, St Mirren 2005.

■ Alan was a talented little midfielder who played his first game against Airdrie in the promotion-winning season. He gradually began to impose himself over the next few seasons until he was being picked with more regularity by Bobby Williamson. Nevertheless, he still required an unbroken run of first-team outings to prove himself, and loan spells with East Fife and Morton suggested that his career lay beyond Easter Road.

REID, Chris

Goalkeeper

Born: Edinburgh, 4 November 1971.
Career: Hutchison Vale BC, HIBERNIAN 1988, Hamilton 1998, Stirling Albion 2000.

■ Standing at 6ft 1in tall, Christopher Thomas Reid was a talented young goalkeeper who won six Scotland Under-21 caps while with Hibernian but ultimately failed to establish himself in the first team despite spending 10 seasons in the east end of Edinburgh. He was, perhaps not surprisingly, unable to oust either Andy Goram or John Burridge from the number-one jersey. He joined Hamilton Accies in the 1998 close-season but suffered a bad injury on his debut there. Nevertheless, he did recover and then became the number-one goalkeeper at Stirling Albion early in the new century.

REID, David

Centre-forward

Born: 23 February 1959.
Career: Leeds United, HIBERNIAN 1979, Shettleston Juniors.

■ Young David played a couple of games in Hibernian's disastrous 1979–80 relegation campaign. His debut came against Morton in a 1–1 draw at Cappielow Park and in truth he never had much chance of establishing himself in what was by any standards a very fragile Hibernian team.

REILLY, Jack

Goalkeeper

Born: 27 August 1945.
Career: Inverurie Locos, HIBERNIAN 1966, Washington Whips, Melbourne Juventus 1970, St George Saints, Melbourne Hakoah, Fitzroy Alexander, South Melbourne Hellas.

■ In the mid-1960s John (to give him his Sunday name) played two games for Hibernian in the League. He was an Australian and eventually was capped 15 times by his country but joined Hibs from Highland League side Inverurie Locos. After playing with Hibs he served Washington and Melbourne clubs. He had 35 international caps for Australia and was with their squad in the 1974 World Cup Finals in Germany.

RENWICK, Michael

Full-back

Born: Edinburgh, 29 February 1976.
Career: Hutcheson Vale BC, HIBERNIAN 1992, Ayr United 2000, Morton (loan) 2001, Cowdenbeath 2002, East Fife 2004, Stenhousemuir 2005.

■ Signed from Hutcheson Vale BC in August 1992, Michael was a red-headed full-back. He was quick and alert going forward. Making his bow in the Premier League he was part of the side that won the First Division Championship in 1999. However, he was less able to hold down a first-team berth when Hibs rejoined the elite and moved down to the First Division with Ayr United. His debut for Hibs had been against Kilmarnock on the final day of the 1994–95 season. He linked up with former Hibees Keith Wright and Mickey Weir at Cowdenbeath in 2002 and this gave him a taste for management that he took to its conclusion at Berwick Rangers in the Scottish Third Division in 2007.

RICE, Brian

Midfield

Born: Bellshill, 11 October 1963.
Career: Whitburn, HIBERNIAN 1980, Nottingham Forest 1985, Falkirk 1991, Dunfermline 1995, Clyde 1997.

LAWRIE REILLY — HERO

Centre-forward
Born: Edinburgh, 28 October 1928.
Career: Edinburgh Thistle, HIBERNIAN 1945.

■ Was this the greatest Hibee of them all? Most would say 'yes'. A legendary centre-forward, and a gentleman to boot, he was a Hibs hero from 1947 until his retirement in 1958. How ironic that just as he faded from the scene a lad called Joe Baker came into the team. Had Hibs been able to field both then surely no defence would have been safe.

Born in October 1928 and raised in Edinburgh, Reilly cut his teeth at juvenile level with North Merchiston and Edinburgh Thistle before joining Hibs. He was a Hibs supporter and had travelled up and down the country watching the club before he joined them. Lawrie made a scoring debut against Kilmarnock in September 1946 when only 17 but was very much a fringe player as the title went to Easter Road in 1948. When Willie Ormond was ruled out with a broken leg the chance came for Lawrie to step into the side and he made such a good job being an outside-left that Scotland capped him in that position in 1949. Prior to playing at full international level Lawrie had made a huge impression in the Scottish League side. In September 1948 he played against the League of Ireland as an outside-left and scored twice in a 5-1 victory. Matches of this nature had a high profile in the post-war calendar and a crowd of 57,600 turned up at Ibrox for a game that was acknowledged as being against weak opposition.

In October 1949 Scotland travelled to Dalymount Park in Dublin for a return fixture and squeezed home 1-0; this time with Gordon Smith at outside-right and Lawrie at outside-left. Eventually the more experienced Willie Ormond returned to the first team at Easter Road and it was decided to try young Reilly at centre-forward. It was a fortuitous switch and the rest, as they say, is history. If Reilly shone as an outside-left then he positively dazzled as a centre-forward. Reilly performed like no other Scottish footballer as a centre-forward. In season 1950-51 he scored 23 League goals and in the next six seasons he netted 27, 30, 15, 15, 23 and 16 League goals. He thus became the first Hibs player to top the Easter Road scoring charts in seven consecutive seasons. His haul of 30 League goals in season 1952-53 was a club record at that time. That 1952 season saw Reilly binge on goals. In October 1952 the Scottish Football League selectors named Smith, Johnstone, Reilly and Ormond in their side to face Ireland. Scotland won 5-1 and Reilly bagged four goals in as emphatic a display of forward play as anyone could wish to see. Physically Reilly was not the archetypal

centre-forward. He was not particularly big, standing at just 5ft 7in, nor was he particularly heavy. Yet Lawrie was a prolific marksman and scored a good number of goals from headers. His explanation was that the other members of the 'Famous Five' delivered such telling crosses and passes. Were he less modest he would have mentioned his own sense of timing and sheer bravery. Reilly could be a terror of individual teams. For example, he scored seven against Motherwell in the two matches in season 1952–53. But like Ormond and Smith his run of success was halted by illness. He was diagnosed as having pleurisy in 1954 and missed the World Cup Finals; although on reflection he may consider himself lucky to have avoided that dreadful trip. Despite that 1954 setback he was an international hero and the darling of the famous Hampden slopes. Scotland's top scorer for three consecutive seasons, he also played five times for Scotland at Wembley and hit five goals…an astonishing feat. It was one of his international goals, a dramatic late counter in 1953, that effectively sealed the

'Last Minute Reilly' tag. However, the 'last minute' title did detract from the real facts which were that Reilly was a handful throughout the 90 minutes! How else could he have bagged no fewer than 22 goals in his 38 internationals? The final word on Lawrie Reilly's remarkable career must be that he was forced to retire when aged only 29. His 253 League games had yielded a sensational 187 goals.

Left to right: Lawrie Reilly, Gordon Smith, Mrs Ormond, Bobby Johnstone and Eddie Turnbull at Easter Road in 1999.

■ Brian was a red-haired midfielder who broke into the Hibs side with such devastating effect in the 1980s that he was soon on his way to the English First Division with Nottingham Forest. Born in Bellshill, this left-sided midfielder graduated from Youth to Under-21 level for Scotland very quickly, indeed at the former level he helped Scotland champion Europe. He made his Hibs debut in an East of Scotland Shield Final against Hearts at Tynecastle and stunned all and sundry with a magnificent goal from 25 yards. That piece of skill was in every sense a taster of what was to come from a very composed and creative midfielder. Sold to Nottingham Forest for £175,000 in August 1985, Brian was on duty for Nottingham Forest on the day of the Hillsborough disaster. On 15 April 1989 Liverpool met Forest at Sheffield Wednesday's ground and in the worst stadium disaster to befall British football 96 people died in a crush. He came back to Scotland to play with Falkirk and then coached at both Clyde and Dunfermline before becoming assistant manager of Morton. The end of his career proved most interesting as he joined Ian McCall when Airdrie battled back from receivership in March 2001 prior to ultimately folding.

RILEY, Paul

Midfield

Born: Edinburgh, 7 August 1975.
Career: Hutcheson Vale BC, HIBERNIAN 1992, Brechin City 1999, Montrose 2003, Bonnyrigg Rose.

■ A solitary outing as a substitute in the 1996–97 season was the extent of Paul's Hibernian career. He had far more success in terms of appearances with Brechin City whom he joined in March 1999. In 2002 Paul helped the little Angus outfit win the Scottish Third Division title. His senior career ended at nearby Montrose.

RIORDAN, Derek

Centre-forward

Born: Edinburgh, 16 January 1983.

Career: Hutcheson Vale BC, HIBERNIAN 2001, Celtic 2006, HIBERNIAN 2008.

■ A remarkably talented young striker, Riordan belied a very slight build. Full of skill and possessed of a goalscorer's uncanny knack of being in the right place at the right time he made a real impact at Hibernian. He was a noted marksman from dead-ball situations and for one so apparently frail possessed a powerful shot. By the time he joined Celtic he had scored 64 goals in 146 appearances. Riordan was brought up in the Muirhouse district of Edinburgh and attended Craigroyston High where his football skills first came to note. A Hibernian supporter, he had once been ejected from the ground when snapping a seat after Paul Wright scored a crucial Cup goal for Kilmarnock in Hibs' relegation season. From Hutcheson Vale he made progress through the Hibernian youth teams until his first-team debut came along in December 2001. It was Franck Sauzee who gave Riordan his debut and in picking a match away to Hearts Sauzee gave a clear statement about Riordan's strength of character. Alas, not long afterward Hibs slumped and Sauzee was shown the door, in came Bobby Williamson and Riordan's career slowly but surely picked up. A loan spell at Cowdenbeath's Central Park was arguably the making of him. He scored four goals in five matches for the Fife club, including a hat-trick in a remarkable 7–5 win at Brechin. Recalled to Easter Road he was soon among the goals and netted a delightful curling effort against Hearts. Sadly, the CIS Cup Final against Livingston went badly for Hibs after the glory of a dramatic semi-final win against Rangers. But little could dent Riordan's confidence and he became a mainstay of Hibs' youthful attack. In the 2004–05 season he was Hibs' top scorer with 20 goals and Young Player of the Month in September, November and December 2004 as well as January 2005. Riordan had well and truly arrived, and he was Hibernian's top scorer three seasons in succession racking up 60 goals. Little wonder he was Scotland's Young Player of the Year by the summer of 2005 and earned his first international cap against Austria. He moved to Celtic in June 2006, with Hibs receiving little by way of compensation, but it was a move that did not really work out. In 18 months he played only a handful of matches and despite scoring regularly did not seem to fit with Gordon Strachan's plans at Celtic. Off-field problems were also causing concern and by 2008 he was training with Celtic's youth team and apparently banned from every nightclub in Edinburgh. Then, in a dramatic switch, he returned to Hibs on a three-year deal in the 2008 summer transfer window.

RIPPA, Juha

Midfield

Born: 12 September 1968.
Career: FC Jazz, HIBERNIAN 1996, FC Jazz.

■ On 16 November 1996 Juha made his only outing as a Hibernian player. Remarkably, it was in the Edinburgh derby at Tynecastle. Hibernian squeezed out a 0–0 draw but it was to little avail for Rippa who never donned the green-and-white jersey again. A 28-year-old midfielder, he was a Finnish trialist and had won a Championship medal with FC Jazz. Still, his single outing was one more than the superbly named Casper Gribskjolo who arrived on trial at the same time.

ROBERTSON, Malcolm

Outside-left

Born: Edinburgh, 7 July 1950.
Career: Penicuik, Raith Rovers 1971, Ayr United 1975, Hearts 1977, Toronto Blizzard 1981, Dundee United 1982, HIBERNIAN 1982, Hamrun Spartans (Malta).

■ Malcolm played in over 300 senior matches in Scotland, but his Hibernian career came at the tail end of that lengthy career and he was only signed on a three-month trial period by Pat Stanton. Robertson enjoyed his best football while with Ayr United and Hearts. He had been a frequent adversary of Hibernian's while with the latter. He was small, dark haired and fairly aggressive in style.

ROCASTLE, Craig

Midfield

Born: London, 17 August 1981.
Career: Kingstonian, Chelsea 2003, Barnsley (loan) 2004, Lincoln City (loan) 2004, HIBERNIAN (loan) 2004, Sheffield Wednesday 2005, Yeovil Town (loan) 2006, Oldham Athletic 2006, Port Vale 2007, Gillingham (loan) 2008.

■ Craig joined Hibernian on loan during the 2004–05 season and impressed with his subtle midfield skills. Lithe and 6ft 1in tall he cut an imposing figure on the field but lacked the determination to really establish himself. Having been with Chelsea (albeit without making the breakthrough) expectations were high but Hibs were unable to offer him a permanent contract and he returned to England in 2005. He then enjoyed a rather nomadic career. Craig was related to the former Arsenal legend David Rocastle.

RODIER, Derek

Centre-forward

Born: Edinburgh, 4 February 1959.

Career: Edinburgh University, HIBERNIAN 1979, Dunfermline Athletic 1982, Berwick Rangers 1983.

■ Stocky and energetic, Derek was with Hibs in the late-1970s and early-1980s. A centre-forward, he combined his footballing duties with full-time study at Edinburgh University. This was perhaps a mistake because in four seasons at Easter Road he failed to score a single League goal. His debut came against Kilmarnock in September 1979 and he had three outings in that first season. Arguably Derek lacked the experience that Hibs required in this particularly testing era. He was clearly drifting out of the picture when Hibernian were relegated in 1980. He later played with Dunfermline and Berwick in the First and then Second Divisions.

ROLLO, Jim

Goalkeeper

Born: Helmsdale, 16 November 1937.
Career: Jeanfield Swifts, HIBERNIAN 1955, Poole Town 1957, Oldham 1960, Southport 1963, Bradford City 1964, Scarborough.

■ With Tommy Younger established as Hibernian number one, openings for the exquisitely named James Shepherd Rollo were limited. Recruited from junior football in Perth he was able to manage only two outings before heading off for Dorset having received a free transfer in April 1957.

ROSS, Louis

Left-back

Born: Dublin, 19 September 1920.
Career: HIBERNIAN 1946, Queen of the South 1947, Walsall 1948.

■ On 24 August 1946 Hibernian entertained Hamilton on League business. On the same day Hibs left-back Davie Shaw was playing in a Scotland versus England game at Maine Road in aid of the Bolton Disaster Fund. This gave Louis Ross his only opening as a Hibs player. He filled in for Shaw and helped the club to a 3–2 win. He had 10 outings while with Queen of the South in the 1947–48 season but by the time the next campaign got underway he was in the English midlands with Walsall.

ROUGH, Alan

Goalkeeper

Born: Glasgow, 25 November 1951.
Career: Sighthill Amateurs, Partick Thistle 1969, HIBERNIAN 1982, Celtic 1988, Hamilton Accies 1988, Ayr United 1999.

■ Alan Rough was arguably the most formidable Scottish goalkeeper of his era. He represented Scotland 53 times, twice in World Cup Finals, and was a huge success at Partick Thistle, Hibs and Celtic. A great talker, he later earned a solid reputation as an after-dinner speaker and radio presenter. They say that a good goalkeeper is the foundation of a successful side and Rough proved that adage. With Partick Thistle he was an incredible asset, foiling club after club with a series of inspired displays. In 1971 he was in goal when Thistle stunned Jock Stein's Celtic by winning the League Cup Final 4–1 at Hampden (being 4–0 to the good at half-time). With his bright yellow top, blond permed hair and model girlfriend he was one of Scotland's best-known players in the late-1970s. Certainly Bertie Auld as manager of Partick Thistle benefited hugely from Rough's consistency and the Glasgow club punched well above their weight with Rough in their ranks. He gave many impressive performances against Hibs, never more so than in October 1976 when he saved time and time again as Hibs were held 0–0 by Partick Thistle. Such was his reputation that it was something of a surprise when Rough was lured to Hibs in 1979 having made over 400 outings for Thistle. When Bertie Auld was sacked as Hibs boss in September 1982 few would have predicted that former Easter Road favourite Pat Stanton would come back to the club, even fewer that one of Stanton's first signings would be Alan Rough. Jim McArthur had been the Hibernian custodian until Rough arrived in late November 1982 and the new man made his debut at home to Celtic. Hibs lost that game but soon rallied with Rough inspirational in goal. His laid back attitude and relaxed manner were often commented on, never more so than in the famous Graeme Souness/George McCluskey match at Easter Road. As mayhem ensued in the middle of the pitch with almost every player involved, Rough was seen to lean against his goalpost and watch the events unfold. As one wag noted: 'See Roughie; come's off his line for nothing!' Rough enjoyed a 10-year career from 1976 as Scotland's number-one 'keeper and from that period stems much of his popularity. He wound his career down with spells at various small clubs but it is as a Partick, Hibs, Celtic and Scotland goalkeeper he is best remembered.

ROUGIER, Tony

Winger

Born: Trinidad, 17 July 1971.

Career: Trinidad Trinity Pros, Raith Rovers 1995, HIBERNIAN 1997, Port Vale 1999, Reading 2000, Brighton 2003, Brentford 2003, Bristol City 2004.

■ Signed from Raith Rovers during the summer of 1997 (in a deal that took Keith Wright and Ian Cameron to Kirkcaldy), it was easy to see why Hibernian wanted Rougier. He had power, pace and an eye for goal. Few wingers were capable of inflicting such delicious and haphazard mayhem on a defence than Rougier in full flight. He had helped Rovers win the First Division Championship in his first season in Scotland and was something of a cult hero in Kirkcaldy. It was unfortunate that he joined Hibs at a time when Jim Duffy's side was badly struggling. He featured little under Alex McLeish and moved on to Port Vale in 1999. The deal that had brought Rougier to Hibs was reckoned to be worth in the region of £250,000; when he moved to Port Vale the transfer fee was £175,000. Unfortunately for Hibs, Rougier's value soared at Port Vale and Reading spent £325,000 to take him south.

RUDGE, Humphrey

Defender

Born: Netherlands, 15 August 1977.
Career: Roda JC 1996, Sparta Rotterdam 2001, Apollon Limassol (Cyprus), HIBERNIAN 2005, Roda JC 2006.

■ A Dutch defender, it was Tony Mowbray who brought Humphrey to Easter Road, largely in response to Gary Caldwell being out injured. Rudge was vastly experienced and as well as being a 28-year-old veteran of the Dutch leagues had played in many UEFA Cup ties. He made his Hibernian debut as a trialist in a pre-season friendly at home to Hartlepool. However, he played only half a dozen games in Edinburgh before returning to the Netherlands.

S

SAR-TEMSOURY, Hakim

Forward

Born: France, 6 March 1981.
Career: Nantes 1994, HIBERNIAN 2000, ESA Brive 2001.

■ Alex McLeish loved to dabble in the transfer market trying to unearth undiscovered gems. Young Hakim was one of his bolder steps. He had a substitute outing at Celtic in 2000 but failed to 'set the heather on fire' and was allowed to return to France shortly thereafter.

SCHAEDLER, Erich

Full-back

Born: Biggar, 6 August 1949.
Career: Melbourne Thistle, Stirling Albion 1969, HIBERNIAN 1969, Dundee 1977, HIBERNIAN 1981, Dumbarton 1985.

■ In two spells with Hibernian Erich became a cult hero. A solid left-back, he had tremendous fitness and was guaranteed to give 100% week after week. The son of a former German prisoner of war, he excelled with Hibs and as well as winning a League Cup-winners' badge he also earned a full Scotland cap. Erich had started out with Peebles Rovers and Melbourne Thistle before joining Stirling Albion and it was from the latter that he joined Hibs in 1969 for £7,000. The link here was Willie MacFarlane who was to be Schaedler's manager at both Albion and Hibs. By the time the 'Turnbull's Tornadoes' era was off and running in the early-1970s, the full-back pairing of Brownlie and Schaedler was a solid foundation in the Hibs team. Throughout the early-1970s he was a regular and rarely missed a match. He was not a frequent goalscorer but he scored from 40 yards when his free-kick eluded the entire Celtic defence for a memorable counter. He moved to Dundee in November 1977 but was back with Hibernian in 1981. He finally moved to Dumbarton on a free transfer in 1985. Sadly Erich took his own life when he was still a young man.

SCHMUGGE, Thorsten

Midfield

Born: Garmisch-Partenkirchen, Germany, 13 October 1971.
Career: Bochum 1990, Wuppertaler SV 1992, Saarbrücken 1994, Bochum 1996, HIBERNIAN 1996, TUS Hordel 1996, Wattensheid 1997, Bayer Uerdingen 2000, Wilmhelmshaven 2002, Kickers Emden 2003, VfB Speldorf 2005.

■ A German midfielder, Thorsten made just one outing as a Hibee and that was as a substitute. The match in question was against Aberdeen at Pittodrie in September 1996 and Hibs recorded a fine 2–0 win thanks to goals by the deadly-duo of Keith Wright and Darren Jackson. A second-half substitute, the right-sided midfielder, who had played with Bochum and won German Under-21 caps, was promptly booked and thus made his one and only Hibernian appearance that little bit more memorable.

SCOTT, Alex

Right-winger

Born: Falkirk, 22 November 1936.
Career: Bo'ness United, Rangers 1953, Everton 1963, HIBERNIAN 1967, Falkirk 1970.

■ A dazzling winger, as a youngster Alex made his name at Rangers, where he won four League Championship medals and 11 Scotland caps before moving to Everton in 1963. While at Goodison he added to his honours collection; winning both League and FA Cup medals and continuing his Scotland career. In September 1967 he became a high-profile Hibs signing and although clearly in the veteran stages of his career he still showed occasional flashes of brilliance. He ended his senior career in his home town of Falkirk. His brother Jim also played with Hibs and the two were at one point business partners in Falkirk. It is worth reiterating that the Scott brothers did not play together at Easter Road or Brockville despite the proximity of their careers there.

SCOTT, Ally

Forward

Born: Glasgow, 26 August 1950.
Career: Glasgow University, Queen's Park 1972, Rangers 1973, HIBERNIAN 1976, Morton 1978, Partick Thistle 1980, Queen of the South 1981.

■ A tall, strong running forward, Ally seemed to fall between two stools and it was never quite clear if he was a winger who enjoyed playing inside, or a central forward who drifted wide. He had started his career at Glasgow University and Queen's Park and then spent a couple of years at Rangers before joining Hibernian in the deal that saw Ian Munro head to Ibrox and Graham Fyfe accompany Ally on the journey to Edinburgh. Ally made his debut for Hibs in the 1976 season and in the League Cup campaign he was among the goals and his clever, often speedy play served Hibs well for a short period. After his stint at Easter Road Ally moved to Morton and in truth he was a much better player in Benny Rooney's doggedly determined side than he had been in the green and white of Hibs.

SCOTT, Jim

Outside-right

Born: Falkirk, 21 August 1940.
Career: Bo'ness United, HIBERNIAN 1958, Newcastle United 1967, Crystal Palace 1970, Falkirk 1972, Hamilton Accies 1973.

■ Brother of the aforementioned Alex, Jim joined Hibs in October 1958 from Bo'ness United. An apprentice painter, he had burst onto the Scottish Junior football scene in the

FRANCK SAUZEE — HERO

Midfield/sweeper

Born: Aubenas, France, 28 October 1965.
Career: Sochaux 1983, Marseille 1988, Monaco 1990, Marseille 1991, Atalanta Bergamo (Italy) 1993, Strasbourg 1994, Montpellier 1996, HIBERNIAN 1999.

■ Raised in the small French fishing village of La Begude near Marseille, Franck was just 17 when he joined Sochaux. He spent five very happy years there and was part of the French Under-21 side that won the European Championship. After 'cutting his teeth' he then moved to Marseille, and although he had a single year with Monaco he returned to Marseille to help in the winning of the French 'double' of League and Cup. The highlight, however, was winning the European Cup in 1993 against AC Milan in Munich. From Marseille, which suffered financially in the wake of owner Bernard Tapie's fall from grace, he joined Atalanta Bergamo in Italy; signed by the renowned Marcello Lippi. Things did not work out in Italy for Franck and he was sold to Strasbourg and stayed there until he was 31 when he moved to Montpellier. He was 33 years old and in dispute with his club when Alex McLeish persuaded him to join Hibernian.

For such a player to come to Easter Road would at one time have been unimaginable. It was not just as a star in French domestic football that Franck had shone. He had 39 caps for France and had scored nine goals. He was, in short, a top class international footballer. Signed in 1999, while Hibs were in the First Division, Franck revelled in the freedom and responsibility he was given at Easter Road. He helped the club win that First Division in 1999 and in 2001 led the club out for the Scottish Cup Final against Celtic. Sauzee had all the skills of a top international star. He could play in midfield or as sweeper and with equal impact. His long range passing was awesome as was his ability from the dead-ball situation and some of his goals for Hibernian were quite thunderous efforts. He genuinely loved his spell as a Hibs player and put much of that down to the mature way in which Alex McLeish handled him. At one point Alex devised an 'open planned' training schedule for the French master. Franck told me at the time: 'I prefer playing and live for the Saturdays. I am lucky at Hibs, however, as Alex McLeish and Andy Watson are so intelligent and recognise that I am 34 years old. They know that I need a different training schedule from the young players of say 18 and 19. Sometimes when I am tired I have a rest and this is better for the team and for me obviously. I am grateful that the club recognise my situation.' Alas, when then Hibs boss Alex McLeish moved to Rangers, Franck was placed in the managerial chair. This was the natural move and it would have been ludicrous for Hibernian not to have offered the post to such a huge international star on their own pay-roll. However, things did not work out and after a sad few months (69 days in total), in which the nadir was losing to First Division Ayr United in a Hampden League Cup semi-final, Franck was sacked as boss. Franck was a very personable man. As programme editor I had the task of speaking to him on Monday nights as we put together his programme notes. Initially these chats were a pleasure and his genuine passion for Hibernian shone through. However, as ignominious results heaped the pressure on he became withdrawn, beleaguered and almost perplexed. For a man used to success as a player and clearly possessed of a wonderful mentality he found such a run particularly hard to bear. The image of him before the press under the main stand at Hampden Park after the League Cup semi-final exit to Ayr Untied was painful to behold. Best to remember him as the truly legendary player he was. The song that rolled down from the terraces 'There's only one Sauzee' is the more fitting memory of a wonderful talent.

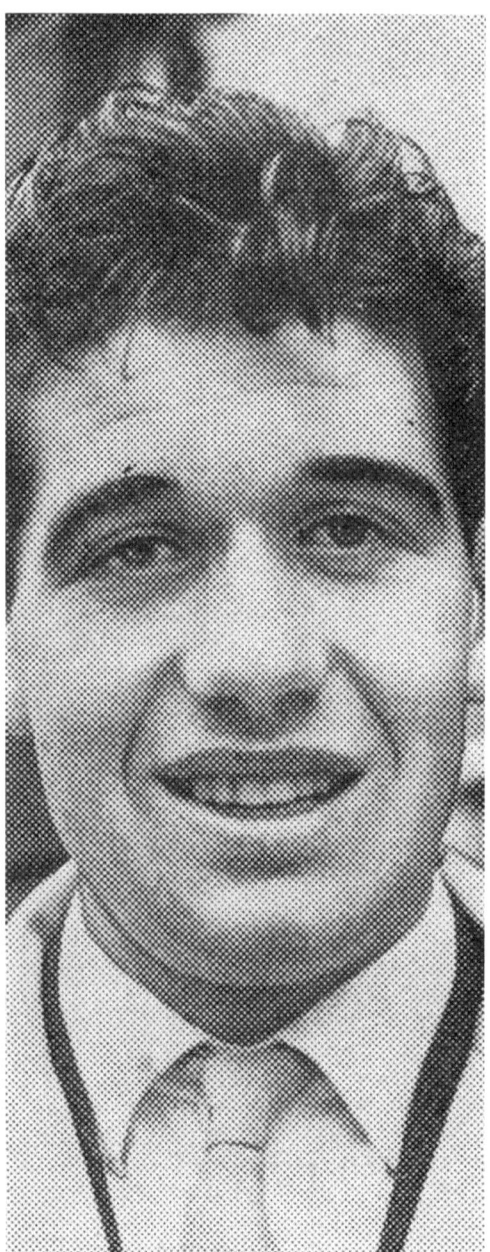

sense of balance. A clever player, he could 'thread the needle' with his accurate passing and was equally capable of beating a man and homing in on goal. Jim made his Hibernian bow at the tail end of the 1958–59 season, making his debut against Dundee and playing in the final three matches of the campaign. He was famously one of two Hibs players to score four goals in an 11–2 rout of Alloa in September 1965, the other being Neil Martin. In August 1967 he was sold to Newcastle United and while on Tyneside he won a Fairs Cup medal when United annexed the 1969 trophy. Later in his career he played for Crystal Palace and Falkirk before retiring and buying a bar in his home town. His Hibernian career had brought 48 League goals in 194 matches and two Scotland caps.

SHANNON, Rab

Full-back

Born: Bellshill, 20 April 1966.
Career: St Columba's BC, Dundee 1982, Dunfermline 1991, Motherwell 1993, Dundee United 1995, HIBERNIAN 1996, East Fife 1999.

■ Rab started his career with Dundee and stayed there for over 250 matches in nine years before moving to Dunfermline. It cost Dunfermline two players (Ian McCall and

summer of 1958 and when Bo'ness exited the prestigious Scottish Junior Cup a number of clubs sought to add him to their squad. Given that Hibs had recently recruited the likes of Jim Harrower and Jackie Wren from Bo'ness the odds were good but manager Hugh Shaw had to fend off Newcastle United, Chelsea and Rangers to lure the 17-year-old to Easter Road. Born in Falkirk he stood at 5ft 8in and although not the strongest he had an uncanny

Eddie Gallacher) plus £125,000 to move him. A former Under-21 cap, he was versatile enough to play either in midfield or as a full-back. He then played for Motherwell for several years before making a 1996 move to Hibernian. It said much for the faith the Hibernian board had in caretaker boss Jocky Scott that they allowed him to spend £100,000 on Rab's signature. He survived the Jim Duffy era but Rab featured only once under Alex McLeish (at Clydebank), and that during an injury crisis. Shannon's career came to an end with a stint as player-manager of East Fife.

SHAW, Davie

Full-back

Born: Annathill, 5 May 1917.
Career: Grange Rovers, HIBERNIAN 1939, Aberdeen 1950.

■ A full-back who could play either right or left-back, he built a wonderful partnership with Jock Govan and both players won a Championship medal in 1948 after losing in the Scottish Cup Final to Aberdeen one year earlier. Indeed, Davie captained Hibs to the 1947–48 Championship. Shaw was a big influence on the Hibernian side, there were times when he seemed to make his area of the field impenetrable and his judgement and nerve were sound when faced with quality opponents. Eventually eclipsed by younger colleagues, he left Easter Road in 1950 to join Aberdeen and played for the Dons until 1953. Unfortunately he lost Scottish Cup Finals with both Hibs and Aberdeen. Upon hanging up his boots he joined the coaching staff and he worked in various capacities at Pittodrie until 1967. Twice Shaw featured for Scotland in sides with two Hibernian full-backs. The first occasion was in April 1948 when he paired with Jock Govan against England and then in October he lined up alongside Hugh Howie for a rare Hibs double. As if that were not a good enough story then consider the fact that he had taken over from his brother (Jock) at full-back, a rare international feat indeed! His older brother was the legendary Jock 'Tiger' Shaw of Rangers. Davie died in October 1976 when

aged only 60 and had spent his final few years working in a paper mill near Aberdeen. Born in Annathill, Davie had worked as a miner before joining Hibs in January 1939.

SHEVLANE, Chris

Full-back

Born: Edinburgh, 6 May 1942.
Career: Edina Hearts, Loanhead Mayflower, Hearts 1959, Celtic 1967, HIBERNIAN 1968, Morton 1971.

■ Signed by Bob Shankly in the summer of 1968, red-headed Chris was a full-back who had captained Scotland at Under-23 level but had been surprisingly released by Celtic. His aggressive, all-energy style was well known to Hibs by dint of a lengthy career with great city rivals Hearts. He went on to make 65 outings as a Hibee between 1968 and 1971 and was the club's Player of the Year in 1970. During that period Chris picked up a League Cup runners'-up badge which complimented an earlier medal gained with Hearts. His capture was

something of a coup in Edinburgh as he had started his career at Tynecastle (making his debut in a shock 7–3 loss at St Mirren) and played for seven years with Hearts before moving to Celtic after apparently retiring through injury. Perhaps observers could have predicted that injury would not beat Chris. He was used to overcoming adversity. In his debut for Hearts reserves he found himself up against Rangers and a certain Willie Henderson, the outcome was an 11–3 defeat and many a full-back would have packed things up at that stage. Not Chris, and he was soon a mainstay of the Gorgie defence and made such a solid job of his Hearts career that he was made club captain and was a fine ambassador for the side. He did not succumb to injury when a floating bone in his knee was diagnosed but instead went to Celtic where not surprisingly he struggled to break into what was the 'Lisbon Lions' side. Thus the record books show that he made only a couple of outings as a Celt, but they do not show that he gained considerable knowledge at the feet of Jock Stein. Ultimately he had proved his ability to come back from injury and he subsequently joined Hibs. In 1971 Hibs freed him and he moved to Morton where he stayed until 1973. When his playing days were over he worked at Thins the Bookshop in Edinburgh and dabbled in the second-hand book market, but nowadays he runs a pub in the east end of Glasgow.

SHIELDS, Jay

Midfield

Born: Edinburgh, 6 January 1985.
Career: HIBERNIAN, Berwick Rangers (loan), Dundee (loan), Greenock Morton 2007, Cowdenbeath 2008.

■ A combative midfielder who was equally at home playing full-back, he found first-team opportunities thin on the ground in Edinburgh. He did play in six League games early in the 2004–05 campaign but as Hibs stuttered and spluttered these were hardly opportunities to convince the management of his long-term future. Loan spells in Berwick and Dundee gave him the confidence to make a move to Morton but he soon switched to Fife and Brian Welsh's Cowdenbeath.

SHIELS, DEAN

Midfield

Born: Magherfelt, 1 February 1985.
Career: Arsenal, HIBERNIAN 2004, Doncaster 2009.

■ Dean was a feisty left-sided midfielder who joined Hibernian from Arsenal's youth ranks in July 2004. He made an almost immediate impact and had five SPL goals in his very first season. A childhood accident had left him blind in one eye and while at Hibs he had the eye removed. This did not impinge on his long-term progress and when returned from surgery he quickly re-established himself. He had a hat-trick against Inverness in 2008 and returned to the Northern Ireland squad later that same year. Sent off against Hearts when scoring a penalty and 'barging' the Hearts goalkeeper in the aftermath, he was noted for his passion.

SIMPSON, Ronnie

Goalkeeper

Born: Glasgow, 11 October 1930.
Career: Queen's Park 1946, Third Lanark 1950, Newcastle United 1951, HIBERNIAN 1960, Celtic 1964.

■ One of the most remarkable stories in post-war senior football belongs to Ronnie. Here was a man who made his senior debut as a 14-year-old and his Scotland debut as a 36-year-old. Born in Glasgow, he joined Queen's Park as a schoolboy and made his League debut for them against Hibernian in August 1946, but he had already kept goal for the Spiders in a first-team game as a 14-year-old. He stayed at Hampden for five years before making the short journey over the hill to Third Lanark and then on to Newcastle United. He won two FA Cup-winners' medals with Newcastle and was 29 years old when Hugh Shaw signed him for Hibernian in October 1960. Agile and a good shot stopper, he was very popular at Easter Road but did not get on with Jock Stein and left for Celtic. Imagine his horror then when Stein duly arrived as Celtic boss a few months later! However, there was an extremely happy ending to this story. Stein and Simpson became reconciled and shared in the remarkable 'Lisbon Lions' triumph as Celtic won the European Cup (and indeed everything they entered) in 1967. Ronnie's father, Billy, had been a centre-half with Rangers so quite clearly his football life was interesting to say the least!

SIMPSON, William 'Billy'

Centre-half

Born: 11 July 1945.
Career: Edina Hearts, HIBERNIAN 1963, Falkirk 1970, Albion Rovers 1971, Alloa 1972, Cowdenbeath 1975.

■ Billy managed a clutch of games in the mid-1960s. However, after little over 40 appearances in seven seasons he moved to Falkirk and from there on to Albion Rovers, Alloa and Cowdenbeath. He was a good B Division player

and was a regular goalscorer for Alloa, scoring eight of his 10 senior goals while with the Wasps.

SKINNER, Justin

Midfield

Born: London, 30 January 1969.
Career: Bristol Rovers, HIBERNIAN 1998, Dunfermline 1999, Brechin 2002, Weston-Super-Mare, Windsor & Eton.

■ A tall, forceful midfielder, Justin was signed by Alex McLeish at the tail end of the 1997–98 season as Hibs struggled in vain to stay in the Premier League. The following season he played his part in helping the club gain promotion, but his aggressive style was never fully appreciated or admired by the Easter Road faithful. He was sent off along with ex-Hibee Gareth Evans in a 3–1 win at Airdrie in the autumn of 1999 as Hibs battled towards promotion, and he tended to enjoy a 'stop-start' career in green. He left Hibernian to join Dunfermline Athletic and served them for two years before joining Brechin City in August 2002. Prior to playing with Hibs he had served Bristol Rovers, Bournemouth, Wycombe and Wimbledon.

SLAVIN, Tommy

Inside-forward

Career: Lesmahagow Juniors, HIBERNIAN 1957, Berwick Rangers 1960.

■ Tommy was an inside-left who joined Hibs in 1957 from Lesmahagow Juniors. Unfortunately he was plagued by injury at Easter Road, crashing his car near Breich and then undergoing a cartilage operation. He played two matches in the 1957–58 season before moving to Berwick in May 1960.

SMART, Allan

Centre-forward

Born: Perth, 8 July 1974.
Career: Inverness CT, Preston North End 1994, Carlisle United (loan) 1995, Northampton (loan) 1995, Carlisle United 1996, Watford 1998, HIBERNIAN (loan) 2001, Stoke City (loan) 2001, Oldham Athletic 2001, Dundee United 2002, Crewe Alexandria 2003, MK Dons 2005, Bury 2006, Portadown 2006.

■ Allan was a slightly nomadic striker who turned up at Hibs briefly but failed to spark and was not signed permanently. Tall and strong, he was a pretty direct striker and seldom had difficulty finding an employer. His best days were arguably spent with Watford where he was a Wembley goalscorer in a 1999 Play-off Final. Allan's was a lengthy if ultimately unspectacular career.

SMITH, Gary

Defender

Born: Glasgow, 25 March 1971.
Career: Duntocher BC, Falkirk 1989, Aberdeen 1991, Rennes 1996, Aberdeen 1998, HIBERNIAN 2000.

■ When Alex McLeish offered Gary a short-term contract in July 2000 few could have imagined what an impact the former Scotland Under-21 international would make. 'Mr. Consistency' would have been a fair title for Gary as he showed considerable experience in his defensive duties. Tall, slim and a very quietly confident player he listed Falkirk, Aberdeen (twice) and Rennes among his former clubs. He scored his first Hibs goal in the Scottish Cup replay win over Stranraer and played in the 2001 Scottish Cup Final against Celtic. With over 500 senior appearances Gary was as dependable as he was consistent. For all Gary was a clean player he was sent off a few times while with Hibernian and by some strange twist most of those were when facing Rangers.

SMITH, Robert 'Bobby'

Inside-forward

Born: Dalkeith, 21 December 1953.
Career: Musselburgh Windsor, HIBERNIAN 1971, Leicester City 1983, HIBERNIAN (loan) 1985, Dunfermline 1987, Partick 1989, Berwick Rangers 1990.

■ Robert Nisbet Smith was to have two spells with the club and was extremely influential in his first spell. A very versatile player, he was equally at home in midfield or at full-back and his mop of curly black hair allied to his bubbly enthusiasm for the game made him a distinctive figure on the field. He made his initial debut against Arbroath in November 1972 and was an industrious midfielder who could play full-back with some style. Bobby was also capable of banging in the odd goal and thus began a 12-year stint at Easter Road that saw him move from fringe player to automatic selection. Jock Wallace had tried to sign Smith for Rangers during his Easter Road career and when Wallace moved to Leicester he tried again. This was a politically more palatable move for the Hibs directors who were wary of selling a talented player to a rival club…Leicester posed no threat to Hibs so Smith was off to England. When Bobby made his Leicester debut he did so alongside another debutant…Gary Lineker. Bobby came back during Pat Stanton's reign in the early-1980s as a loan signing.

SMITH, Tom

Full-back

Born: Glasgow, 12 October 1973.
Career: Partick Thistle 1991, Portadown 1996, Ayr United 1996, Clydebank 1998, HIBERNIAN 1999.

Gary Smith

GORDON SMITH — HERO

Outside-right
Born: Edinburgh, 25 May 1924.
Career: Dundee North End, HIBERNIAN 1941, Hearts 1959, Dundee 1961.

■ Arguably the silkiest-ever Scottish footballer, there was an undeniable majesty about Smith. Gordon joined Hibs in April 1941 and stayed until 1959. He won three League titles at Easter Road, then amazingly won Championship badges with both Hearts and Dundee. An outside-right, Smith was as elegant and athletic a player as has ever graced the Scottish football scene. He was born in Edinburgh in May 1924 and was a Scottish Schoolboy international before joining Hibs. He went on to win a host of Scotland caps and 10 League caps. His Hibernian career brought 310 League games and 122 goals. With Hibs he lost in both League and Scottish Cup Finals, but with Hearts he won the League Cup. He retired from football in 1964 having played his last senior game in Scotland against Aberdeen on New Years Day. An astute businessman, he promptly opened a pub called, rather fittingly, 'The Right Winger'. One of the great gentlemen of Scottish football, his name inevitably crops up whenever the more mature Scottish football writers speak of the truly magnificent players. Signed in April 1941, Smith had caught the eye with Dundee North End and scored a hat-trick for a Scottish Junior select against a Hibs-Hearts XI before his 17th birthday. Snatched from under Hearts' noses, the gifted youngster responded with a hat-trick for Hibs in a 5–3 wartime victory over Hearts on his debut. Thus began one of the greatest Hibs careers of them all. With his ability to run at players with pace and carry the ball beyond them, he was feared even as a youngster. He then benefited from playing in Hibs' wartime team which frequently included experienced guests from south of the

border such as the legendary Matt Busby. When football returned to normality after the war he was already evolving into an international-class player. The icing on the cake was his ability to despatch chances with a powerful shot, a knack that made him one of the highest scoring wingers in the history of the Scottish game. Smith was not only an effective player but also pleasing on the eye. He displayed great close control and supreme grace to baffle his opponents and was always a delight to watch with many observers reckoning him to be the most charismatic player in Scotland. His goalscoring became legendary, he rattled in 170 competitive goals for Hibs, and there were 17 hat-tricks or better. When he topped the Hibs scoring charts in 1950 he capped a sequence that had seen him finish as Hibs' top scorer in seven out of eight seasons. Not bad going for a wide player. He scored five in an 8–0 win over Third Lanark in 1947 and by the early-1950s was popularly appointed club captain. In 1951 he was widely acclaimed as 'Scotland's Player of the Year'. Two years on and Smith had reached the 100-goal mark for Hibs and clocked up his 500th appearance. A testimonial was richly deserved and a 7–3 win over Manchester United was the outcome in one of the most memorable games ever to take place in the capital city. Sadly he broke a leg in December 1953 and was lost to the game for several months. Injury it seemed was the only thing that could apply the brakes to a remarkable career. Yet he bounced back and even in his mid-30s Smith was revered throughout Scotland and a popular choice as national captain in 1955. Surprisingly, Gordon was given a free-transfer by Hibs in 1959 and he went on to win League Championship badges with both Hearts and Dundee…a truly remarkable feat. Never before, or since, has a player won Championship medals with three different clubs – none of them being based in Glasgow. Immensely popular, he was welcomed back to Easter Road in the 1961–62 season as a visiting player and scored directly from a corner as Dundee won 3–1. If evidence of Smith's remarkable fitness and longevity were needed then it surely came in the bald facts that he turned professional in 1941 and did not retire until 1964…a 23-year career! Sadly Gordon passed away in 2004.

■ A bad injury ended 27-year-old Tom's career just as he was making himself a feature in the Hibs side at left-back. Doctors advised him that he had a degenerative knee injury and that to continue playing football would be to run the risk of permanent disability. He had played 33 League games in his short Hibernian career. Signed by Alex McLeish from Clydebank, Tom had been a Second Division Player of the Year and his career had started well with Partick Thistle. Much of his Thistle football was played in the Premier League before he moved to Ayr United where he won a Second Division Championship medal. It was then over to the Bankies where he played only 22 matches before Hibs came calling in January 1999. Alas, his career was to be cut short by an injury sustained against Aberdeen.

SNEDDON, Alan

Full-back

Born: Ballieston, 12 March 1958.
Career: Larkhall Thistle, Celtic 1977, HIBERNIAN 1981, Motherwell 1992, East Fife 1993.

■ Not many players break the 300 appearance mark at Easter Road; Alan was one of that small, select band. Signed from Celtic in 1981 for a bargain £40,000, Alan won both Premier and First Division Championship medals in his first season with Hibernian due to his split of games between Celtic Park and Easter Road. He was signed by Bertie Auld, and few could deny that Auld knew a good defender when he saw one. Sneddon, who was 22 when he joined Hibs, quickly justified the faith placed in him although he did concede a penalty in his debut at Raith! However, Hibernian were heading for promotion that season and Alan played his part alongside such veterans as Jackie McNamara and Ally MacLeod. There was a change of manager when Pat Stanton replaced Bertie Auld but Alan continued to play with his usual mix of determination and verve. This was also the case when Pat was succeeded by his former teammate John Blackley. It was during this reign that Hibs knocked Celtic out of both the League and Scottish Cups. Such triumphs were not enough to keep John Blackley as Hibs boss when League form slumped and Alex Miller entered the manager's office. Soon Hibs were back in Europe for the first time in a decade. In all, Alan made over 300 League outings for Hibs and his reward came in 1991 when he enjoyed a testimonial match against Aston Villa. Never a great goalscorer, he scored his first in Arthur Duncan's testimonial match, but in a League Cup tie in 1989 against Alloa Alan scored twice in a 2–0 win! A junior with Larkhall Thistle, Alan started his senior career in 1977 with Celtic and was signed by the great Jock Stein. He won a Scottish Cup-winners' badge in 1980 and had the enviable task of taking over at Parkhead from the truly legendary Danny McGrain. His career after Hibernian took him to Motherwell in July 1992, before bringing the curtain down on his senior career with a spell at East Fife.

SOUNESS, Jimmy

Outside-right

Born: Edinburgh.
Career: Edinburgh Thistle, HIBERNIAN 1949, Falkirk (loan) 1950, Hearts 1953.

■ What a debut Jimmy had! Pitched into the first team against Clyde at Shawfield in April 1951, he promptly scored twice as Hibs won not just the match but the League title itself.

PAT STANTON — HERO

Half-back
Born: Niddrie, 13 September 1944.
Career: HIBERNIAN 1963, Celtic 1976.

■ Pat was one of the 'all time greatest Hibees' who guided the club to League Cup and Drybrough Cup triumphs during the Eddie Turnbull era. He played for Hibernian between 1963 and 1976 and was quite simply a most accomplished performer. In amassing 399 League appearances he proved his value to the team over an extended period. Signed provisionally in 1961, he had a wonderful link with the club's past being a direct descendent of the first-ever Hibernian captain – Michael Whelahan. Pat was farmed out to Bonnyrigg Rose before being called-up by Walter Galbraith. He made his debut against Motherwell in 1963 and scored in a 4–3 defeat. His career never looked back and there were to be many highs in a Hibs jersey. As a midfield general, capable of assisting both attack and defence, he scored and captained the club to the 2–1 League Cup Final win over Celtic in 1972 and was also part of the side that mauled Hearts 7–0 on New Years Day 1973. The League Cup Final was a seminal moment for the Turnbull era and Pat played a huge role. 'The achievement stands out,' he noted, 'because I don't think Hibs had won a Cup in Glasgow for around 70 years. I scored a goal and it was a great feeling. I actually thought we won that Final far more convincingly than the 2–1 scoreline suggested.' Yet he was quite clear about what he considered one of the best Hibs performances. It came in the European Cup-Winners' Cup in a second-leg match. Hibs had lost 2–1 to Sporting Lisbon in Portugal but played sufficiently well to pave the way for an incredible 6–1 home triumph. But Europe gave Pat his bitterest disappointment too when Leeds United ousted Hibs on penalties after two goalless draws. The shoot-out ended up 5–4 for Leeds with Pat missing the first spot kick and as a result retiring from penalty taking there and then. The final sighting of Stanton in a Hibernian top came in August 1976 and a few days later he left Hibs to join Celtic. That transfer marked the end of a year-long pursuit by Celtic supremo Jock Stein, a long-term admirer. Turnbull had begun to question the value of Stanton to his team, suggesting his performances were notably sub-standard, but it appears the great manager was beginning to chop and change too readily at Easter Road. Proof that Stanton was still a top player was swift in coming. He collected a League Championship medal and a Scottish Cup badge at Celtic and in 1978 he returned to Easter Road for a testimonial match which was attended by over 20,000 appreciative fans. When his playing career was over he moved into coaching as assistant boss at Aberdeen (to the famous Alex Ferguson) and success there earned him a move to Cowdenbeath as manager. From Central Park (after a mere 17 games) it was on to Dunfermline. He managed Hibernian in the early-1980s when the club nurtured promising youngsters such as Collins, Weir and Hunter, but in a period of transition Pat was unable to arrest a gradual decline. Reflecting on that spell in charge later he would say: 'Actually I did enjoy it although it was perhaps the wrong time to be in charge of the club. I was aware that it was a chance that might never come along again and I was desperate to take it when it emerged. The one aspect I certainly did appreciate was seeing a crop of good youngsters breaking through.' He would return to Easter Road to host hospitality tables and his support for the club did not waver despite occasional fall-outs.

This 5ft 10in winger also enjoyed a four-goal salvo against Manchester City in a prestige friendly. He went on loan to Falkirk in January 1950 and joined Hearts in a permanent deal in January 1953. He was something of a sporting all-rounder enjoying both cricket and rugby in Edinburgh's thriving post-war sporting environment. When his football days were over, and he retired early, Jimmy made a considerable mark in the insurance industry.

SOWUNMI, Thomas

Forward

Born: Lagos, Nigeria, 25 July 1978.
Career: Vasas Budapest, Dunaferr, Ajaccio, Ferencváros 2003, FC Slovacko, HIBERNIAN 2007, Vasas Budapest 2007.

■ Thomas came to Hibernian in February 2007 and made his debut as a substitute at Dundee United in a 0–0 draw. He was in for the next five matches (scoring in the Scottish Cup quarter-final win at Queen of the South) but failed to impress and was released by John Collins in September 2007 to pursue a career in Hungary.

SPALDING, Derek

Centre-half

Born: 20 December 1954.
Career: Butterburn YC, HIBERNIAN 1971, Chicago Sting 1978.

■ Derek was a young centre-half who was a product of Hibernian's own youth system and who was given his debut in an East of Scotland Shield match against Berwick Rangers in 1972. Dangerous at set pieces, he grabbed a couple of goals in Hibs' Cup run of 1976 that saw replays aplenty. Derek travelled to America to play with Chicago Sting after his Hibernian career ended, which could probably have been hinted at from 1975 when he married a girl from Chicago.

SPROULE, Ivan

Winger

Born: Omagh, 18 February 1981.
Career: Institute, HIBERNIAN 2005, Bristol City 2007.

■ Possessed of electric pace, Ivan Sproule burst onto the Scottish football scene with a wonderful hat-trick against Rangers at Ibrox in 2005. When he followed up with a goal at the same venue as Hibs knocked Rangers out of the Scottish Cup his reputation was made. As if the above were not enough he then contrived to make his Northern Ireland full international debut in the very match in which they defeated England 1–0 in Belfast. Shocks, it seemed, were part and parcel of Sproule's early career development. He had joined Hibs under Tony Mowbray for £5,000 from Institute (a part-time Northern Irish side) in January 2005. Debut day came away to Inverness and his first goal was in a surprise 3–1 win at Celtic. His impact was therefore pretty swift, so much so that Dnipro of Ukraine allegedly made a £1 million bid for his services, having faced him in a UEFA Cup tie. Sproule was eventually lured away from Hibernian in June 2007 when newly promoted Bristol City convinced him to swap Edinburgh for the West Country in a £350,000 deal. He had the perfect frame and build for a winger being 5ft 9in and a very speedy 10st 8lb.

STEIN, Colin

Centre-forward

Born: Linlithgow, 10 May 1947.
Career: Armadale Thistle, HIBERNIAN 1965, Rangers 1968, Coventry City 1972, Rangers 1975, Kilmarnock 1977.

■ Centre-forward Stein joined Hibernian in 1965 from Armadale Thistle. Bustling, direct and a sharp finisher, he scored 40 League goals for Hibs in just 69 starts and was every bit the 'darling' of the Easter Road terraces. However, all of that changed in the early days of November 1968. Stein by then was 21, had been capped at Under-23 and League level by Scotland and as well as some 30 goals in the previous season was sitting with nine strikes in what was, in truth, a rather poor Hibs side. Clubs hovered on the fringes coveting the young striker and Everton were first to make a move offering £90,000 for his services. However, Stein proved most capable of negotiating his own transfer and turned down the Goodison club, confirming that: 'I stated my terms and they are certainly not in the fortune class. No matter where I go, the terms have to be my terms.' And indeed that is what transpired. Hibs contacted Rangers and negotiations got underway. On 1 November Stein left training while Hibs and Rangers directors met at 11.00am. By midday Easter Road chairman Harrower emerged to say that a deal had been done…by which time Stein was on the train home to Linlithgow. A Rangers car met him and whisked him back to Edinburgh to tie up the deal. *The Dundee Courier* of the day noted the impact this transfer would have on Hibs: 'Stein in a Rangers jersey would always be a reminder to Hibs fans that he was once at Easter Road – and he would be a constant danger too, to any ambitions of the Edinburgh club, even this season with both Gers and Hibs in the Fairs Cup competition'. And so it proved. A couple of weeks later Stein lined up against Hibs at Ibrox Park in a League fixture. He ran riot and scored three in a 6–1 rout. The love affair between Hibs supporters and Colin Stein was definitely over. He would come back to Easter Road in 1975, during his second spell at Rangers, and score the goal that won the League title for the Ibrox men.

STEVENS, Tommy

Full-back/inside-forward

Career: Dunbar United, HIBERNIAN 1973, Hamilton Academical 1974, Berwick Rangers 1974, East Fife 1976, Forfar Athletic.

■ Late in season 1972–73 Tommy made his debut in a match at Easter Road against Motherwell. Alas, it was his only League game for the club. He played that single game as a right-back when Hibernian had lost John Brownlie to a broken leg. From Edinburgh it was off to various clubs in the lower Leagues but there was a chance to represent Scotland in the 'semi-professional' grade. Ultimately Tommy managed Cowdenbeath.

STEVENSON, Eric

Inside-forward

Born: Bonnyrigg, 25 December 1942.
Career: HIBERNIAN 1960, Ayr United 1971.

■ An outside-left, rather slightly built at 5ft 8in, Eric forged a link with Neil Martin which gave Hibs supporters one of their finest pairings to admire. Stevenson's crosses allied to Martin's heading prowess was a potent combination indeed. Eric was raised in Bonnyrigg and despite being a Hibs fan he all but joined Hearts only for the deal to falter at the 11th hour. Hearts were to regret this in one particular derby when both he and Jim O'Rourke scored twice in the first 10 minutes of a 4–0 win at Tynecastle. As John Campbell noted in the Hibernian match programme: 'Eric Stevenson could barely watch teammate Joe Davis taking penalties. As Davis set himself to take the penalty, Stevenson had a habit of walking to the half-way line, near the dug out, before turning his back on play while crouching down and placing his forearms on his knees, waiting for the crowd reaction to see if we'd scored and with Joe Davis an ace from the spot he was rarely disappointed'. He was capped once by the Scottish Football League, in a match against their Northern Ireland counterparts at Ibrox which Scotland won 5–2 with Stevenson lining up alongside fellow Hibees Pat Stanton and Peter Cormack. Also playing that night (and scoring twice) was Joe

Harper, then of Aberdeen but later to star with Hibs. Eric clocked up 256 League outings as a Hibee and netted 53 goals before he left Hibs to join Ayr United in 1971, ironically just as his early mentor Eddie Turnbull was returning to the club.

STEVENSON, James

Wing-half

Born: Bellshill, 4 August 1946.
Career: HIBERNIAN 1963, Southend United 1967.

■ James was a Scotland Schoolboy international. He was signed by Hibernian in August 1963 but managed only 13 League outings for the Hibees before falling out of the picture. He moved to Southend in July 1967 and played 33 League games for them.

STEVENSON, Lewis

Full-back

Born: Kirkcaldy, 5 January 1988.
Career: Hibernian Youths, HIBERNIAN 2005.

■ Although only 5ft 7in Lewis was a natural footballer who convinced manager John Collins 'within minutes of seeing him play' that he was a genuine talent. A Man of the Match performance in the 5–1 League Cup Final victory over Kilmarnock cemented his reputation and Scotland Under-21 honours followed. By 2008 he was less of an automatic pick at Hibs and was having to re-establish his credentials.

STEVENSON, Morris

Inside-forward

Born: Tranent, 16 April 1943.
Career: Musselburgh Windsor, Motherwell 1960, HIBERNIAN 1962, Morton 1963, Luton Town 1968, Dundee United 1970, Berwick Rangers 1972.

■ Morris was released by Hibs in June 1963 and enjoyed the last laugh against the club, being part of the Greenock side that surprisingly won the League Cup semi-finals of 1963. Essentially an inside-forward, he had skill and pace but lacked consistency. He fared much better in Greenock where he was a regular for six seasons before going to England in November 1968

STEWART, George

Centre-half

Born: Edinburgh, 29 August 1947.
Career: Tynecastle Boys Club, Dundee 1964, HIBERNIAN 1976, Cowdenbeath 1981.

■ Edinburgh born, George started his career with Tynecastle Boys Club then joined Dundee in 1964. His commanding displays won a band of admirers and he was a regular in a very good Dundee side that could boast talents such as Jocky Scott and John Duncan. Stewart, a vocal Hibs supporter, was eventually lured to Easter Road in 1976. His move to Hibs coincided with Dundee's slip from the Premier League. A move to Edinburgh was ideal as he lived in the city and had a dry-cleaning business in Gorgie. He came to Hibs for £40,000 as a 28-year-old

and made his debut against Bohemians of Dublin in a pre-season friendly. George made over 100 League outings for Hibs and formed a wonderful partnership in defence with firstly John Blackley and then Gordon Rae.

STEWART, Michael

Midfield

Born: Edinburgh, 26 February 1981.
Career: Manchester United, Nottingham Forest (loan) 2003, Hearts 2004, HIBERNIAN 2005, Hearts 2007.

■ Michael was hugely controversial in some quarters because of the switches he made between the green and maroon halves of Edinburgh. Stewart clocked up over 50 outings as a Hibee before deciding he was fundamentally unhappy with coach John Collins's approach to the game. Labelled a 'trouble-maker', he was invited to leave and promptly returned to Hearts to set up camp at Tynecastle Park. His career had begun promisingly at Manchester United but like many youngsters he was unable to make the break through; although that did not stop him establishing a Scotland Under-21 career that would yield 29 awards at that level. He moved to Hearts and then made the first of his cross-Edinburgh switches. Clever, creative and combative, he was occasionally on the wrong side of referees both at Hibs and Hearts.

STIRLING, Robertson

Centre-forward

Career: Queen's Park 1946, Dumbarton (loan) 1947, HIBERNIAN 1947, Third Lanark 1948, Dundee 1948.

■ When you play two matches in your first season and score two goals you are entitled to think you have found your niche. Alas, this was not the case for Robert (as he was better known) who fleetingly occupied a spot in Hibs' first team in the 1946–47 season. His goals came in the last two games of the campaign away to Third Lanark (unusually in a game played at Hampden Park) and Falkirk. Given that Hibernian lost the title by a mere two points he was unlucky not to celebrate a Championship success. Stirling played just one game for Queen's Park before moving to Dumbarton and creating quite a stir with nine goals in only eight games. He was likewise prolific at Third Lanark where he bagged five goals in only six outings in the 1948–49 season. Indeed, his haul of 17 goals in 23 League matches is quite outstanding, what is not so clear is why he was able to muster less than two dozen matches at senior level.

SZAMOTULSKI, Grzegorz

Goalkeeper

Born: Poland, 13 May 1976.
Career: Lechia Gdansk 1991, Legia Warsaw 1995, PAOK 2000, Slask Wroclaw 2001, Amica Wronki 2001, Admira Wacker 2004, Sturm Graz 2005, Dundee United 2007, Preston North End 2008, FC Ashod (Israel) 2008, free agent, HIBERNIAN 2009.

■ Signed as a 32-year-old in the January transfer window by Mixu Paatelainen, Grzegorz brought great experience to his role. He had sampled the Scottish game before joining Hibs; early in the 2007–08 season he earned a short-term contract with Craig Levein's Dundee United, making 18 League appearances. But the bulk of his experience was gained in Polish football where he graduated from youth football within the shipyard city of Gdansk before moving to Legia Warsaw. He made over 100 appearances for the capital city club before embarking on a series of moves, a couple of which were in Austria. After a successful spell at Tannadice, Grzegorz attracted interest from several clubs and he opted to move south to Preston North End in February 2008, but neither there nor with FC Ashdod in Israel was Grzegorz able to make an impact. When he joined Hibs he was actually enjoying the status of being a free agent.

T

TEMPERLEY, Willie
Forward

Born: 4 October 1958.
Career: Bo'ness United, Celtic 1977, HIBERNIAN 1978, Bo'ness United (loan) 1979, Alloa 1979, Meadowbank 1980, Linlithgow Rose 1980, Dunipace 1982, Bo'ness United 1983.

■ Willie came to Hibs in 1978 from Celtic having been an 'S' form signing at Parkhead who was loaned out to Bo'ness for experience. His career at Celtic never got off the ground and he therefore must have been a happy man indeed when he scored the Hibs goal that beat Celtic at Parkhead in September 1978. It was Hibs' first win their in nine years so Temperley really did make the most of his return. However, in the bigger picture Temperley failed to sparkle and he left Hibs at the end of the season having made only eight outings.

THICOT, Steven
Utility

Born: Montreuil-sous-Bois, France, 14 February 1987.
Career: Clairefontaine 2002, Nantes 2003, Sedan 2006, Nantes 2007, HIBERNIAN 2008.

■ Steven joined Hibs in July 2008 and made an impressive competitive debut against Kilmarnock at Rugby Park a few weeks later. Sadly, his debut was cut short when he was injured after only half-an-hour and had to be replaced. The problem was a thigh strain and he thus missed the first few crucial weeks of the campaign.

THOMSON, Darren
Midfield

Born: Edinburgh, 31 January 1984.
Career: Hibernian Youth, HIBERNIAN, Inverness Caledonian Thistle 2003.

■ Bobby Williamson gave Darren a couple of outings at the tail end of the 2002–03 season. One of them was against Livingston at Almondvale and Williamson was quite open that he was 'giving the boy a shop window in which to sell himself'. At Livingston Darren played with enough enthusiasm to convince Inverness to sign him.

THOMSON, Jimmy
Left-half

Career: Edinburgh City, HIBERNIAN 1950, Ayr United 1959, Cowdenbeath 1960.

■ A left-half, Jimmy made his first-team debut against Sheffield United in a friendly in March 1954. Indeed, he ended the season on a high and scored against Aberdeen in one of his three League outings that term. He was in and out of the side over the next few seasons and between 1953 and 1959 he played in 55 League games for Hibs and contributed eight goals. He represented Scotland Under-23s *against* Hibs in January 1956.

THOMSON, Kevin
Midfield

Born: Edinburgh, 14 October 1984.
Career: Hibernian Youth, HIBERNIAN 2003, Rangers 2007.

■ Kevin's move to Rangers in early 2007 was just one part of a frenetic spell of transfers from Easter Road to Glasgow. Kenny Miller, Ulrik Laursen, Didier Agathe, Ian Murray, Gary Caldwell, Derek Riordan, Scott Brown, Chris Killen and Steven Whittaker all made switches out of Edinburgh to the Old Firm as Hibs cashed in big-style. He broke into the side during the 2003–04 season and was impressing all and sundry when he suffered a cruciate ligament injury at the tail end of the season. Absent for almost a year, he was back to his best by 2006 and was soon appointed Hibernian captain. A good box-to-box midfielder he was also creative, the only weakness perhaps being a low scoring ratio. Thomson made 80 appearances for Hibs before Rangers came calling with a cheque for £2 million in January 2007.

THOMSON, William 'Bobby'

Forward

Born: Glasgow, 21 March 1955.
Career: Glasgow United, St Johnstone 1974, Morton 1978, Middlesbrough 1981, HIBERNIAN 1982, Morton (loan) 1985, Blackpool 1985, Hartlepool 1987, Hamilton Academicals 1987, Queen of the South 1988.

■ Bobby was one of Scotland's more controversial, and dare one say it notorious, players. Bobby's downfall was a temper that was both swift and purposeful. Nevertheless, between the 'incidents' were some displays in both midfield and attack that were highly praiseworthy. He started his career with Glasgow United and showed sufficient promise to earn a move to St Johnstone. He was a hit in Perth bagging goals with rapidity. He moved from St Johnstone to Morton for a Greenock record fee of £30,000 in July 1978 and the transfer was the making of him. He quickly won a Scottish League cap and Morton were able to turn down a £130,000 offer from Oldham Athletic for his services. Very versatile, he was comfortable playing as a striker or an attacking left-sided midfielder. However, he was plagued by indiscipline and frequently missed matches through suspension. After playing with Middlesbrough, whom he joined in 1981, he journeyed to Hibernian and in 68 games was only sent off twice but the second of those dismissals was one too many for the SFA who slapped a six-month ban on him. His career with Hibs was followed by spells with smaller clubs such as Blackpool, Hartlepool, Hamilton Academicals and Queen of the South.

TIERNEY, Lawrie

Midfield

Born: Leith, 6 March 1981.
Career: Salveson BC, Hearts 1976, HIBERNIAN (loan) 1980, Wigan Athletic 1980.

■ Lawrie joined Hibs in March 1980 having spent several seasons with Hearts and then drifted out of the game. A former Scotland Youth international, he made his Hibs debut in a 3–0 defeat at Dundee. His stay at Easter Road was short (just eight games) and the midfielder soon returned to running his sandwich bar in the Roseburn district of Edinburgh. It was perhaps unfortunate that he arrived in the relegation campaign of 1979–80.

TONER, Willie

Centre-half

Born: Glasgow, 18 December 1929.
Career: Queen's Park, Celtic 1948, Sheffield United 1951, Kilmarnock 1954, HIBERNIAN 1963, Ayr United 1963, Dumbarton 1964.

■ Born in 1928, Willie enjoyed an interesting and lengthy career, playing with Walter Galbraith's Hibs from the tail end of the 1962–63 season until November 1963 and managing nine outings in that time. With five Scottish League caps he was a player with a solid reputation. His early clubs were St Pauls BC in the Shettleston district of Glasgow and Queen's Park before he joined Celtic then moved on to Sheffield United in May 1951. In 1953 he picked up a Division Two Championship medal with United and when he came back to Scotland with Kilmarnock he managed an outing in the 1957 Scottish Cup

Final. He repeated that feat in 1960 then joined Hibs in April 1963. It is interesting to note that Toner started his Kilmarnock career as a centre-forward but was then moved back to central defence and truly found his niche. Much was expected of Willie in Edinburgh but he struggled to break into the side and Hibs only avoided relegation by two points in his first season. Worse was to follow in the next campaign as Willie made only one outing. Not surprisingly he moved on, and a return to Ayrshire was on the cards, with Ayr United securing his services before he entered football management with Dumbarton. Willie's son, Kevin, made his mark on Scottish football as a Grade One referee.

TORRANCE, Bobby

Inside-forward

Born: Glasgow, 12 August 1958.
Career: Anniesland Waverely, St Mirren 1976, HIBERNIAN 1980, Partick Thistle 1980, Stirling Albion 1981, Brechin City 1984, Arbroath 1985, Alloa Athletic 1987.

■ An attacking midfielder, Bobby was signed from St Mirren in March 1980. His career at Easter Road was short lived. He scored just one goal and managed only 13 League outings. Nevertheless, he arrived with a sound reputation. He had indeed scored several goals against Hibernian in the course of his career which started at Anniesland Waverly then took in Paisley's St Mirren. He scored twice on his Saints debut in a side managed by Alex Ferguson. He left Hibs to join Partick Thistle then had stints with Stirling Albion, Brechin City, Arbroath and Alloa. He continued his career as an apprentice quantity surveyor while with Hibs but when he gave the game up he opened his own travel agency and indulged in his passion for scuba diving.

TORTOLANO, Joe

Midfield

Born: Stirling, 6 April 1966.
Career: West Bromwich Albion, HIBERNIAN 1985, Falkirk 1996, Clyde 1997, Stirling Albion 1999, East Stirling 2000.

■ After two years as an apprentice at West Bromwich Albion Hibs signed Joe in 1985. Capable of playing at either full-back, midfield or even out wide he gained two Under-21 caps in 1987 against West Germany and Eire. Joe was among the goals early in his career but he struggled to impose himself in the first team and tended to be more of a squad player than an automatic selection. He quickly became a victim of the 'boo-boys', a state of affairs that was hardly helped when he contrived to get himself sent off in a testimonial match against Manchester United (the foul incidentally against Gordon Strachan – a dyed-in-the-wool Hibs supporter!).

TOSH, Paul

Forward

Born: Arbroath, 18 October 1973.
Career: Arbroath Lads' Club, Arbroath 1991, Dundee 1993, HIBERNIAN 1997, Partick (loan) 1998, Raith Rovers 1999, Forfar Athletic 2001.

■ Signed from Dundee by Jim Duffy in March 1997 there were high hopes for Paul Tosh. After all he was aged just 23, stood 6ft tall and had bagged goals for both Arbroath and Dundee. A change of manager saw Jim Duffy give way to Alex McLeish and as the new manager brought in his own men it was clear Paul was surplus to

EDDIE TURNBULL — HERO

Inside-forward
Born: Falkirk, 12 April 1923.
Career: HIBERNIAN 1946.

■ Eddie was just out of the Royal Navy and playing junior football in the Grangemouth area when he was recruited by Hibernian in 1946. A physically impressive man he had the happy knack of possessing both aggression and creativity. What is more, he was a thinking footballer and he followed a clutch of honours as a player with a raft of successes as a manager. Born in Falkirk in 1923 he was to be the 'engine room' of the 'Famous Five' forward-line. In his very first season with the club he tasted the drama of a Scottish Cup

HIBERNIAN: The Players and Managers 1946–2009

Final, and with his excellent work-rate and thunderous shot he became a huge favourite with the Hibs fans. When Willie Ormond arrived as outside-left a Hibernian partnership was forged that would last Hibs a decade. Turnbull played as an inside-left and became the 'enforcer' for the lighter players in a side that was high on flair but less so on aggression. Turnbull's debut for Hibs came in a mid-season friendly against Sparta Prague of (the then) Czechoslovakia. Hibs lost the game 1–3 (despite Turnbull's autobiography suggesting Hibs 'easily won the match') but Turnbull did well enough to retain his first-team spot and made his League debut against Third Lanark on 2 November at Easter Road. Hibernian romped home 4–1 and Turnbull, with a brace of goals, was the star of the show. His first season was a complete triumph. He had a hat-trick in a 5–3 win at Kilmarnock and two against Queen's Park (when he missed a penalty and the opportunity of a hat-trick). He even scored in the epic Scottish Cup semi-final win over Motherwell that was played to a finish and lasted an incredible 147 minutes. From that opening season in which Hibs had lost the Cup Final and finished just two points away from the title better times would flow. In 1948, 1951 and 1952 the League title would end up at Easter Road and in each and every season Turnbull made a huge impact. In February 1950 Turnbull stepped firmly in to the limelight when he scored all four Hibs goals in a magnificent 4–1 League triumph over Celtic. Three of those goals were penalties and Turnbull had a routine approach to spot-kicks – he simply blasted them. He did have an aggressive streak and proved this in December 1950 when he was sent off against Third Lanark (a fairly rare achievement in those days!) when clashing with Staroscik of the Glasgow club. Club captain by 1954, in addition to his major Scotland representative outings he also earned one Scotland B cap but pride of place went to his collection of three League Championship badges. Indeed, the only item missing from his trophy cabinet was a Cup-winners' medal; despite playing in two Scottish Cup Finals. Nevertheless, he addressed that absence as a manager. From coaching at Queen's Park he moved to a struggling Aberdeen in 1965 and by 1970 steered them to a Scottish Cup triumph over Celtic. When Tom Hart became Hibs chairman he lured Eddie to Edinburgh in July 1971 and the club was suddenly on the up. His impact was almost immediate. By 1972 Hibs were in the Scottish Cup Final and Turnbull's old adversaries – Celtic – lay in wait. Strangely the players froze and were thumped 6–1, but Turnbull was determined they would bounce back and they did…twice. A few weeks later the same sides contested the Drybrough Cup at the same venue and Hibs won 5–3, then in the early winter they met in the League Cup Final. Again Hibs came out on top. Turnbull was by now boasting a famous forward line of his own – Edwards, O'Rourke, Gordon, Cropley and Duncan. He moulded Hibs into the second force in Scotland and had it not been for an exceptionally powerful Celtic side they would have been the top club in Scotland. All the same with Scottish Cup, League Cup and Drybrough Cup Final appearances (and a 7–0 win over Hearts) Eddie more than did his bit for the club. His managerial reign at Easter Road ended when the club were relegated for the first time in 49 years in 1980 having won just six matches in a 36-game campaign. Even the introduction of the world famous George Best had been unable to save Hibs. Turnbull never returned to football and thus was lost to the game at the ludicrously young age of 57.

requirements. He spent a brief spell on loan to Partick Thistle and joined Raith and ultimately Forfar in permanent deals soon afterwards. He really shone at Forfar hitting 63 League goals over a four-year spell that was rightly rewarded with the Second Division Player of Year award for season 2003–04. It is clearly a case of what might have been for Hibs.

TOWNSLEY, Derek

Forward

Born: Carlisle, 21 March 1973.
Career: Gretna, Queen of the South 1996, Motherwell 1999, HIBERNIAN 2001, Gretna 2004, Annan Athletic 2008.

■ Standing at 6ft 5in, Derek cut an imposing figure on the field. He was an apprentice at Carlisle United but left the senior ranks to play in the Unibond League with Gretna. He did well enough there to tempt Queen of the South and the highlight of his stay in Dumfries was a Challenge Cup Final outing in 1997. Two years later he moved to Motherwell where his versatility made him a valuable squad member. Signed for Hibs by Alex McLeish in July 2001, he made his Hibs debut against Dundee in August that year. He quickly won over the Hibernian supporters and ended the 2001–02 season with a glut of goals. Moreover, he proved his adaptability a few months later when he was fielded as an emergency sweeper to good effect. Derek played a role in Gretna's amazing rise in the early-2000s and was in their side that lost the 2006 Scottish Cup Final to Hearts; alas missing one of the spot-kicks in the penalty shoot-out. When Gretna folded he was able to shift across to the team that replaced them in the League – Annan Athletic.

TURNBULL, Stuart

Full-back

Born: 22 August 1961.
Career: Dundee 1975, HIBERNIAN 1981, Hamilton Academicals 1984, Bush Bucks (South Africa).

■ Stuart could play either in defence or midfield and had done so for Dundee when Hibernian signed him in the early-1980s. He stayed at Hibs for three years in which time he seemed to be little more than a fringe player. In 1984 he moved on, joining Hamilton Accies, but he left there after only 15 League outings to take a position with a club in South Africa. Upon retiring from playing he worked with Dundee United.

TWEED, Steven

Centre-half

Born: Edinburgh, 8 August 1972.
Career: Hutcheson Vale BC, HIBERNIAN 1990, Ionikos (Greece) 1996, Stoke City, Dundee, Duisburg, Yokohama (Japan) 2004, Livingston, East Fife 2007.

■ A commanding central-defender, Steven was signed in 1990 from Hutcheson Vale BC. He made his debut in 1992 against St Mirren and gradually forced his way into the first team. With the departure of Tommy McIntyre to Airdrie the way seemed clear for 6ft 3in Steven to establish himself at Easter Road. Alas, it did not work out that way and he moved from Hibernian to Greece in 1996 in one of the earliest Bosman moves. There he played with Ionikos, linking up with Craig Brewster, before returning to Britain with Stoke City. Jocky Scott, himself a former Hibernian manager (albeit as a caretaker), then took Steven to Dundee for £80,000 and the big defender did well to hold his place during the Bonetti revolution which brought many overseas stars to Dens Park. Clearly he gelled well with overseas players for his next move carried him to the Bundesliga and Duisburg where he impressed former German World Cup winner and Duisburg boss Pierre Littbarski. Nevertheless, he truly came into his own when he joined East Fife as a 35-year-old and helped them win the Third Division Championship (the Fifers' first title in some 60 years!).

V–W

Van ZANTEN, David

Left-back

Born: Dublin, 8 May 1982.

Career: Celtic 1999, St. Mirren 2003, HIBERNIAN 2008.

■ In October 2006 Hibs lost 1–0 to St Mirren with Van Zanten scoring a wonder winner for Saints. Clearly Hibs took notice of this strike and in the summer of 2008 Mixu Paatelainen made the St Mirren full-back one of his recruits. As a 17-year-old David had joined Celtic but in four years with the Glasgow club failed to make the breakthrough and moved to St Mirren where he ended up making over 200 appearances. He made his Hibs debut in a UEFA Intertoto Cup tie at home to Swedish side Elfsborg in July 2008.

VINCENT, Stan

Centre-forward

Career: Haddington Athletic, Cowdenbeath 1962, HIBERNIAN 1964, Falkirk 1966, South Africa 1968, Raith Rovers 1969.

■ In February 1964 the club went to Cowdenbeath to sign a centre-forward of some bulk. Although showing promise in flashes, and winning a Summer Cup medal, he was unable to command an automatic spot so moved to Sammy Kean's Falkirk in order to secure a more regular first-team berth. He had not been at Falkirk long when he popped up at Easter Road in November 1966 and scored for Falkirk against Hibs. Stan had scored 27 goals in 61 matches for Cowdenbeath and bagged 15 in 31 Hibs matches; which on reflection is a very useful return. His career with Falkirk was slightly less prolific returning only seven goals in 31 starts there.

WALDIE, Simon

Centre-half

Career: Inverness CT, HIBERNIAN 1945, Queen of the South 1950, Ross County.

■ Signed from Highland League football in 1945 by Willie McCartney, Simon was a powerful centre-half. He stayed with Hibs for five years, making nine appearances and an impressive debut in a 5–1 win over Clyde. Essentially, however, he was reserve to Peter Aird and Hugh Howie so openings in the first XI were severely limited. One of the games he did play in was a 6–0 rout of Queen of the South and clearly the Dumfries side were impressed for they offered Simon first-team football. He was at Palmerston Park for almost four years before being freed, playing against Hibs in a League Cup semi-final, before returning to the Highlands where he played with Ross County and worked with British Rail.

WALKER, Andy

Centre-forward

Born: Glasgow, 6 April 1965.

Career: Ballieston Juniors, Motherwell 1984, Celtic 1987, Newcastle (loan) 1991, Bolton 1992, Celtic 1994, Sheffield United 1996, HIBERNIAN 1997, Raith 1998, Ayr United 1998, Partick Thistle 1999, Alloa Athletic 1999.

■ Signed on loan from Sheffield United in December 1997, Andy was best known for his prolific scoring stints with Motherwell, Celtic and Bolton Wanderers. Indeed, prior to joining Hibs he had scored 120 League goals and won three Scotland caps, pride of place was probably his spell at Bolton where he had scored 44 goals in just 67 matches. He grabbed goals while at Hibs (three in eight games) but no permanent move was forthcoming. Later in the same season he spent a period on loan to Raith Rovers and he grabbed a couple of First Division goals for them too. Upon retiring he moved into the media and proved a most able radio and television reporter.

WARD, Joe

Centre-forward

Born: Glasgow, 25 November 1954.

Career: St Rochs Juniors, Clyde 1974, Aston Villa 1978, HIBERNIAN 1979, Dundee United 1980, Ayr United 1981, Stirling Albion 1984, St Johnstone 1985.

■ Joe Ward will be remembered as a Hibernian player who threatened to score often but ultimately fell short of his own targets. His debut came in a 0–2 home reversal to St Mirren in September 1979 and Hibernian never won a match in which Joe featured. In all he was given nine games in the 1979–80 season but failed to score in any of them. Elsewhere he built up his 51-goal collection, by far the bulk of them coming when he played with Clyde.

WARD, Pat

Wing-half

Born: Dumbarton, 28 December 1926.
Career: Renton Guild, Glasgow Perthshire Juniors, HIBERNIAN 1948, Leicester City 1955, Crewe Alexandria 1958.

■ In season 1950–51 Hibernian won the Scottish Championship in a canter, leaving second placed Rangers trailing by 10 points. Pat Ward made his debut in this thrilling season, replacing the imperious Bobby Combe in a 1–0 win at St Mirren on 24 March. Alas, openings in such a good Hibs side were few and far between and this energetic wing-half was forced to look elsewhere for regular first-team football. He was sold to Leicester City in September 1955, his best season at Easter Road being the 1953–54 campaign when he played in two dozen League games. Prior to coming to Hibs he had worked as an engineer at the huge Babcock & Wilcox plant in Dumbarton.

WATSON, Andy

Left-midfield

Born: Aberdeen, 3 September 1959.
Career: Aberdeen Sunnyside, Aberdeen 1977, Leeds United 1983, Hearts 1984, HIBERNIAN 1987.

■ One of the select band of players to have served both Hearts and Hibernian, Andy eventually became assistant manager at Hibs. The latter appointment owed much to his solid relationship with Alex McLeish, the two had played together at Aberdeen and then Watson became McLeish's assistant at Motherwell, Hibernian, Rangers, Scotland and Birmingham City. Born in Aberdeen in 1959, Andy was with the Pittodrie side for several years (winning four Scotland Under-21 caps) before joining Leeds United. Hibernian kept tabs on his midfield talents but it was Hearts who snapped him up for a £70,000 fee in 1984. Never fully appreciated by the Hearts support he moved to Hibernian for £30,000 and gave solid service before beginning a coaching career that brought many highs.

WEIR, Jock

Centre-forward

Born: Fauldhouse, October 1923.
Career: Leith Renton, HIBERNIAN 1942, Blackburn Rovers 1947, Celtic 1948, Falkirk 1952, Llanelly, Dumbarton 1953, Portadown 1954.

■ A native of Fauldhouse, Lanarkshire, John Weir (known as Jock) joined Hibernian in 1942 from Leith Renton and was a fine outside-right who developed into an even better centre-forward. During the war he guested with Cardiff City and Brighton and he was an instant success when football returned in the post-war era. Indeed, in Hibs' first post-war League game they hammered Queen of the South 9–1 and Weir blasted in four goals, including a first half hat-trick. He was an ever present in the first post-war campaign until his departure to Blackburn Rovers on the last day of January 1947. Newspapers struggled to find the exact fee but called it 'substantial'. It was fitting that Blackburn paid good money for Weir as he had netted 14 goals in the 19 League matches played, five in six League Cup games and four in his only Scottish Cup tie! Had he stayed he would surely have led the line in the Scottish Cup Final against Aberdeen; and to this days rumours persist as to why Hibs sold him so abruptly. He only stayed in Lancashire for a year and in February 1948 returned to Scotland with Celtic for £7,000. He won a Scottish Cup medal there

Mickey Weir

and later turned out for Falkirk, Llanelly and Dumbarton. Interestingly, his Falkirk debut came against Hibs.

WEIR, Mickey

Winger

Born: Edinburgh, 16 January 1966.
Career: Portobello Thistle, HIBERNIAN 1982, Luton Town 1987, HIBERNIAN 1988, Motherwell 1997.

■ Signed in 1982 by John Blackley, Mickey was a Hibs supporter whose love for the club in turn endeared him to the Easter Road support. A tricky winger, his diminutive stature did not hamper him in any way. He was a capable goalscorer, even with his head, and when in possession of the ball a buzz of excitement would sweep around Easter Road. Standing at just 5ft 4in Mickey made his debut in a League Cup-tie in season 1983–84 and two seasons later was regularly featuring on first-team duty. However, a contractual dispute in 1987 saw him head to Luton for £200,000. He was unable to settle in Bedfordshire and for the same fee returned to Hibs just three months later. His second spell at Easter Road was arguably more profitable than the first and he played a major role in helping Hibs win the League Cup in 1991. It was from his cross that Wright headed home the winner against Rangers in the semi-final, and he was fouled to earn Hibs their penalty in the Final. He finally left Hibs in March 1997 (having played in over 200 League games) to join Motherwell on a free transfer and scored against Hibs in a 6–2 reversal at Fir Park in January 1998 which ultimately cost Jim Duffy his job as Hibs boss. At Fir Park Mickey graduated from playing to coaching and spent the bulk of his time with the younger players at Motherwell. By 2002 he was working as assistant manager to former Hibee Keith Wright at Cowdenbeath.

WELSH, Brian

Centre-half

Born: Edinburgh, 23 February 1969.
Career: Tynecastle Boys Club, Dundee United 1985, HIBERNIAN 1996, Stenhousemuir 2000, Valur (Iceland) 2000, Cowdenbeath 2000, Clydebank 2000, Cowdenbeath 2001.

■ Although born in Edinburgh, it was with Dundee United that Brian started his senior career. A powerful and towering centre-half, he had the job of succeeding the likes of Gough, Hegarty and Narey at Tannadice and made over 100 appearances before moving to Hibernian in 1996. The highlight of his Tayside decade was landing the Scottish Cup. His Hibs debut came against Kilmarnock at Easter Road but Hibs lost that game and soon afterwards Brian picked up the first of several injuries that curtailed his career with the club. This was a great shame because at 6ft 3in and possessing great strength in the air he was a highly impressive left-sided pivot. He was released by Alex McLeish and began to drift down the Leagues, playing with lowly Stenhousemuir at one stage. By 2008 he was manager of Cowdenbeath and he used his Hibs connections well while in that post.

WELSH, Peter

Defender

Born: Coatbridge, 19 September 1959.
Career: Leicester City 1977, Nuneaton Borough, HIBERNIAN 1982, Falkirk (loan), Alloa Athletic (loan).

■ Peter played for Hibs in the 1982–83 season and scored a League Cup goal before making a dozen League outings. Sadly, his career was effectively over in 1983 due to a cartilage operation. Born in Coatbridge he joined Hibs from Leicester City.

WHITTAKER, Steven

Full-back

Born: Edinburgh, 16 June 1984.
Career: Hutchison Vale BC, HIBERNIAN 2001, Rangers 2007.

■ In August 2007 Hibernian sold this talented young wing-back to Rangers for just over £2 million. He was only 23 at the time and in joining Kevin Thomson and Ian Murray at Ibrox revealed not just the prolific nature of Hibs' youth system but the fact that the club were addressing what had been an unhealthy debt situation. In the space of a year the club had taken in somewhere in the region of £8.9 million in transfer fees and seen a debt figure drop from £16 million to nearer £7 million. John Collins, while sad to lose Whittaker, was philosophical about the move: 'We weren't looking to sell Steven, but were offered a good fee for a player who has been a good servant to this club. This offer will set Steven and his family up for life and in Kevin McCann and Thierry Gatheussi I believe I have excellent replacements.' Whittaker had made classic progress through the Hibs youth system before establishing himself in the first team. He grabbed his first senior goal against Partick Thistle and eventually forced himself into the Scotland Under-21 side. Although perhaps not as well known as Scott Brown or Derek Riordan there was a feeling that he had the best

Steven Whittaker

temperament of all the young Hibernian players in the Mowbray–Collins era. A CIS Cup winner against Kilmarnock, his aim was clearly to progress his chances of adding further silverware to his collection. In March 2008 Steven was a playing substitute as Rangers won the CIS Insurance Cup against Dundee United, thus repeating the feat of one year earlier with Hibernian. He also played for Rangers in the 2008 UEFA Cup Final.

WHYTE, Hugh

Goalkeeper

Born: Kilmarnock, 24 July 1955.
Career: Hurlford United, HIBERNIAN 1972, Dunfermline Athletic 1976.

■ Hugh was with Hibs in the mid-1970s but had to play second fiddle to Jim McArthur and eventually left Hibernian to play with Dunfermline Athletic. A native of Kilmarnock, he joined Hibs from Hurlford United, turning down Crystal Palace and Huddersfield in favour of Hibs. He was part time for most of his Easter Road career due to the fact that he was a medical student at Edinburgh University. He did indeed graduate and at one time dove-tailed his interests neatly by being club doctor at Dunfermline when his playing days were over. He certainly found his niche in Fife for the vast bulk of his 300 senior outings were made while with the Pars.

WILKINS, Ray

Midfield

Born: London, 14 September 1956.
Career: Chelsea 1973, Manchester United 1979, AC Milan 1984, Paris St Germain 1987, Rangers 1987, Queens Park Rangers 1989, HIBERNIAN 1996, Millwall 1997.

■ A marvellously talented midfielder, Ray had been a star with England, Manchester United and AC Milan before he joined Hibs. Indeed, his list of previous clubs also included the likes of Paris St Germain and Rangers so clearly Ray was as cosmopolitan as he was cultured. Few players could pass the ball with such unerring accuracy or control the midfield with such zeal and authority. He had won 84 England caps by the time he joined Hibernian and it showed. His play was a delight to watch and although it was but a brief goodnight in his career it was nevertheless immensely enjoyable to see such a talent at Easter Road. In all he played in 16 League games and fans loved to see his meticulous and studied approach. Ray later managed QPR, worked on Channel 4's Italian football programme and continued to be a highly respected figure within the game. In 2008 Ray was appointed assistant to Luiz Felipe Scolari at Chelsea.

WILKINSON, Ian

Centre-half

Career: Wallhouse Rovers, HIBERNIAN 1968, Raith Rovers 1970.

■ Ian played three times in the 1968–69 season and once in the following campaign in his short Hibernian career. A wing-half, his greatest difficulty was finding himself in opposition to the likes of Stanton, Blackley and Cousin.

WILSON, Mick

Wing-half

Career: HIBERNIAN 1972, Dunipace Juniors 1977.

■ A midfielder, Mick played three matches in the 1975–76 season (against Celtic, Aberdeen and Rangers). However, he faced stiff competition for a first-team spot from men such as Des Bremner, Iain Munro, Alex Edwards and Bobby Smith. He left the club before the start of the 1977–78 campaign.

WILSON, Terry

Utility

Born: Dunfermline, 20 December 1959.
Career: Oakley United, Aston Villa, Cowdenbeath 1977, Arbroath 1978, HIBERNIAN 1980, Dunfermline Athletic 1981, Dunedin (New Zealand) 1981, Hamilton Academicals 1981, Dunfermline 1983, Lochgelly Albert.

■ Signed from Arbroath in 1980 under freedom of contract, Terry, who was a combative midfielder, ultimately cost Hibs £35,000. He had been with Aston Villa and Cowdenbeath before joining Arbroath and although a versatile player was best known as a full-back. As a Hibs supporter he naturally enjoyed moving to Easter Road but in truth his transfer did not really work out. He lived in Dunfermline and was a part-time player working in the mining industry. His transfer to Hibs had a degree of controversy in that Hibs fielded Tommy in a reserve fixture with Aberdeen in the belief that he had earned a free transfer. This was not the case and he could not be properly signed until later. He also played with Dunfermline, Dunedin (New Zealand) and Hamilton Accies in a fairly nomadic career.

WILSON, Willie

Goalkeeper

Born: Wallyford, 9 October 1941.
Career: Musselburgh Windsor, HIBERNIAN 1959, Berwick Rangers 1969, Cowdenbeath 1974.

■ Although perhaps not the greatest-ever Hibernian goalkeeper there is no doubt that Willie played in some of the most memorable Easter Road nights. He was in goal when Hibs trounced Napoli (Dino Zoff and all) 5–0 in the Fairs Cup in 1967 and had kept a clean sheet against Real Madrid three years earlier. Willie came from Wallyford and joined Hibs from Musselburgh Windsor in 1959. His debut was the stuff of nightmares coming as it did in a 6–1 reversal against Rangers! He vied with the likes of Lawrie Leslie and Ronnie Simpson for a first-team berth at Easter Road. When he did get in he showed himself to be agile and a fine shot stopper. He won a Summer Cup medal in 1964 but was also the 'keeper when Ian St John scored a hat-trick against Hibs in just two and a half minutes. When he retired from playing he continued his connection with football as an early example of the goalkeeping coach working with the likes of Berwick, Falkirk and Hearts.

WISS, Jarkko

Midfield

Born: Tampere, Finland, 17 April 1972.
Career: TPV Tamper 1993, FF Jaro Pietarsaari 1996, HJK 1997, Molde 1999, Lillestrom 1999, Moss FK 2000, Stockport County 2000, HIBERNIAN 2002, Tampere 2004.

■ Signed from Stockport County in January 2002, Jarkko made his Hibernian debut as a substitute against Aberdeen in a 3–4 defeat at Easter Road. He was Franck Sauzee's second signing following on from the arrival of Kevin Nicol of Raith Rovers. A full Finnish international, Jarkko had earned 38 full caps and scored three goals. He joined Stockport from Norwegian side Moss FK for £350,000 and in 47 outings for the English club scored seven times. Jarkko, who made his international debut against Denmark in February 1996, sounded out ex-Hibee Mixu Paatelainen and Hearts' Finnish star Tommi Gronlund in the lead up to his transfer to Hibernian. It would be fair to say that he took time to settle at Easter Road in Bobby Williamson's side.

KEITH WRIGHT — HERO

Centre-forward

Born: Edinburgh, 17 May 1965.
Career: Melbourne Thistle, Raith Rovers 1983, Dundee 1986, HIBERNIAN 1991, Raith Rovers 1997, Morton 1998, Stenhousemuir 2000, Cowdenbeath 2000.

■ When bought from Dundee in 1991 Keith was Hibs' record signing – it had taken a cheque for £500,000 to prise him from Dens Park. It was ironic he should cost half a million pounds because he had been an 'S' form signing at Easter Road but failed to make the mark. He then played with Melbourne Thistle and in 1983 joined Raith Rovers. He became a scoring sensation in Kirkcaldy and grabbed 61 League goals in only 127 starts. In December 1986 he joined Dundee and while there he forged a wonderful partnership with Tommy Coyne, indeed Keith managed 62 goals in his 167 League outings. A life-long Hibs fan, his July 1991 move to Easter Road was a dream come true. He scored 17 goals in his first season as a Hibee and pride of place was reserved for his League Cup performances; goals in the semi-final and Final brought the Cup back to Easter Road. So impressive was Keith as a Hibee that he was capped by Scotland (against Northern Ireland). From Hibs he moved to Raith Rovers then Morton. Keith brought the curtain down on his senior career with Cowdenbeath and by the start of the 2002–03 season was settled as the Fife club's manager.

WOOD, Robert

Centre-half

Born: Elphinstone, 15 February 1930.
Career: Haddington Athletic, Musselburgh Union, HIBERNIAN 1947, Barnsley 1951.

■ Robert scored two goals in only five matches in the Championship-winning 1950–51 season and suggested there were more to come. His debut was at home to St Mirren on 16 December 1950 and Hibs not only romped home 3–1 but Robert scored the opening goal. A few weeks later he had a goal in a 6–2 win at home to Aberdeen and his success seemed assured. The trouble was other clubs agreed and Hibs reluctantly sold him to Barnsley in July 1951. This was a something of a mistake as he went on to make 336 appearances for the Tykes and bagged a very useful 41 goals. With Hibs he played as an inside-forward but he moved to wing-half in south Yorkshire. He had also played rugby at one stage for Preston Lodge.

WREN, Jackie

Goalkeeper

Born: Bonnybridge, 26 April 1936.
Career: Gairdoch Juveniles, Bo'ness United, HIBERNIAN 1956, Southend 1960, Rotherham 1960, Stirling Albion 1961, Falkirk, 1962, Dundee United 1962, Berwick Rangers 1963.

■ John 'Jackie' Mackie Wren was an athletic and agile goalkeeper, who made 31 outings between 1956 and 1960. He moved about in his later career but with little sense of staying at any club for a notable period of time.

WRIGHT, Alexander

Inside-forward

Born: Kirkcaldy, 18 October 1925.
Career: Bowhill Rovers, HIBERNIAN 1946, Barnsley 1947, Tottenham Hotspur 1950, Bradford Park Avenue 1951, Falkirk 1955, Stenhousemuir.

■ Alexander Mason Wright played just two League games for Hibernian in the 1946–47 season and moved to Barnsley in August 1947. He served the south Yorkshire club well with 30 goals in 80 matches; sufficient to earn him a move to Tottenham Hotspur. That move never quite worked out and he went on to have greater success with Bradford Park Avenue between 1951 and 1954. He came back to Scotland in August 1955 with Falkirk. He was joint top scorer for the Bairns in his first season with 11 goals and collected a Scottish Cup-winners' badge in 1957. He also scored a hat-trick for Falkirk in a remarkable 5–5 draw with Rangers.

WRIGHT, Paul

Centre-forward

Born: East Kilbride, 17 August 1967.
Career: St Andrews HS, Aberdeen 1983, Queens Park Rangers 1989, HIBERNIAN 1990, St Johnstone 1991, Kilmarnock 1995, Falkirk 2001, Morton 2002.

■ Paul joined Aberdeen on schoolboy forms and showed great promise while at Pittodrie. First-team football and goals, however, did not come regularly enough and he moved to Queen's Park Rangers where he scored five goals in just 15 appearances. However, he could not settle in west London and Hibs snapped him up in a £250,000 deal in March 1990. Capped by Scotland at Youth and Under-21 level, he made his Hibs debut against, of all teams, Aberdeen and came off the bench to score in the final minute of a 3–2 win! Hibs beat Rangers 1–0 in the very next game but in a 1–2 defeat to Hearts saw Paul pick up a bad injury and his season was over. He bounced back in the 1990–91 season and was top scorer at the end of the season with six goals, but it was a disappointing campaign for the club and only the presence of a very ordinary St Mirren side prevented Hibs propping up the table. St Johnstone made him their record buy in a £285,000 deal in 1991. He was similarly a Kilmarnock record signing when Alex Totten paid £330,000 for him in March 1995. He took a while to settle in Ayrshire then burst on the scene with a welter of goals. From a Hibs perspective he was noticeable when netting a brace when Killie dumped Hibs 2–0 in a Scottish Cup tie and when scoring for the Ayrshire club in the Final against Falkirk.

Y

YANTORNO, Fabian

Defender

*Born: Montevideo, Uruguay, 4 September 1982.
Career: Bella Vista 1999, Sambenedettese 2005, Miramar Misiones 2006, Gretna 2007, HIBERNIAN 2008.*

■ This fabulously named (Fabian Rodrigo Yantorno Blengio to give him his full moniker) 25-year-old full-back made his debut for Hibs against Kilmarnock on the opening day of the 2008–09 season. He had been sacked by Gretna when they folded a few weeks earlier following the departure of Brookes Mileson. A few trial matches for Hibs convinced Mixu Paatelainen to offer him a two year contract.

YOUNG, John

Defender

Career: Loanhead Mayflower, HIBERNIAN 1957, St Johnstone 1962.

■ John broke into the Hibernian first team in the 1958–59 season, playing in two League matches and a clutch of friendlies. Big and strong, he could play either full-back of wing-half and very quickly showed the benefits of full-time training. He moved to St Johnstone in September 1962 but played only a handful of matches there, and apparently his refusal to move to Perth was an issue. Nevertheless, with 41 League appearances while a Hibee it is clear he was no mean player in his heyday.

YOUNGER, Tommy

Goalkeeper

*Born: Edinburgh, 10 April 1930.
Career: Hutchison Vale BC, HIBERNIAN 1948, Liverpool 1956, Falkirk 1959, Stoke City 1960, Leeds United 1961, Toronto 1962.*

■ A gregarious, fun-loving person, golden-haired Tommy was always popular with fans and players alike. In serving the club as a player and director then holding high office in the SFA he amply illustrated his versatility. He won 24 Scotland caps and made a huge impression with both Hibs and Liverpool. Indeed, while a Hibee Tommy kept goal in 176 League matches. Signed after helping Scotland Juveniles beat their English counterparts, he had been a star of Edinburgh schools football, making quite a splash while with Tynecastle School. Tommy made his debut for Hibs in April 1949 at home to Partick Thistle and

defended the Hibernian goal for the last four games of that season. In the 1949–50 season he was in goal for all League games bar one and helped the club reach the League Cup Final. He was much closer to honours the next season, collecting a League Championship medal and playing in the League Cup Final. Unfortunately Hibs lost that Final 0–3 to Motherwell and Tommy in coming off the field in floods of tears earned the nickname 'The Greetin' Goalie'. A cheque for £9,000 made out by Liverpool in June 1956 was sufficient to prise him away to Merseyside and as part of that deal Hibs met Liverpool in a floodlit friendly. Later in his career he played with Falkirk but in March 1960 he returned to England to play with Stoke City. He made only 10 outings for them but following a stint in Toronto, Canada, joined Leeds United and played 37 League matches before coming home to settle in Scotland. In 1970 Tommy joined the board of directors at Easter Road and 13 years on from that he was president of the SFA. Alas, he died in January 1984 when aged only 53.

Z

ZAMBERNARDI, Yannick

Defender

Born: Ajaccio, Corsica, 3 September 1977.
Career: Bastia, AC Ajaccio, ES Troyes, HIBERNIAN 2002, La Lourviere 2004, Dunfermline 2005.

■ Born in Ajaccio on the French island of Corsica he started his senior career with Bastia. Yannick then moved to AC Ajaccio where he impressed sufficiently to earn a move to Troyes where he was a teammate of Freddy Arpinon. In due course Arpinon joined Hibs and he was instrumental in Zambernardi's transfer to Hibernian. Signed as a 24-year-old by Bobby Williamson during Hibs' disastrous start to the 2002–03 season, Yannick made his debut in a 1–2 defeat at Dundee. Soon his sliding tackles (which were excellent when they came off and disastrous when mis-timed) and long range passing were making an impact. Following a good debut season Yannick was plagued by a thigh-injury and moved back to the continent. By 2005 Yannick was playing with Dunfermline and he was sent-off against Hibernian in a 2–1 win for the Hibees in Fife.

ZARABI, Abderraouf

Full-back

Born: Algeria, 26 March 1979.
Career: NA Hussein Dey 1997, AC Ajaccio 2003, FC Gueugnon 2005, HIBERNIAN 2008, Nimes Olympique 2008.

■ Signed by Mixu Paatelainen, the 28-year-old defender was intended to replace David Murphy who had gone to Birmingham. With 26 caps for Algeria he clearly had a wonderful pedigree but his transfer was unusual in that Paatelainen confessed he had never seen or met Zarabi in the flesh before signing him: 'I haven't seen Abderraouf playing live but I have watched him on DVDs and thankfully it is the same player.' Zarabi played just eight games for Hibs before it became clear that domestic issues were proving insurmountable and Hibs allowed him to return to Europe on compassionate grounds.

ZEMMAMA, Merouanne

Midfield

Born: Morocco, 7 October 1983.
Career: Raja Casablanca, HIBERNIAN 2006, Al-Shaab (UAE) 2008.

■ A controversial transfer to Hibernian in 2006 temporarily put the little winger's international career on hold. He had played in the 2004 Olympics for Morocco and impressed with his industry and trickery. His Hibernian debut came at Inverness in August 2006 and he had a goal against Hearts in a 2–2 draw a couple of months into his Edinburgh career. Thereafter he flitted in and out of the side, his cause hardly helped by a broken bone in his foot. In September 2008 Hibs allowed him to join Al-Shaab of the United Arab Emirates in a loan deal, drawn up on compassionate grounds when his wife Zineb fell pregnant and as she was under 18 unable to acquire an entry permit to Britain.

ZITELLI, David

Forward

Born: France, 30 October 1968.
Career: AS Nancy 1985, FC Metz 1992, RC Strasbourg 1995, Karlsruher 1998, RC Strasbourg 1999, HIBERNIAN 2000, FC Istres 2002.

■ David was a clever French striker who was lured to Easter Road by Alex McLeish…and the fact that his great friend Franck Sauzee was already on Hibs' books. Zitelli had been a notable striker and had caught British attention when scoring UEFA Cup goals against both Liverpool and Rangers. His impact at Hibernian was significant. An early goal proved to be the winner against Rangers and he scored in the Scottish Cup semi-final win against Livingston when Hibs reached the 2001 Scottish Cup Final. His powerful shooting

and shrewd positional sense made him a dangerous striker, and he scored in the 6–2 rout of Hearts and the never-to-be-forgotten UEFA Cup classic against AEK Athens. David left Hibernian in the summer of 2002 and joined Istres in France, and Hibs fans were left wondering just what might have happened had the Zitelli prowess been available a few years earlier. As it was his 52 games yielded 10 goals in the League.

HIBERNIAN MANAGERS

Hibernian have had 20 managers in the post World War Two period. The profiles below serve as an introduction, although for those who served Hibs as players as well as a manager their story can be found earlier in the book. I've not included those who have acted as caretaker managers at various points in the club's history but such as list would include the likes of Donald Park, Jocky Scott, Mark Proctor and Tommy Craig.

1. Willie McCartney 1936 to 1948

Willie's father, John, was a football manager of some repute. He had managed St Mirren and Hearts, and Willie followed in his footsteps; managing the Maroons for an incredible 16 years from 1919 until leaving Tynecastle in 1935. If his tenure at Hearts had been remarkable then his 'defection' to Hibs was even more so! He gradually improved Hibernian and was responsible for recruiting players of the calibre of Arthur Milne, Jimmy Kerr, Matt Busy, Gordon Smith and Eddie Turnbull.

A 'dapper' man, he was always dressed in his bowler hat, wore a flower in his button-hole and was recognised as a superb administrator. He had made Hearts one of the most attractive sides in Scotland, taking men like Massie and Walker to Tynecastle. There was an air of the sensational when he resigned and for 10 long months he was out of football. Even more stunning, however, was his return to senior football at, of all places, Hibernian. With the staunch support of Hibs' chairman Harry Swan he sought to revolutionise the way the club operated.

Of course his ability to recruit top quality players continued, even in the war years. Indeed, so successful was he in bringing the best to Easter Road that Hibernian were able to hand Rangers a record 8–1 thumping at Easter Road before seizing the 1944 Southern League Cup. The good work continued after the war as Hibs improved year on year, contesting the Scottish Cup Final in 1947 before finally landing the League title in 1948.

Alas, Willie McCartney died in January 1948, just months before the title was won, thus he died having failed to see Hibernian winning the biggest domestic prize of them all. He had collapsed while Hibs were winning a Scottish Cup tie at Albion Rovers and never regained consciousness.

2. Hugh Shaw 1948 to 1961

A former player, who had been an uncompromising defender, Hugh Shaw brought both local knowledge and pride to the post of Hibs boss. Of course, rather like a predecessor – Davy Gordon – he became manager in most unfortunate circumstances.

Hugh came from footballing stock, although he made faltering progress in his own playing career. He started out with a club in Leith but as an apprentice engineer at the famous Clydeside shipyard of John Brown this was far from ideal and he was soon on his way to Clydebank. There he played with Clydebank Corinthians and Clydebank Juniors before joining Hibs in 1918. Indeed, it was Davy Gordon (then Hibs boss) who signed the young centre-forward and persevered when the youngster didn't really show up well as a striker. Gordon moved Shaw into defence and ultimately Shaw became a solid half-back.

He served Hibernian until 1926, making over 200 outings and playing in the 1923 and 1924 Scottish Cup Finals...both of which Hibs lost. Shaw then joined Rangers for the 1926–27 season before moving to Hearts where he spent three seasons. As a Hearts player he scored against Hibs in a 1927 clash and in total he made 141 outings for the Tynecastle club. However, this did not impinge on his popularity at Easter Road where he remained fondly remembered.

As his playing career drew to a close he joined Elgin City as player-coach and this helped him secure a move to Hibernian as assistant trainer to the legendary Willie McCartney. Shaw was thus settled as McCartney's trainer when Hibs were cruelly robbed of their boss in January 1948. That Hugh Shaw was able to maintain the club's run to the title confirmed his status as the correct choice as the next Hibernian manager.

Filling McCartney's shoes cannot have been easy. Throughout the 1950s Shaw worked closely with chairman Harry Swan to make Hibernian both successful and innovative. One little known fact is that he tried strenuously to sign Dave Mackay before he opted for Hearts. Given what Mackay subsequently achieved at Tottenham Hotspur he would have been a classic signing for Hibs.

Hugh Shaw enjoyed what can only be called a significant Hibs career. He was a player in the 1920s, a coach in the 30s and ultimately a successful manager in the 40s and 50s. Under his stewardship the club won League titles, contested the European Cup and the 'Famous Five' flourished, in short his association with the club brought nothing but good to Easter Road.

3. Walter Galbraith 1961 to 1964

Walter Galbraith, who was born in Glasgow in 1918, had managed extensively, albeit unspectacularly, in England before coming to Hibernian in 1961. He stayed until 1964. His list of previous employers read like a who's who of traditional small northern English clubs, listing as it did Accrington Stanley, Bradford Park Avenue, New Brighton and Tranmere Rovers. Rather ominously only the latter of those clubs was to survive without mishap in the modern era!

As a player Walter had played in Scotland with Queen's Park and Clyde before sampling life in England from 1948 onwards with New Brighton, Grimsby Town and finally Accrington Stanley. It was with Accrington that he learned his managerial trade. Appointed their boss in 1953 he relied heavily on Scots in his team (indeed, in April 1955 he famously fielded an entire Scottish team against York City).

When he made the move to Hibs there are those who say the club really wanted Dunfermline's Jock Stein as boss, but that would come later. Galbraith moved quickly to strengthen the squad and added Johnny Byrne from Tranmere within days or arriving. As the months rolled by Galbraith revealed himself to be an astute judge of players and spent wisely to bring Neil Martin, Pat Quinn, John Parke and Willie Hamilton to the club. Alas, the results that such foresight deserved did not arrive and Galbraith resigned having failed to lift the club above mid-table mediocrity.

4. Jock Stein 1964 to 1965

On 1 April 1964 Jock Stein took over as Hibernian manager following a four year spell with Dunfermline Athletic that earned nothing but praise. Unfortunately he was a former Celtic captain and with the Bhoys going through a bad spell it was a fact of life that if he did well for Hibernian then the call to Glasgow would come.

Stein had been a centre-half with Celtic and had steered his team to victory over Hibs in the 1953 Coronation Cup Final. When his playing career ended he coached the Celtic reserve side for three years. Then came his stint with Dunfermline which began in March 1960 and during which time he led them to Scottish Cup success including a semi-final victory over Hibernian. When Dunfermline won the Scottish Cup in 1961 Stein began to earn rave reviews for his tactical genius and he further enhanced that reputation when he led the Pars on memorable European clashes with the likes of Valencia and Ujpest Dosza.

He came to Hibernian in 1964 and within months of being at Hibs he had landed the Summer Cup. Celtic stepped in and Stein, having learned his craft at East End Park and Easter Road, reached his true potential at Parkhead. He steered the Bhoys to the European Cup in 1967, and to an astonishing nine consecutive League titles. In short he became a Celtic legend.

5. Bob Shankly 1965 to 1969

Fifty-four-year-old Bob Shankly succeeded Jock Stein as Hibs boss in 1965 and lasted in the hot seat for four years. He had previously managed Third Lanark with some note in the 1950s, then led Dundee to the League Championship in 1962 and was a solid, if somewhat rugged, player with Falkirk before that.

He was a member of a notable footballing family, brother Bill being the most famous, earning an international reputation as manager of all-conquering Liverpool, while another brother, Johnny, played for both Morton and Alloa. Like his brother Bill, Bob started his playing career with the famous Glenbuck Cherrypickers, six of that side going on to represent Scotland. He then sampled life in England with Tunbridge Wells before joining Alloa Athletic. In 1933 he joined Falkirk and thus began a long association with the Brockville club. Bob was capped once by the Scottish Football League and stayed with Falkirk for 15 years.

While his coaching career had its roots at Stenhousemuir he honed his skills at Falkirk, whom he rejoined in 1950. After five years in charge of the Bairns came a stint with Third Lanark and then the move to Dundee in 1959 which was to make his name. He eclipsed all of his earlier achievements while at Dens Park, especially in 1962 when his wonderfully gifted Dundee team, with Alan Gilzean as spear-head, romped to the Scottish title then took Europe by storm, reaching the European Cup semi-final stage.

At Hibernian Bob managed with some skill, leading the club in European campaigns and overseeing the 5–0 humbling of Napoli at Easter Road. When Shankly left Hibs it was to retire, however he was tempted out of retirement in March 1971 by Stirling Albion. He managed them for two years before being promoted to a position 'upstairs' and latterly on to their board. He held that post until 1982 when he sadly died while representing Albion at an SFA meeting in Glasgow.

One of the grandstands at Dundee's Dens Park is named after Shankly.

6. Willie Macfarlane 1969 to 1970
(See entry under player section)

7. Dave Ewing 1970 to 1971
In June 1949 Dave moved from Perthshire's Luncarty Juniors to Manchester City and there followed 11 solid years in English football. A teammate of former Hibernian legend Bobby Johnstone during much of his Maine Road career, he proved a distinguished centre-half in Manchester, making over 300 outings and playing in the 1955 and 1956 FA Cup Finals. When he left City it was to join Crewe Alexandria in 1962 and he guided them to promotion before entering coaching with some gusto.

He coached with passion and drive at Ashton United, Bradford, Crystal Palace and Sheffield Wednesday and was earning plaudits at the latter when he was lured to Hibernian in early December 1970. What followed was a quite controversial promotion to the managerial office in the aftermath of Willie Macfarlane's bizarre sacking.

When the Hibernian board interfered in team selection on the eve of Hibs' eagerly awaited Fairs Cup tie with Liverpool it led to a standoff that saw Macfarlane sacked and Ewing promoted to manager literally hours before the big game. It was hardly the ideal scenario for Ewing and it was clear he would inherit a board which had an overzealous approach to running the club. Hibs lost the game 1–0 and Ewing's slow start badly hampered his hopes of retaining the job for any length of time.

Ewing was soon busy in the transfer market, bringing former hero Joe Baker back to the club, but when he described Rangers as 'rubbish' on the eve of a Cup semi-final, which Hibs subsequently lost, it was one faux pas too many and he left Hibs soon afterwards. Some said that chairman Tom Hart had been set on this course for some time and harboured ambitions to bring his good friend Eddie Turnbull back to the club from the outset of his chairmanship.

Ewing returned to England to coach the reserves at Manchester City and earned considerable respect for brining a talented crop of youngsters into the City first team.

8. Eddie Turnbull 1971 to 1980
(See entry under player section)

9. Willie Ormond 1980
(See entry under player section)

10. Bertie Auld 1980 to 1982

(See entry under player section)

11. Pat Stanton 1982 to 1984

(See entry under player section)

12. John Blackley 1984 to 1986

(See entry under player section)

13. Alex Miller 1986 to 1996

In 1991 Alex Miller steered Hibernian to success in the League Cup and for that alone he deserves enormous credit, but such was the cautious nature of his side that he rarely earned the praise he deserved. Indeed, there were those who suspected that his Rangers background went against him with some elements within the Hibs support. Alas, only when he was gone did some fans realize just how good he had been.

Born in Glasgow in 1949, Miller joined Rangers in 1967 from Clydebank Juniors and served the Ibrox club for a lengthy period of 17 years without ever being in the limelight in his 300-plus games. However, as a coach he quickly achieved success. He steered Morton to the First Division Championship in his first season, then moved to St Mirren where again he caught the eye. That was enough for the Hibernian directors who moved swiftly to bring him to Easter Road in December 1986. This broke a run of five consecutive managers who were former players.

There is an enigma about Alex's career at Hibs. He was never universally accepted by the fans…that much is true. Yet the cold facts show that he stayed for a decade and won the League Cup; Hibs' first trophy in 19 years. In comparison to the higher profile Stein, Shankly, and Galbraith his spell in charge must be considered an outstanding success.

He resigned as Hibs boss in 1996 following a heavy home defeat to Hearts that had fans on his back. When Miller left Hibernian chairman Douglas Cromb was extremely upset and said 'When we were close to liquidation Alex had several opportunities to go elsewhere but he chose to stay at Hibs. He stood by the club in its darkest days when we were threatened by the Hearts takeover. When I first arrived at Hibs I was a football novice and Alex was my crutch. He had been in football all his life and helped guide me through some difficult times. Alex helped us win the League Cup, took us to another Final and to our best ever Premier League finish. Alex will go on to higher and better things.' How right he was.

Miller, who had spent two years as part-time assistant to Scotland boss Craig Brown, briefly coached at Coventry City before becoming a highly respected head coach at mighty Liverpool; at Anfield he played a key role in a range of trophy successes including a Champions League triumph, and on reflection Hibernian were rather hasty in dispensing with his services.

14. Jim Duffy 1996 to 1998

Jim Duffy had been a notable centre-half as a player. Although he started out with Celtic he made his reputation with Greenock Morton, to the extent that he was named Scottish Players' Player of the Year for 1985 despite playing with a relatively minor club. Transferred to Dundee, he saw his career cut short by a knee injury and officially retired to become boss of Falkirk, only to make a remarkable recovery and resume playing with Dundee.

His second career began at Dundee where he was player-manager from 1993 until concentrating solely on management. He joined Hibernian at the tail end of December 1996 but his stay at Easter Road – announced by his arrival in a helicopter on the pitch – was not a success. In 1997 the club needed to defeat Airdrie in the Play-offs to secure Premier Division status and the following season things had not improved. After a particularly damaging 6–2 defeat at Motherwell (when Hibs led 2–0 after 10 minutes!) he was relieved of his duties. Able to acquire coaching work at Chelsea and then Portsmouth, he was a manager in his own right again by 2002 – once more at Dundee. He steered them to the 2003 Scottish Cup Final but one year on the Dens Park side were relegated and Jim left Dundee early the following season. He then held various posts at Hearts and Norwich City

(Director of Football at the former and caretaker boss at the latter in October 2007) but was earning greater fame for his television work when he surprisingly returned to football management with Brechin City in January 2009.

15. Alex McLeish 1998 to 2002

Alex was known as 'Big Eck' in a playing career that scaled the heights with Aberdeen. He joined the Dons in 1976 and went on to win 77 Scotland caps (a record only Kenny Dalglish could better) as well as a European Cup-winners' badge and a host of domestic honours.

A tall, red-headed centre-half he formed a marvelous partnership with Willie Miller at Pittodrie and they were the spine on which Alex Ferguson built his successful Aberdeen side.

In 1994 he was appointed Motherwell manager and he did sufficiently well there to pick up the Hibs job in 1998 following the departure of Jim Duffy from the hot seat. Unable to prevent relegation he nevertheless steered the club back to the top flight at the first attempt. His recruitment of quality overseas players such as Russell Latapy, Franck Sauzee and David Zitelli took the club to new heights and in 2001 they contested the Scottish Cup Final. Back in Europe Hibs were clearly on the verge of bigger and better things when Rangers came calling.

In 2001 McLeish was off to Rangers where he enjoyed some success but by 2007 he was Scotland manager. Given his Scottish playing record this seemed like an ideal appointment, and the swashbuckling European Championship qualifying campaign of 2007 merely confirmed this. Late in 2007 after Scotland had narrowly failed to reach Austria/Switzerland he moved to manage English Premiership club Birmingham City.

16. Franck Sauzee 2002 to 2004

(See entry under player section)

17. Bobby Williamson 2002 to 2004

A powerful and direct centre-forward, Bobby Williamson enjoyed a lengthy playing career that saw him overcome injury to make a mark on the game both north and south of the border. However, he had greater impact as a manager, steering Kilmarnock to a Scottish Cup win and building a strong young team at Rugby Park which tasted European football on a regular basis.

Born in Glasgow in August 1961 his first senior club was Clydebank, whom he joined from Auchengill Boys Club. He proved himself to be a clever forward while at Kilbowie and in 1983 was signed by Rangers for £100,000. There is no doubt that his time at Rangers was hindered a broken leg he suffered in 1984, and while he recovered from that injury he was nevertheless allowed to join West Bromwich Albion in 1986.

Williamson scored 11 goals in 53 matches for the West Midlands club then joined Rotherham in 1988. His move to South Yorkshire proved more successful; indeed his figures of 49 goals in only 93 matches go a long way to explaining his popularity at Millmoor.

Never quite forgotten in Scotland, he was lured to Kilmarnock in 1990 by a £100,000 deal. However, that was proved to be money well spent by a sleeping giant of the Scottish game that was slowly but surely stirring to life. By 1993 Williamson was leading the line for Kilmarnock in the Premier League and he scored in a notable 2–1 win at Ibrox that not only brought great personal satisfaction but also confirmed that Kilmarnock were back near the top of the Scottish game.

In December 1996 the Kilmarnock manager Alex Totten left the club and Bobby Williamson succeeded him into the hot seat. By this time his coaching ambitions were to the fore and the award of a UEFA Professional coaching licence was just rewards for his endeavour. In 1997 he steered Kilmarnock to victory in the Scottish Cup Final over Falkirk, the first such trophy success for Killie since 1929.

A CIS League Cup Final outing against Celtic in 2001, and consistent appearances in Europe, ensured that Bobby was one of the Scottish game's most highly sought-after bosses. The departure of Franck Sauzee in February 2002 from the Easter Road hot seat paved the way for Williamson to become the 17th Hibernian manager since the war.

His initial task was to keep Hibs in the top flight and this he did, with a vital win against St Johnstone all but clinching survival. Thereafter he led the club to safer waters but his rather taciturn and dour manner did not endear him to the Hibernian support, which was by now welded to the open and attacking style displayed by his predecessors McLeish and Sauzee. Occasionally defensive when facing the Press (and it must be said frequently very funny) he once famously remarked that entertainment was the objective of the cinema, not football. It was more than likely a piece of dry wit but it damaged his standing with a section of the club's support.

Bobby left to join Plymouth Argyle in April 2004 with Hibs working on a much reduced budget that was making it almost impossible for him to repeat the excellent work he had carried out at Rugby Park. By one of the bizarre twists so beloved of football his first game in charge in Devon saw Plymouth promoted to the First Division!

18. Tony Mowbray 2004 to 2006

Tony Mowbray was appointed Hibs manager on 24 May 2004. He came into the role with little previous experience in coaching but with an impressive CV as a player and having given a superb interview.

Between 1981 and 1991 Mowbray was a rock at the heart of the Middlesbrough defence, forming a super partnership for much of it with Gary Pallister, and it cost Celtic £1 million to lure him north of the border. He spent four seasons in Glasgow before moving to Ipswich Town and it was in Suffolk that he made his first foray into coaching.

For all Mowbray had been a big, strong, physical centre-half he was a total contrast as a manager. His entire philosophy was one of playing attacking football with the emphasis on purposeful passing, swift movement and cultured play. In his first season he steered Hibs to third place in the League and the Scottish Cup semi-final. Leading 1–0 against Dundee United the loss of two late goals robbed the club of a Final appearance. Hibs were back for the 2006 Scottish Cup semi-final too, but this went even worse as the side folded to local rivals Hearts in an embarrassing 4–0 reversal that saw two Hibs players (G. Smith and I. Sproule dismissed). It was a sad ending to a season that had started full of promise with Hibernian winning 10 of their opening 14 League games. Holding on to such a charismatic and inspirational leader proved too much for Hibs when the lure of on English opportunity surfaced.

Mowbray was 42 when he succeeded Bryan Robson in the West Brom hot seat. They lost out on promotion to the Premiership in his first season in the Play-offs but were champions the very next season and he then set about trying to ensure their survival in arguably the toughest League in Europe.

19. John Collins 2006 to 2007
(See entry under player section)

20. Mixu Paatelainen 2008
(See entry under player section)

HIBERNIAN STATS

Arthur Duncan holds the appearance record for Hibernian. Indeed, his League total alone stands at a most impressive 448 outings. By a strange twist of fate the man with the next highest number of outings was a teammate in the bulk of those matches, Pat Stanton. As you might expect, the 'Famous Five' feature strongly in the list of Hibernian all-time appearances. Eddie Turnbull and Willie Ormond are third and fourth respectively while Gordon Smith slips in as number nine on the list. However, the 'Famous Five' themselves were always quick to praise their colleagues and they would be delighted to see that men such as John Paterson and Bobby Combe, true Hibee legends, feature not only in that chart but also in the list of players to have gone through a season ever present. More recent additions to the top dozen Hibernian list are Gordon Hunter and Pat McGinlay. Pat, rather like John Blackley, spread his Hibs appearances over two stints at the club. Defenders feature strongly in the list with Stanton, Blackley, Paterson, Schaedler, Sneddon, Hunter and Rae all having amassed the bulk of their matches while on defensive duties, indeed Arthur Duncan spent many of the later matches in his career as a left-back despite having started out a flying left-winger. Testimonial recipients are well represented in the list with Pat Stanton, Alan Sneddon, Gordon Rae, Arthur Duncan, Gordon Smith and Gordon Hunter all having been rewarded with testimonial fixtures by a grateful Hibernian.

The top dozen Hibernian appearances

Player	Hibs Career	Appearances Start (Subs)	Total
A. Duncan	1969–84	436 (12)	448
P. Stanton	1963–76	397 (2)	399
E. Turnbull	1946–59	349	349
W. Ormond	1946–61	348	348
G. Rae	1977–90	337 (11)	348
G. Hunter	1983–97	333 (6)	339
P. McGinlay	1988–2000	299 (23)	322
A. Sneddon	1980–92	303 (9)	312
G. Smith	1946–59	310	310
E. Schaedler	1969–78, 1981–85	291 (8)	299
J. Paterson	1948–59	283	283
J. Blackley	1967–78, 1983–84	278 (1)	279

Ever present

Below are the Hibernian players who have been ever present in a League season:
* Full-back Joe Davis was ever present for four consecutive seasons.
* John Paterson who was ever present in three seasons, was joined by his son Craig who was ever present in season 1981–82.
* Club record appearance maker Arthur Duncan only managed the feat of being ever present twice while Joe Davis, who was ever present for four consecutive seasons, does not feature in the top 12 Hibees list.
* Goalkeepers feature strongly on our list of ever presents with Ronnie Simpson, Jim Herriot, Mike MacDonald, Alan Rough, Andy Goram, Jim Leighton, and Ole Gottskalksson all having enjoyed at least one season as an ever present.

* In season 1951–52 Hibernian had three players ever present – John Paterson, Jock Govan and Hugh Howie. In 1966–67 the feat was repeated when Joe Davis, Bobby Duncan and Alan Cousin did likewise. However, in season 1976–77 the record of four ever-present players was set when Mike MacDonald was joined by John Brownlie, Des Bremner and Bobby Smith.
* Since World War Two there have been 53 occasions of players being ever present on League duty for Hibernian. Some of the players on that list are a little surprising. Take Alan McGraw for example whose career was blighted by injury yet he managed to go through season 1967–68 without missing a League match. Others whom you might not expect to have made it through a season without missing a game are Alan Cousin, Willie Hamilton and Johnny MacLeod.
* Both of Hibs' Ally MacLeods (the one who became Scotland manager and the one who played up front in the late-1970s) feature on the list.

Players who were ever present at least twice

Player	Seasons
Joe Davis	1965–66, 1966–67, 1967–68, 1968–69
John Paterson	1950–51, 1951–52, 1954–55
Alan Sneddon	1981–82, 1982–83, 1984–85
Jim Leighton	1993–94, 1994–95, 1995–96
Bobby Combe	1949–50, 1952–53
Bobby Johnstone	1952–53, 1953–54
Pat Stanton	1965–66, 1974–75
Arthur Duncan	1975–76, 1980–81
Mike MacDonald	1976–77, 1977–78
Ally MacLeod	1977–78, 1978–79

Goalscorers

The leading goalscorers for Hibernian in all competitions are as follows:

League: Lawrie Reilly, centre-forward (ultimately) in the 'Famous Five' side scored 187 goals for Hibernian in 12 seasons at the club. Given that he retired when aged just 29 it is reasonable to assume that he would have broken the 200 goal barrier had injury not intervened.

However, the most goals scored in a single season by a Hibernian player was Joe Baker, who bagged 42 in season 1959–60.

Scottish Cup: Joe Baker has 22 Scottish Cup goals to his name, this includes a haul of nine in one match against Peebles Rovers and four in one game against Hearts Willie Ormond scored 18 Scottish Cup goals.

League Cup: Gordon Smith and Eddie Turnbull each scored 35 League Cup goals for Hibs.

Europe: Both Arthur Duncan and Joe McBride have eight European goals for Hibs.

The top dozen Hibernian scorers

Player	Hibs Career	Games	Goals
L Reilly	1946–58	253	187
E Turnbull	1946–59	346	147
W Ormond	1946–61	349	132
G Smith	1946–59	310	122
J Baker	1957–61;1970–72	138 (1)	113
R Johnstone	1948–55;1959–61	195	100
J O'Rourke	1962–74	202 (8)	81
P Cormack	1962–70;1979–81	197 (3)	77
A Duncan	1969–84	436 (12)	73
A MacLeod	1974–82	201 (7)	72

Player Stats

Appearances and Goals (Substitute appearances after plus sign)
Statistics up to date as of 5 January 2009

	League		League Cup		Scottish Cup		Europe	
Player	Apps	Gls	Apps	Gls	Apps	Gls	Apps	Gls
Adair, G.	4	0	0	0	0	0	0	0
Adams, W.	0	0	0	0	0	0	1	0
Agathe, D.	5	4	0+1	0	0	0	0	0
Aird, P.	44	0	20	0	5	0	0	0
Aitken, A.	35	11	11	5	5	4	0	0
Aitkenhead, J.	22	10	6	2	1	0	0	0
Allan, T.	70	0	13	0	6	0	5	0
Allen, W.	1	0	0	0	0	0	0	0
Allison, K.	5	4	0	0	0	0	0	0
Anderson, B.	1	0	0	0	0	0	0	0
Anderson, Derek	6	0	0	0	0	0	0	0
Anderson, Des	2	0	0	0	0	0	0	0
Andersson, D.	41	0	5	0	1	0	0	0
Andrews, L.	4+9	0	2	0	0+1	0	0	0
Antoine-Curier, M.	8+5	3	1	1	0+1	0	0	0
Archibald, S.	39+5	15	3	2	4	1	0+2	0
Arpinon, F.	25+10	2	0+1	0	1+3	0	0	0
Auld, B.	8+3	3	3+1	0	0+1	0	0	0
Bailey, L.	1	0	0	0	0	0	0	0
Baillie, J.	4+1	0	1+1	0	2	0	0	0
Baines, R.	23	0	0	0	1	0	4	0
Baird, S.	39	5	6	0	5	1	7	0
Baker, G.	59	27	15	11	4	2	6	3
Baker, J.	138+1	113	23	16	25	22	5	6
Bamba, S.	15	0	0	0	0	0	0	0
Bannerman, S.	2+14	0	0	0	0	0	0	0
Bannon, E.	1	0	0	0	0	0	0	0
Barry, R.	36	0	8	0	3	0	2	0
Baxter, J.	208	22	47	4	27	2	11	2
Beaumont, D.	64+6	2	4+2	0	3	0	2	1

HIBERNIAN: The Players and Managers 1946–2009

Player	League Apps	Gls	League Cup Apps	Gls	Scottish Cup Apps	Gls	Europe Apps	Gls
Beedie, S.	9	2	3	1	0	0	0	0
Benjelloun, A.	23+31	8	4+1	5	5+4	3	0	0
Bell, D.	24+8	3	1+1	0	1	0	0	0
Best, G.	17	3	2	0	3	0	0	0
Beuzelin, G.	85+14	10	7+2	0	7	0	2	0
Black, I.	2	0	0	0	0	0	0	0
Black, J.	151+1	0	44	0	16	0	15	1
Blackley, J.	278+1	6	64	1	28	2	26	1
Blair, J.	15+2	5	2+1	0	0	0	0	0
Boco, J.	29	0	2	0	1	0	0	0
Bogie, M.	3	0	0	0	0	0	0	0
Bottiglieri, E.	0+1	0	0	0	0	0	0	0
Boyle, G.	11	0	6	0	0	0	0	0
Bradley, J.	0	0	1	0	0	0	0	0
Brazil, A.	188+17	7	22+1	1	22+1	1	0	0
Brebner, G.	113+19	7	10+1	2	12+3	5	2+1	0
Bremner, D.	199	18	36+2	2	25	2	15	0
Brewster, C.	23+2	3	1	2	0	0	2	0
Brogan, J.	2+3	1	2	0	0	0	0	
Brown, A.	0+1	0	1	0	0	0	0	0
Brown, J. (1)	40+4	0	6	0	2	0	0	0
Brown, J. (2)	14+1	1	0	0	0+1	0	0	0
Brown, John	12	0	1	0	0	0	0	0
Brown, J.T.	3	0	1	0	0	0	0	0
Brown, Scott	101+8	13	9+1	3	10	3	5	0
Brown, Simon	49+1	0	3	0	8+1	0	4	0
Brown, Steve	14+4	0	0	0	1+2	0	0	0
Brownlie, J.	212+1	14	45+1	6	24	0	17	3
Bruce, A.	1	0	0	0	0	0	0	0
Bruce, W.	4	0	0	0	0	0	0	0
Buchanan, A.	203	15	59	4	23	2	2	0
Buchanan, J.	13	6	0	0	1	0	1	1
Burridge, J.	65	0	5	0	5	0	2	0
Byrne, G.	0+2	0	0	0	0	0	0	0
Byrne, J.	23	5	8	1	0	0	3	3
Caig, T.	13	0	2	0	5	0	0	0
Cairns, J.	55	1	21	0	5	0	0	0
Caldwell, G.	97+2	5	7	0	8	1	3+1	0
Callachan, R.	207+13	26	31+1	4	23	5	0	0
Cameron, A.	15	0	0	0	0	0	0	0
Cameron, I.	9+8		1+1	0	1+1	0	0	0
Campbell, C.	32+6	5	3+3	0	8	0	0	0
Campbell, J.	2	0	0	0	0	0	0	0
Campbell, R.	4+7	0	0	0	0+1	0	0+1	0
Canning, M.	12	0	0	0	0	0	0	0
Carroll, P.	13+6	0	0	0	2+1	0	0	0
Carson, T.	2	0	0	0	0	0	0	0
Caughey, M.	5+9	0	1	0	0	0	0	0
Charnley, J.	26+3	4	2	1	2+1	0	0	0

HIBERNIAN STATS

	League		League Cup		Scottish Cup		Europe	
Player	Apps	Gls	Apps	Gls	Apps	Gls	Apps	Gls
Chisholm, G.	57+2	4	6+1	1	5	1	0	0
Chisholm, R.	22+11	0	1	0	0+1	0	1+1	0
Clark, W.	17	1	3	0	6	0	0	0
Colgan, N.	121	0	8	0	16	0	2	0
Collins D.	39+1	0	2+1	0	6	1	0	0
Collins, J.	155+8	16	8+3	1	17	3	4	0
Combe, R.	263	53	64	9	27	5	6	1
Connolly, J.	30+4	8	6	0	3	0	0	0
Conroy, M.	31+1	2	6	2	1+1	0	0	0
Cooper, N.	38	0	5	0	3	0	4	0
Cormack, P.	194+8	77	38	13	17	4	13	3
Cousin, A.	84+5	2	15	0	7	1	6	0
Cowan, S.	64+6	23	0+1	6	6	3	0	0
Craig, T.	10+1	0	0	0	0	0	0	0
Crawford, S.	64+9	23	5+1	1	2+1	0	0	0
Cropley, A.	123+4	29	30+5	14	10+1	1	15	6
Cuthbert, I.	1	0	0	0	0	0	1	0
Cuthbertson, J.	33	29	11	6	10	6	0	0
Dacquin, F.	2+2	0	0	0	0	0	0	0
Dalglish, P.	4+8	1	0	0	0	0	1+3	1
D'Arcy, T.	3	0	5	5	0	0	0	0
Davidson, K.	15+4	4	0	0	3	2	3+1	0
Davin, J.	17	1	4	0	1	0	6	0
Davis, J.	157	34	38	4	14	2	15	3
De La Cruz, U.	25+7	2	2	0	2+1	0	2	0
Dempsie, A.	4+2	0	0	0	0	0	0	0
Dempsie, M.	15+4	0	0+1	0	2	0	0	0
Dennis, S.	61+3	4	4	0	6	0	0	0
Dietrich, K.	1	0	0+1	0	0	0	0	0
Dobbie, S.	7+27	2	2+5	5	1	0	0+2	0
Docherty, P.	2+1	0	1+1	0	0	0	0	0
Dods, D.	61+4	1	4	0	2	0	0	0
Donald, G.	17+26	5	1+2	1	0	0	0	0
Donaldson, A.	0	0	6	0	0	0	0	0
Donaldson, C.	11+8	5	2	1	0+1	0	0	0
Doumbe, M.	46	1	5	0	2	0	0	0
Dow, A.	50+14	3	5	1	2	0	0	0
Duchart, A.	3	0	0	0	0	0	0	0
Duncan, A.	436+12	73	84+7	23	48+2	7	26+1	8
Duncan, B.	82+1	0	12	0	7	0	8	1
Durie, G.	45+2	14	6	8	5	0	0	0
Easton, J.	79	1	21	0	6	0	8+2	2
Edge, R.	20	0	4	0	0	0		
Edwards, A.	137+5	5	36+1	3	11	3	14+1	1
Elliot, D.	17+2	0	3	0	1	0	0	0
Evans, G.	176+81	30	13+7	6	12+6	1	4+2	1
Falconer, D.	48	14	0	0	1	0	3	1
Farm, G.	7	0	0	0	2	0	0	0
Farmer, J.	2+1	0	1	0	0	0	0	0

HIBERNIAN: The Players and Managers 1946–2009

Player	League Apps	Gls	League Cup Apps	Gls	Scottish Cup Apps	Gls	Europe Apps	Gls
Farrell, D.	89+21	2	6+1	0	0	0	0	0
Fellinger, D.	30+16	4	0+1	0	0+2	0	0+1	0
Fenwick, P.	83+1	4	7	0	11	0	2	0
Findlay, W.	66+53	7	8+2	0	2+5	0	0	0
Finnigan, W.	41	1	11	2	7	0	0	0
Flavell, R.	30+6	3	8	1	4	4	0	0
Fleming, R.	11+1	0	4	0	0	0	2	0
Fletcher, S.	100+43	38	6+5	5	10+5	3	5+1	1
Fox, D.	32	8	10	3	7	3	0	0
Franks, M.	1+1	0	0	0	0	0	0	0
Fraser, J.	195	25	39	6	20	5	13	2
Fraser, R.	5	0	1	0	0	0	0	0
Frye, J.	20	1	7	0	4	0	0	0
Fulton, M.	38+1	0	7	0	4	0	0	0
Fyfe, G.	9+1	1	6+1	0	0	0	0+1	0
Gallacher, M.	49	0	6	0	12	0	0	0
Gatheussi, T.	18+5	1	1	0	1	0	1	0
Gibson, D.	41	8	7	2	7	0	5	0
Glass, S.	68+17	3	5+1	1	6+1	1	1+4	0
Goram, A.	138	1	8	0	13	0	4	0
Gordon, A.	83+1	51	28+1	10	12	4	13	7
Gottskalksson, O.	63	0	7	0	4	0	0	0
Govan, J.	163	0	53	0	27	0	0	0
Graham, J.	42+2	14	7+1	4	3	1	2+1	1
Grant, B.	11+7	0	0+2	0	4	0	0	0
Grant, C.	14+8	4	7+1	6	1	0	3	1
Grant, John	224	2	37	0	23	0	13	0
Grant, Johnny	13	1	0	0	0	0	0	0
Gray, D.	2+3	1	0	0	1+1	0	0	0
Gray, E.	1	0	2	0	0	0	0	0
Grof, D.	0	0	0+1	0	0	0	0	0
Guggi, P.	7+1	2	2	0	0	0	0	0
Gunn, B.	12	0	0	0	0	0	0	0
Gunning, J.	1	0	0	0	0	0	0	0
Hall, A.	1	0	2	0	0	0	0	0
Hamill, H.	6+1	0	3	1	2	0	0	0
Hamilton, B.	183+11	9	12+5	2	13	1	5+1	0
Hamilton, D.	23	0	0	0	3	0	0	0
Hamilton, J.	53+5	11	20+2	5	7	0	2+1	0
Hamilton, W.	50	15	6	2	6	4	0	0
Hanlon, P.	8+2	1	0	0	2	0	2	0
Harper, J.	69	26	18	16	3	2	6	3
Harper, K.	73+24	15	4+5	0	9+1	3	0	0
Harris, C.	12+15	4	0+3	1	0+3	0	0	0
Harrower, J.	36	11	7	1	0	0	0	0
Hartley, P.	18+15	6	1+1	1	2+3	1	0	0
Harvey, G.	21+12	3	2+1	2	1+1	0	0	0
Hazel, J.	35+9	3	10+1	1	3+2	1	0+2	0
Henderson, M.	4+2	0	0	0	0	0	0	0

HIBERNIAN STATS

Player	League Apps	Gls	League Cup Apps	Gls	Scottish Cup Apps	Gls	Europe Apps	Gls
Hendry, I.	1	0	0+2	0	0	0	0	0
Henry, F.	6+3	0	0	0	0	0	0	0
Herriot, J.	57	0	18	0	9	0	6	0
Higgins, A.	91+12	23	20+5	8	13+2	4	11+2	3
Higgins, H.	10	0	6	0	0	0	1	0
Higgins, J.	10	0	11	0	0	0	0	0
Higgins, L.	1	0	0	0	0	0	0	0
Hilland, P.	3	0	0	0	0	0	0	0
Hogg, C.	86+1	1	5	0	10	0	6	0
Hogg, D.	11	1	3	0	0	0	0	0
Holsgrove, P.	9+9	1	2	0	0	0	0	0
Houchen, K.	51+6	11	5	1	6	4	4	1
Howie, H.	139	0	50	0	18	1	0	0
Huggins, D.	3	0	0	0	0	0	0	0
Hughes, J.	72+2	4	6	0	5	0	0	0
Hughes, P.	68	0	5	0	3	0	6	0
Hunter, G.	333+6	7	35	1	29	0	4	0
Hunter, W.	11+1	1	0	0	0	0	1	0
Hurtado, E.	4+8	1	0	0	1+1	1	0	0
Hutchinson, B.	57+10	13	8	0	9+2	0	3+1	0
Irvine, W. (1)	8+7	2	0+2	0	0+1	0	0	0
Irvine, W. (2)	82+3	26	6+1	5	2+1	0	0	0
Jack, M.	102+7	4	4+1	0	9+1	1	2	0
Jackson, C.	53+17	2	3+2	0	5+1	0	0	0
Jackson, D.	162+12	50	12+1	3	16	3	2	1
James, C.	20+2	2	1	0	2	0	0	0
Jamieson, W.	87+30	25	7+2	2	6+2	0	0	0
Jean, E.	0+5	0	0	0	0	0	0	0
Johnston, L.	9	8	5	4	0	0	0	0
Johnstone, B.	195	100	40	28	21	9	0	0
Joneleit, T.	0+2	0	1	0	0	0	0	0
Jones, M.	30	0	1	0	4	0	2	0
Jones, R.	82+6	6	6	3	9	1	6	1
Kane, J.	0+1	0	0	0	0	0	0	0
Kane, P.	235+12	33	25+2	6	15+2	2	4	0
Kean, S.	58	0	15	0	14	1	0	0
Keenan, J.	8+1	0	1	1	0	0	0	0
Kelly, C.	2	0	1	0	0	0	0	0
Kerr, B.	23+2	1	3	0	2	0	1	0
Kerr, J.	72	0	28	0	13	0	0	0
Kilgour, R.	5	0	3	0	0	0	0	0
Killen, C.	23+2	15	2	0	1+1	2	3	1
Kinloch, R.	17	12	11	5	3	3	3	2
Kirkwood, W.	26	1	3	0	0	0	0	0
Konde, O.	9+5	0	0	0	0+2	0	0+1	0
Konte, A.	4+23	1	0+1	0	0+1	0	1+1	2
Laing, D.	6	0	4	0	0	0	0	0
Lambie, D.	13+3	0	1+1	0	7	2	0	0
Larusson, B.	3+4	1	0	0	0	0	0	0

HIBERNIAN: The Players and Managers 1946–2009

Player	League Apps	Gls	League Cup Apps	Gls	Scottish Cup Apps	Gls	Europe Apps	Gls
Latapy, R.	82+2	22	2+2	3	2	4	0	0
Laursen, U.	52+1	3	3	0	5	1	2	0
Lavety, B.	37+28	9	5	3	1+1	0	0	0
Lehmann, D.	27+33	9	3+2	1	2+4	3	0	0
Leighton, J.	153	0	13	0	12	0	0	0
Leishman, T.	30	1	2	0	2	0	2	0
Lennon, D.	19+18	2	0	0	0	0	0	0
Leslie, L.	76	0	12	0	11	0	0	0
Libbra, M.	7+4	5	0	0	2+1	0	0	0
Linwood, A.	36	22	10	6	5	4	0	0
Love, G.	33	6	0	0	3	0	0	0
Lovell, S.	75+13	17	4+2	1	7+3	1	0	0
Lovering, P.	26+1	1	2	0	2	1	0	0
Luna, P.	28+14	9	3+1	1	2	1	2	2
Lynch, S.	2+3	0	0	0	1+1	0	0	0
McAllister, K.	92+17	12	11+2	2	4	1	0	0
McArthur, J.	217	0	38	0	25	0	8	0
McBride, J. (Jun)	66+15	11	8	1	2+2	0	0	0
McBride, J. (Sen)	66	44	12	6	1+1	0	9+1	8
McCabe, T.	13	0	0	0	1	0	0	0
McCaffrey, D.	0+2	0	0	0	0	0	0	0
McCaffrey, S.	0+2	0	0	0	0	0	0	0
McCann, K.	26+3	2	1+2	0	3+1	0	0	0
McClelland, J.	183	2	37	0	25	0	12	0
McCluskey, G.	61+22	15	2+5	1	3+1	0	0	0
McCluskey, J.	1+18	0	1+2	1	0+5	0	1	0
McCormack, D.	2+3	0	3	0	5	0	1	0
McCreadie, H.	9	3	0	0	0	0	0	0
McCurdy, P.	1+4	1	1+1	0	0	0	0	0
McDonald, K.	0+5	0	0+2	0	0+1	0	0	0
McDonald, M.	109	0	16	0	11	0	8	0
MacDonald, T.	16	6	1	0	3	3	0	0
McEwan, W.	59+2	2	3	0	1	0	4	0
Macfarlane, W.	78	2	9	0	5	0	5	1
McGachie, J.	3+8	1	0+1	0	0	0	0	0
McGhee, A.	22+3	6	0	0	4	1	0	0
McGinlay, P.	299+23	60	21	8	23+1	10	2+2	1
McGlinchey, P.	10+5	0	0	0	2	0	0	0
McGlynn, T.	3	2	0	0	0	0	0	0
McGovern, P.	1+2	1	1	0	0+2	0	0	0
McGraw, A.	60+3	17	15	4	2	0	6	0
McGraw, M.	21+28	3	4+2	0	1+2	0	0	0
McGurk, D.	1	0	0	0	0	0	0	0
McIntosh, M.	13	0	3	0	2	0	0	0
McIntyre, T.	121+5	9	12+1	2	12+1	1	0	0
McKay, J.	3+1	1	0	0	0	0	0	0
McKee, K.	30+7	0	6+1	0	0	0	0	0
McKenzie, R.	7	0	4	0	0	0	0	0
McLaren, W.	36+2	0	6	0	3	0	0	0

HIBERNIAN STATS

	League		League Cup		Scottish Cup		Europe	
Player	Apps	Gls	Apps	Gls	Apps	Gls	Apps	Gls
McLaughlin, J.	18	0	1	0	1	0	0	0
MacLeod, A.	200+8	72	28+1	11	27	13	5	1
MacLeod, A.	52	6	6	2	2	0	9	0
McLeod, J.	34	27	9	4	5	3	5	2
MacLeod, M.	73+5	2	6	1	9	0	2	0
McManus, M.	0+1	0	0	0	0	0	0	0
McManus, T.	58+50	21	6+3	2	4+3	2	1+2	0
McNamara, J.	231+5	2	38	0	22+1	1	4	0
McNamee, J.	77	4	22	6	7	1	3	1
McNeil, A.	29+2	0	3	0	5	0	1	0
McNeil, G.	1	0	0	0	0	0	0	0
McNeil, M.	1	0	7	0	0	0	0	0
McQueen, T.	3	0	0	0	0	0	0	0
McQuilken, J.	10	0	0	0	1	0	0	0
McWilliams, D.	0	0	0	0	0	0	0	0
McWilliams, W.	2	1	0	0	0	0	0	0
Madsen, J.	71	0	7	0	7	0	8	0
Malkowski, Z.	50+1	0	4	0	1	0	2	0
Ma-Kalambay, Y.	44	0	2	0	3	0	1	0
Marinello, P.	42	5	13	4	2	0	2	1
Marinkov, A.	10	1	1	0	0	0	0	0
Marjoribanks, B.	5	3	0	0	0	0	0	0
Marshall, G.	47	0	14	0	5	0	2	0
Martin, L.	1	0	0	0	0	0	0	0
Martin, N.	65	53	25	19	6	2	2	0
Martis, S.	27	0	4	0	2	0	0	0
Mathisen, S.	2	0	1	0	0	0	0	0
Mayos, J.	14	0	1	0	0	0	0	0
May, E.	88+21	10	4	1	7+4	4	0	0
Millen, A.	49+3	0	5	0	3	0	0	0
Miller, Graeme	1+2	0	0+1	0	0	0	0	0
Miller, Greg	4+8	1	0+1	0	2+2	1	0	0
Miller, K.	29+16	12	1+2	1	5	1	0	0
Miller, W.	3	0	0	0	0	0	0	0
Miller, W. (2)	239+7	1	21	0	17+1	1	2	0
Milne, A.	3	1	0	0	0	0	0	0
Milne, C.	70+9	0	4+1	0	2	0	1	0
Mitchell, G.	258+7	3	19	0	27+1	0	5	1
Morais, F.	19+13	1	2+1	1	1+1	0	1	0
Moran, D.	3	1	0	0	0	0	0	0
Morrow, S.	5+17	1	3+1	0	2+2	2	1+2	0
Muir, G.	49	0	10	0	0	0	1	0
Muir, L.	10+8	1	6	2	2+3	0	2	0
Muirhead, W.	21	0	6	0	3	0	1	0
Mulkerrin, J.	16	8	2	1	1	0	3	1
Munro, I.	85+8	11	21+3	2	7	0	6	2
Munro, J.	1	0	0	0	0	0	0	0
Murdock, C.	37	3	6	1	1	0	2	0
Murphy, D.	107+1	4	9	1	12	1	6	1

HIBERNIAN: The Players and Managers 1946–2009

Player	League Apps	Gls	League Cup Apps	Gls	Scottish Cup Apps	Gls	Europe Apps	Gls
Murphy, J.	8+4	1	4+1	2	0	0	0	0
Murray, A.	10+2	0	0	0	1+1	0	0	0
Murray, G.	68+11	16	12+5	3	3+1	0	0	0
Murray, I.	159+16	13	9	2	15+2	2	4	0
Murray, W.	63+14	7	1+3	0	7+3	0	5+1	0
Nelson, D.	1	0	0	0	0	0	0	0
Nicholls, D.	6	0	0	0	0	0	0	0
Nicol, K.	11+7	1	0+1	0	0+1	0	2	0
Nicol, R.	37	2	9	0	1	1	0	0
Nish, C.	29+5	10	1	0	0	0	1+1	0
Noubissie, P.	4	0	0	0	0	0	0	0
Nutley, R.	1	0	0	0	0	0	0	0
O'Brien, A.	13+22	0	0+1	0	1+2	0	1	0
O'Brien, G.	2+5	0	2	0	0+1	0	0	0
O'Connor, G.	116+23	45	9+1	4	9+5	6	4	1
Ogilvie, J.	35	0	11	0	6	0	0	0
O'Neil, J.	82+4	9	5	0	7+2	3	2	0
O'Neil, M.	96+2	19	9	3	6	2	0	0
Orman, A.	78+7	4	7+1	1	3+1	0	4	0
Ormond, W.	348	132	90	37	50	18	8	1
O'Rourke, J.	204+19	81	39+3	17	23+1	15	14+2	6
Orr, N.	151+16	3	11+3	1	17+2	2	5+1	0
Paatelainen, M.	103+14	39	3+2	0	12+2	1	0	0
Parke, J.	21	0	4	0	0	0	0	0
Paterson, C.	104	4	11	1	13	1	0	0
Paterson, J.	283	0	54	0	29	0	6	0
Paterson, W.	2+9	2	0	0	0+2	0	0	0
Paton, E.	11	3	0+1	0	0	0	0	0
Peat, W.	11	3	2	0	0	0	0	0
Peters, A.	0+1	0	0	0	0	0	0	0
Pinau, S.	0+8	0	0+1	0	0	0	0	0
Plenderleith, J.	123	0	18	0	14	0	4	0
Plumb, A.	7	7	0	0	3	3	0	0
Power, L.	10+3	2	1	0	0	0	0	0
Prenderville, B.	13	2	0	0	0	0	0	0
Preston, T.	228	34	52	11	24	1	12	3
Pringle, A.	7+3	0	0	0	2	0	0	0
Quinn, P.	109+3	17	26	4	12	1	15	1
Rae, G.	337+11	47	42+4	7	29+4	5	4	0
Rae, R.	13	0	1	0	2	0	0	0
Rankin, J.	30+5	4	1	0	2	0	1+1	0
Raynes, S.	2+1	0	0	0	0	0	0	0
Refvik, I.	5	0	2	2	0	0	0	0
Reid, A.	16+14	1	2	1	0	0	0	0
Reid, C.	35	0	3	0	4	0	0	0
Reid, D.	0+1	0	0	0	0	0	0	0
Reilly, J.	2	0	3	0	0	0	0	0
Reilly, L.	253	187	55	33	23	16	3	1
Renwick, M.	38+11	0	4	0	2	0	0	0

HIBERNIAN STATS

Player	League Apps	Gls	League Cup Apps	Gls	Scottish Cup Apps	Gls	Europe Apps	Gls
Rice, B.	75+10	11	8+2	1	2+1	0	0	0
Riley, P.	0+1	0	0	0	0	0	0	0
Riordan, D.	110+27	61	9+3	7	7+3	2	1	1
Rippa, J.	1	0	0	0	0	0	0	0
Robertson, M.	2+3	0	0	0	0	0	0	0
Rocastle, C.	11+2	0	1	0	0	0	0	0
Rodier, D.	13+18	0	6+2	2	1+3	1	-	0
Rollo, J.	2	0	0	0	0	0	0	0
Ross, L.	1	0	0	0	0	0	0	0
Rough, A.	175	0	21	0	10	0	0	0
Rougier, T.	34+11	4	4	0	0	0	0	0
Rudge, H.	4+2	0	2	0	0	0	0	0
Sar-Temsoury, H.	0+1	0	0+2	0	0	0	0	0
Sauzee, F.	76+1	13	2	0	10	3	1	0
Schaedler, E.	291+8	2	67	2	28+2	1	25	0
Schmugge, T.	1	0	0	0	0	0	0	0
Scott, A.	38+2	2	1	0	2	0	8	0
Scott, Ally	28+10	4	8	5	1+1	0	3	0
Scott, J.	171+1	47	43	16	10	4	12	0
Shannon, R.	6	0	0	0	0	0	0	0
Shaw, D.	85	0	19	0	12	0	0	0
Shevlane, C.	65+1	1	17	0	1	0	8	0
Shiels, D.	80+36	24	10+1	4	9+2	3	3+4	0
Shields, J.	10+7	0	1+1	0	0	0	0	0
Simpson, R.	123	0	22	0	9	0	14	0
Simpson, W.	45+1	0	9	0	3	0	3	0
Skinner, J.	30+2	2	3	1	2	0	0	0
Slavin, T.	2	0	0	0	0	0	0	0
Smart, A.	2+3	1	0	0	0	0	0	0
Smith, G.	154+4	1	9+1	0	18	1	2	0
Smith, G.	310	122	80	35	36	12	5	0
Smith, R.	144+23	20	29+6	6	11+2	2	10+1	1
Smith, T.	32+2	0	3+1	0	6	0	0	0
Sneddon, A.	303+9	7	33+1	2	22	0	4	0
Souness, J.	4	3	5	1	0	0	0	0
Sowunmi, T.	2+3	0	0+1	1	0	0	0	0
Spalding, D.	70+4	1	10	0	8	2	5	0
Sproule, I.	35+36	12	5+1	0	10+1	4	4+2	2
Stanton, P.	397+2	51	102+1	14	38	4	36	8
Stein, C.	69	40	20	8	3	3	8	4
Stevens, T.	1	0	0	0	0	0	0	0
Stevenson, E.	255+1	53	72+1	15	15	2	23	5
Stevenson, J.	13	1	4	0	0	0	0	0
Stevenson, L.	39+8	0	5+1	0	3+2	0	0+2	0
Stevenson, M.	20	4	6	2	2	1	5	3
Stewart, G.	107+2	2	14	1	16	1	6	0
Stewart, M.	47+7	2	2+1	0	6	2	6	0
Stirling, R.	2	2	0	0	0	0	0	0
Temperley, W.	3+5	1	0+1	0	0	0	1	1

	League		League Cup		Scottish Cup		Europe	
Player	Apps	Gls	Apps	Gls	Apps	Gls	Apps	Gls
Thicot, S.	8+2	0	0	0	0	0	0	0
Thomson, B.	55+6	13	14	1	2	0	0	0
Thomson, D.	2	0	0	0	0	0	0	0
Thomson, J.	52	8	10	0	1	0	6	0
Thomson, K.	73+7	2	7	1	4+2	0	6	0
Tierney, L.	7+1	0	0	0	0	0	0	0
Toner, W.	9	0	0	0	0	0	1	0
Torrance, R.	10+3	1	0+1	0	1	0	0	0
Tortolano, J.	154+68	13	8+4	1	15+7	2	1	0
Tosh, Paul J.	13+11	3	0+2	0	0	0	0	0
Townsley, D.	22+20	9	3	0	5+1	0	0	0
Turnbull, E.	349	147	86	35	40	9	6	3
Turnbull, S.	54+8	1	11	0	2	0	0	0
Tweed, S.	105+3	3	9	1	9	1	0	0
Van Zanten, D.	18	0	1	0	0	0	0	0
Vincent, S.	17	8	1	0	2	0	0	0
Waldie, S.	9	0	1	0	0	0	0	0
Walker, A.	7+1	3	0	0	1	0	0	0
Ward, J.	9	0	2	0	0	0	0	0
Ward, P.	46	1	5	0	3	0	0	0
Watson, A.	23+8	3	1	0	1	0	0	0
Weir, J.	19	14	6	5	1	4	0	0
Weir, M.	161+46	30	20+2	0	15+1	4	3	0
Welsh, B.	34+2	1	3	0	0+1	0	0	0
Welsh, P.	10+2	0	5+1	1	0+1	0	0	0
Whittaker, S.	125+15	4	6+3	0	15	1	8	0
Whyte, H.	5	0	0	0	1	0	0	0
Wilkins, R.	15+1	0	1	0	0	0	0	0
Wilkinson, I.	4	0	5	0	0	0	0	0
Wilson, M.	3+1	0	0	0	0+1	0	0	0
Wilson, T.	4+3	1	1+1	1	0	0	0	0
Wilson, W.	116	0	27	0	9	0	10	0
Wiss, J.	40+8	0	4	0	1	0	0	0
Wood, R.	5	2	0	0	0	0	0	0
Wren, J.	31	0	7	0	2	0	0	0
Wright, A.	2	0	0	0	0	0	0	0
Wright, K.	183+14	60	15	9	17+1	7	2	0
Wright, P.	33+3	7	1	0	0+1	0	0	0
Yantorno, F.	1+6	0	0	0	0	0	0	0
Young, John	41	2	7	0	4	0	0	0
Younger, T.	177	0	48	0	17	0	5	0
Zambernardi, Y.	35+1	0	2	0	1	0	0	0
Zarabi, A.	7	0	0	0	1	0	0	0
Zemmama, M.	35+17	8	2+3	0	2	0	0	0
Zitelli, D.	31+21	10	3	0	4+3	2	0+2	1

BV - #0145 - 100426 - C0 - 240/170/16 - PB - 9781780911168 - Gloss Lamination